CAHSEE

CALIFORNIA HIGH SCHOOL EXIT EXAM

MATHEMATICS

Available Online

TAKE THE ONLINE DIAGNOSTIC QUIZ

Go to kaptest.com/cahsee.

The address is case sensitive, so enter it carefully. Choose Mathematics. To register, you will need to have your book in front of you because you will be prompted for a word found in the text. Type that word when prompted by the computer.

Registering your program online is important because it gives you access to the diagnostic quiz, as well as any late-breaking information on the CAHSEE. Once you have registered, it's simple to access your Online Companion whenever you want.

FOR ANY TEST CHANGES OR LATE-BREAKING DEVELOPMENTS

kaptest.com/publishing

The material in this book is up-to-date at the time of publication. However, the test makers may have instituted changes in the test after this book was published. Be sure to carefully read the materials you receive when you register for the test. If there are any important late-breaking developments—or any changes or corrections to the Kaplan test preparation materials in this book— we will post that information online at kaptest.com/publishing.

RELATED TITLES FOR HIGH SCHOOL STUDENTS

SAT Comprehensive Program 2008

SAT Premier Program 2008

SAT Strategies for Super Busy Students, 2007

ACT Strategies for Super Busy Students, 2007

ACT Comprehensive Program 2008

ACT Premier Program 2008

AP Series 2008

CAHSEE
CALIFORNIA HIGH SCHOOL EXIT EXAM

MATHEMATICS
2008 Edition
by the staff of Kaplan

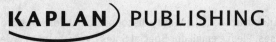

KAPLAN PUBLISHING

New York

This publication is designed to provide accurate and authoritative information in regard to the subject matter covered. It is sold with the understanding that the publisher is not engaged in rendering legal, accounting, or other professional service. If legal advice or other expert assistance is required, the services of a competent professional should be sought.

Vice President and Publisher: Maureen McMahon
Editorial Director: Jennifer Farthing
Acquisitions Editor: Allyson Rogers Bozeth
Development Editor: Janell Lantana
Production Editor: Karina Cueto
Interior Book Designer: Ivelisse Robles Marrero and Sokie Lee
Typesetter: Pamela Beaulieu
Cover Designer: Carly Schnur

Published by Kaplan Publishing, a division of Kaplan, Inc.
1 Liberty Plaza, 24th Floor
New York, NY 10006

Printed in the United States of America

January 2008
10 9 8 7 6 5 4

978-1-4277-9601-1

Kaplan Publishing books are available at special quantity discounts to use for sales promotions, employee premiums, or educational purposes. Please email our Special Sales Department to order or for more information at kaplanpublishing@kaplan.com, or write to Kaplan Publishing, 1 Liberty Plaza, 24th Floor, New York, NY 10006.

Table of Contents

How to Use This Book

If you're a high school sophomore, junior, or senior, or an adult learner, you are approaching the California High School Exit Examination (CAHSEE), the exam that all California students must pass in order to get their high school diplomas.

For many students, facing a high-stakes test like the CAHSEE can be intimidating. But you already have a head start: You've bought this book, putting yourself on the best path to mastering the topics on the exam—and succeeding on test day.

This chapter will provide you with information about how the CAHSEE Mathematics Exam is structured, and how you can best study for it. The rest of the chapters in this book will examine in detail the skills that the test measures, providing you with a solid foundation for success.

Introduction

What You Will Be Tested On

The Mathematics exam is one of two exams that make up the CAHSEE, a test that all high school seniors in California must pass in order to graduate. The other half of the test is the CAHSEE English-Language Arts exam.

The CAHSEE Mathematics exam includes 80 multiple-choice questions that test your understanding of essential mathematical concepts in the following areas:

> *Number Sense (14 questions)*
> *Statistics, Data Analysis, and Probability (12 questions)*
> *Algebra and Functions (17 questions)*
> *Measurement and Geometry (17 questions)*
> *Mathematical Reasoning (8 questions)*
> *Algebra I (12 questions)*

You may find that your exam includes more than 80 multiple-choice questions. Many administrations of the CAHSEE Mathematics exam have 92 questions, 12 of which are experimental test questions that are not scored. You have no way to distinguish these experimental items from the questions that will be scored, however, so it's important to approach each question with your full attention.

This may sound intimidating, so you will be glad to hear that unlike many standardized tests, the CAHSEE Mathematics exam has no set time limit. Students are generally expected to finish within one full school day, but you have a good deal of time to really evaluate, work through, and answer each question without watching the clock.

How Do I Prepare for The CAHSEE Mathematics Exam?

Just looking at this book means that you've begun preparing for the CAHSEE Mathematics exam. The book will help you determine what topics you have a good grasp on and in what areas you need some practice. Once you know where to focus your studying, you can use the techniques we provide to ensure that your studying and preparation are well-rounded.

You probably have many day-to-day responsibilities and commitments already. Finding time to study can feel difficult and challenging, but you're willing to take the time. Some of this material will feel like a review, and you'll ace the questions. For other topics, you may have to give the content some more consideration. You know yourself better than anyone, so you know how you prefer to study and prepare for exams. To help you maximize your study time and minimize the hours needed, we've made a few suggestions for how to study with this book. We realize you like having options—the option of when to study, where to study, and most of all—how to study. That's why the CAHSEE English Language Arts program contained here is your program—flexible and adaptable to your needs. What's unique about it is that you control the variety and amount of study to fit your busy life.

First, we know you want practice, but to make sure that you don't get bored with a big book of lessons, quizzes, and tests, we've made this program interactive. We encourage you to go online to take a mini-diagnostic quiz. You will see what you know, and where you could improve. Once you do that, you aren't forced to go in a predetermined order. Jump around all you want—to a specific chapter in the book, or straight to a full-length practice test!

Here's the plan, step-by-step.

STEP 1: REGISTER YOUR PROGRAM ONLINE

Go to kaptest.com/cahsee.

The address is case sensitive, so enter it carefully. Choose Mathematics. To register, you will need to have your book in front of you because you will be prompted for a word found in the text. Type that word when prompted by the computer.

Registering your program is important because it gives you access to the diagnostic quiz, as well as any up-to-date information on the CAHSEE. Once you have registered, it's simple to access your Online Companion whenever you want.

STEP 2: TAKE THE ONLINE DIAGNOSTIC QUIZ

The first thing you need to do is take the short diagnostic quiz. It will help you to figure out your strengths and weaknesses. With that information, you can customize and focus your study time.

 GOING ONLINE

If you don't have access to a computer at home, don't worry! You can access this at the library, a school, or a friend's house. If getting online is impossible, it's still OK — the diagnostic quiz is good to take, but it doesn't mean you can't skip it and dive right into the lessons and practice in the book.

STEP 3: IDENTIFY YOUR WEAKNESSES

Check your answers to the Diagnostic Quiz, noting how many questions you got right and how many you got wrong. Look for patterns. Did you ace the number sense questions? Did the tough statistics questions trip you up?

Don't limit your initial review to the questions you missed. Read all of the explanations—even those you answered correctly—to reinforce key concepts and sharpen your skills. As time permits, go back to the question types that you aced so you can keep that material sharp.

STEP 4: CUSTOMIZE YOUR STUDY PLAN

The best study plan will adapt to your individual needs and should start with a review of content weaknesses and include practice on weaker topics to boost skills and understanding. However, only you can determine the course of study that's right for you. We suggest the following:

- If you were able to do the online practice, target your chapters to the order of what you need to work on the most—are you stronger in algebra than geometry? Start with geometry. If you aced the measurement parts but struggled with mathematical reasoning, start there. Use the detailed Table of Contents to point yourself in the right direction. Devote time to reinforcing content strengths within the chapters through lessons and practice quizzes.

- If you weren't able to go online, start going through the book in order of the areas you know are sometimes a struggle for you. Once you've gotten through the chapters you've targeted for skill-building, try the first full-length practice test. This is your first milestone. How did you do? Did you improve since the diagnostic quiz?

- Think about the topics on which you need to focus, and go back to the chapters, if needed. Plan to read the remaining lessons in the book and take the quizzes at the end of each chapter. As time permits, go back to the question types that you aced so you can keep that material sharp.

- When you've finished the chapters, take the other full-length practice test.

STEP 5: REVIEW, REINFORCE, AND BUILD SKILLS

Again, you know what you need to do, so feel confident that the content you need to practice to pass the CAHSEE is right here. Go ahead and skip to the first practice test and find out what you know. Or, start on the first page, and dive into the material in sequential order, leaving no sentence unread, if that's what you need to prepare. Whatever your study needs happen to be, make a study plan, and then commit to following it. Block time out of your day to study, and give yourself rewards for sticking to your schedule. Don't push yourself too hard, but do try to keep a good long-term perspective on your goals and the work you need to do.

Take a look at the Table of Contents for the topics covered in each chapter. When you've assessed your skills and the areas where you need work, make a study plan—and make a commitment to see it through. Schedule some time each day to study, and give yourself rewards for maintaining your commitment. It's not healthy to push yourself too hard, but you should try to take small steps every day toward achieving your long-term goal.

How Do I Find The Time to Study?

Most students, especially adult learners and graduating seniors, have busy lives, with many commitments outside of school. The prospect of taking several hours out of your day to study can be a real challenge, and might discourage you from preparing at all. Think instead about committing just a small period of time each day: You probably don't have four hours free to study, but you can surely find an extra 20-30 minutes in your day.

- Create a timeline. Making a timeline of your study plan will give you a concrete way to see the progress you're making as test day approaches, keeping you encouraged and on track.

- Make outlines and mind maps. As you read and evaluate the material in this book, create your own outlines and notes that review the important concepts you want to remember. For many people, writing down notes or formulas can cement those concepts in our minds, helping us to remember them later.

- Get help from your friends and family. Studying alone can get old—and studying with another person can be just as productive, if not more so. Ask a friend or family member to help you review notes, formulas, or flashcards. If you are in high school, you're in an especially good position, since many of your classmates will also be preparing for the CAHSEE exams.

- Make flashcards. Flashcards are one of the simplest and most effective study tools you can use. They are key in helping you learn formulas, memorize important terms and concepts, and fortify your understanding of material you already know.

- Find creative times to study. If you have a free moment, you have time to be preparing for the CAHSEE Mathematics exam. Waiting for a ride? Review the flashcards you've made and test your knowledge of geometry concepts. Commercial break during your favorite show? Ask a family member to give you a quick quiz on number sense.

- Enjoy yourself! Graduating from high school will open up a world of possibilities for you—in your career and your further education. If you can envision the CAHSEE as a stepping stone on the way to your ultimate goals, rather than just a requirement for school, you might find that you can get excited about studying for the test, passing it, and moving on to the next stage in your life. This is a great chance to learn essential basic skills, hone your study habits, and make a commitment to do your best for the future.

KAPLAN'S 4-STEP METHOD FOR MULTIPLE-CHOICE QUESTIONS

Step 1: Read the question carefully.

Step 2: Rephrase the question.

Step 3: Read all the answer choices.

Step 4: Eliminate any remaining incorrect choices.

STEP 1: READ THE QUESTION CAREFULLY

One of the mistakes that test-takers make the most is that they misunderstand or misinterpret the question, and answer a question that isn't the one being asked. Most of us think we're too careful to make this mistake—but are you sure? In a tense situation like a high-stakes exam, it's easy to let stress push you into working faster. But working faster doesn't mean that you're doing better or getting a higher score. The important thing is not to hurry through the test, but to be well prepared and approach each item carefully and thoughtfully.

Your awareness of language will be essential in understanding the clues that are contained in each question. Many test-takers find it helpful to mark key words and phrases as they read. These important terms are what make a question unique, setting it apart from other questions and leading to one unique correct answer. The terms you've marked could point to a particular relationship (e.g., which scatterplot shows a negative correlation... or which statement is MOST strongly supported...), or they may qualify or limit the range of correct answers (e.g., between which two integers... or after three hours of travel...).

As you work through the practices in the book, practice this method. That way, marking up your book will be second nature to you on test day.

When a chart or graph is followed by a set of questions, try skimming over the questions before you look at the figure itself. Questions might direct you to a specific part of the chart (e.g., after 3 minutes) or ask for a more general evaluation of a set of figures (e.g., which graph shows the relationship...). If you have an idea of what to look for in the chart or table, you'll be more focused and directed as you review it, and be able to make the most effective use of your time.

STEP 2: REPHRASE THE QUESTION

For example, a question that starts with "which of the following" might be difficult to rephrase. If the question is "which of the following is the approximate weight on Mars of an astronaut who weighs 175 pounds on Earth?," you could rephrase it so that you think to yourself, one of these (answers) says how many pounds an astronaut will weight on Mars if she weighs 175 pounds on Earth. This helps you approach the answer choices with a clear knowledge of exactly what you're looking for. Once you've reworded the question, see if you can predict what a correct answer might look like, without looking at the answer choices—for example, if you know that the astronaut should weigh less on Mars, then you can approach the choices prepared to rule out any number above 175. This will help you to recognize the correct answer from among choices that might seem plausible, but are actually incorrect.

STEP 3: READ ALL OF THE ANSWER CHOICES

You may be tempted to choose the first answer that looks like what you're looking for, then move along to the next problem—especially if you've already predicted an answer, and you think you've found a match. Be aware, though, that there are frequently two very similar choices in a set, only one of which is the correct answer. If you stop at choice B, you will never see choice D, which might be the right answer. Rather than settling on the first one you like, mark off the choices you don't like as you read through. Crossing off answers that are incorrect means that you never have to think about them again; every time you cross off an incorrect answer, you narrow the field of possible correct answers from which you'll choose.

STEP 4: ELIMINATE ANY REMAINING INCORRECT CHOICES

You may have eliminated two choices, but find yourself unable to choose between the remaining two possible correct answers. In order to find the truly correct choice, you'll need to return to the question. Look at the words or phrases you marked the first time you read it, and reread, marking any additional words or phrases you might have missed.

Now reread the remaining answer choices, and look for the one that gives the best answer to the question that is being asked. If you are still unsure, it's a good idea to run through the problem again and redo your calculations—often, one or more incorrect answer choices are the products of common mathematical errors.

CAHSEE MATHEMATICS EXAM EXPLAINED

The questions on the Mathematics exam will test your understanding of six strands—groups of standards that are included in California's K-12 curriculum. Questions on five strands of the CAHSEE Mathematics exam cover only material that is taught through the eighth grade, while the Algebra I strand includes material taught in Algebra I classes.

NUMBER SENSE (14 QUESTIONS)

The questions in this strand will test your ability to perform basic mathematical calculations without using a calculator, on percents, integers, whole numbers, fractions, and decimals. You may be asked to multiply, divide, add, or subtract quantities; understand and use scientific notation; estimate the square root of a whole number; or solve a problem by applying a proportion or ratio.

STATISTICS, DATA ANALYSIS, AND PROBABILITY (12 QUESTIONS)

For the questions in this strand, you will need to show that you can examine and interpret displays of data, such as tables, bar graphs, and scatterplots. You will be asked to work with measures of central tendency such as the median, mode, and mean of a data set. Additionally, you should be able to determine whether events are dependent or independent, and express an event's probability in multiple forms (percent, decimal or ratio).

MEASUREMENT AND GEOMETRY (17 QUESTIONS)

The Measurement and Geometry strand tests your knowledge of rates, measurement, and geometric properties. Specifically, you will be asked to show that you can convert a measurement or set of measurements from one measurement system to another (e.g., meters to feet). You must demonstrate knowledge of the geometric principles of congruency, scale, translation, and reflection. You may be provided with an object's dimensions and asked to calculate its volume.

Although some formulas will be provided to you on the test, you will need to have memorized the following formulas in order to complete this strand successfully:

- Adding lengths of all sides (calculating the perimeter of a polygon)

- $C = \pi d$ or $C = 2\pi r$ (circumference of a circle, where d is the diameter or r is the radius)

- $A = bh$ (area of a parallelogram or rectangle; A = area; b = base; h = height)

- $A = \frac{1}{2} bh$ (area of a triangle; A = area; b = base; h = height)

- $V = lwh$ (volume of a rectangular prism; l = length; w = width; h = height)

You will also need to know the Pythagorean theorem ($a^2 + b^2 = c^2$) and its converse, and understand its applications.

ALGEBRA AND FUNCTIONS (17 QUESTIONS)

This strand tests knowledge of algebra and functions based on grade 7 standards (more advanced algebraic concepts are covered in the Algebra I strand). Questions in this strand will test your ability to generalize a numerical or geometric pattern; represent such patterns in a table, graph, or other form; and compare these representations. You will also be asked to solve linear equations and to distinguish between a function and a relation.

MATHEMATICAL REASONING (8 QUESTIONS)

Questions in this strand evaluate how well you understand the logic of mathematics. You might be asked to decide whether a conjecture is valid, to recognize a pattern within a set of numbers, or to decide what pieces of information would be necessary to solve a given problem.

ALGEBRA I (12 QUESTIONS)

The Algebra I strand of the CAHSEE Mathematics exam is the only one that covers material taught in California after grade 7. You will be asked to solve various algebraic problems, including systems of two equations with two variables; linear equalities; and problems that involve percent, rate, and work. These questions will test your knowledge of essential algebraic concepts, including evaluating polynomials and tackling problems that deal with time, distance, and speed. You must demonstrate an understanding of important terms such as absolute value, reciprocal, and root. You will also need to solve graphing problems, showing that you understand how to find a line's slope and intercepts and determine whether two lines are parallel.

RESOURCES

The chapters that follow will provide you with more detailed information about, and strategies for, preparing for these types of questions. However, if you would like more information or background in a particular area, here are some resources that are available online.

http://www.cde.ca.gov/ta/tg/hs/documents/math05guide.pdf

Preparing for the California High School Exit Examination: A Mathematics Study Guide. Published by the California Department of Education, this guide provides guidelines on the content strands covered on the test, as well as sample questions for each strand.

http://www.thatquiz.com

Create a customized math test to hone your skills in any of twenty areas, including geometry, fractions, exponents, basic arithmetic, and graphs.

http://www.math.com/homeworkhelp/Algebra.html

A helpful primer and review on algebraic principles and vocabulary, and explanations of how practice problems are solved.

Scoring The CAHSEE Mathematics Exam

The Mathematics component of the CAHSEE has 80 possible points. Your score report will convert this raw score to a scaled score between 275 and 450. In order to pass this portion of the CAHSEE, you must receive a scaled score of at least 350, or roughly 44 of the 80 possible points.

CAHSEE Mathematics Test Dates

The CAHSEE Mathematics exam will be administered on these dates for the 2008 school year:

February 6, 2008	*November 5, 2008*
March 12, 2008	*December 13, 2008**
May 7, 2008	*February 4, 2009*
July 30, 2008	*March 18, 2009*
October 8, 2008	*May 13, 2009*

*Saturday administration.

Students who plan to graduate in June 2008 should plan to take the CAHSEE prior to the May administration so that their scores are received before graduation.

NOTE ON RETESTING:

High school seniors and adult students may take the part(s) of the CAHSEE that they have not passed up to three times during the school year, and may take the test on two successive test dates.

Juniors may take the part(s) of the CAHSEE that they have not passed up to two times during the school year. However, grade eleven students may not take the CAHSEE on two successive test dates (e.g., December and February).

Sophomores are required to take the CAHSEE, and may take the test only once during the school year.

Section 1
Mathematical Concepts

Number Sense

HOW TO APPROACH MATH QUESTIONS

Before we dive into the actual math, let's take a step back and build some strategies for how to approach math problems in general. You've most likely seen most of the math concepts you'll encounter on the CAHSEE. However, you need to approach the math on the test a little differently than you would in class or another situation. Below are four strategies for approaching multiple-choice math problems.

Kaplan's 4 Strategies for Multiple-Choice Math Problems

STRATEGY 1: Practice in test-like conditions—do your arithmetic by hand.
STRATEGY 2: Be careful with negative numbers.
STRATEGY 3: Factor numbers to simplify fractions.
STRATEGY 4: Backsolve to avoid complicated calculations.

ARITHMETIC

One of the most important foundation skills tested on the CAHSEE is arithmetic. Some questions test your arithmetic skills directly, and some just require you to add, subtract, multiply, or divide along the way to the answer. Many questions involve situations you might run into in your daily life where arithmetic skills will come in handy.

Make your practice sessions as similar to the test as you can. No calculator on the test? No calculator while you practice!

You can't use a calculator on this test (unless you need special testing arrangements), so if you're used to relying on one, you might need a little practice doing arithmetic by hand to feel totally comfortable without it. But don't worry! You've been adding, subtracting, multiplying, and dividing since you first stepped into a classroom, so this will all come back to you soon.

7.6 + 4.4 =

A   11.10

B   12.00

C   13.00

D   13.60

 Work carefully to get all the points you can.

The correct answer is choice **B**. You might have selected choice A or choice C if you regrouped incorrectly. Remember, on the CAHSEE, you have a whole test booklet to work in and all the time you need, so write everything down and don't rush. Start adding from the right-hand side:

$$\begin{array}{r} {}^{1}7.6 \\ +\ 4.4 \\ \hline .0 \end{array}$$

Remember to regroup 10 ones into a ten!

$$\begin{array}{r} {}^{1}7.6 \\ +\ 4.4 \\ \hline 12.0 \end{array}$$

If you hurry through the arithmetic, you might accidentally leave something out and get the wrong answer to a question you really know how to do. Take your time to make sure you get all the points you can.

Three friends are going to an amusement park. If each friend buys a ticket for $20.00 and a souvenir hat for $15.00, how much money did all three friends spend at the amusement park?

A $35.00

B $60.00

C $75.00

D $105.00

Each friend spent $20.00 + $15.00 = $35.00 at the park. All three of them together spent $35.00 × 3 = $105.00. You could also calculate this the other way around: the friends bought three tickets for 3 × $20.00 = $60.00, along with three hats for 3 × $15.00 = $45.00, so the total amount they spent was $60.00 + $45.00 = $105.00. Either way, choice **D** is correct.

Dave, his sister Sally, and their friends Javier and Martha are running a lemonade stand. They earned $26.48 on Monday. If the four children divide the money equally, how much money will each child get?

A $6.12

B $6.48

C $6.62

D $22.48

The correct answer is choice **C**. There are two ways to solve this problem. You should try both methods while you're practicing to determine which one is easier for you to use without making any mistakes. Use the method that you feel most comfortable with on the test.

The first way to solve this problem is to do just what it says: divide $26.48 by 4. Don't even try to divide complicated numbers like this in your head—writing it down will make sure you get the points you need! If it's been a while since you've done long division by hand, get plenty of practice before you take the test.

```
  .
4)26.48
```

Copy the decimal point above where it appears in the number you're dividing. Start dividing by figuring out what you could multiply 4 by to get the largest possible number that's less than 26. Multiplying 6 by 4 is equal to 24, so write 6 above the line and 24 below the number you're dividing.

```
    6.
4)26.48
  24
```

26 – 24 = 2, so there are 2 left over. Move down the 4 from 26.48 to get 24.

```
    6.
4)26.48
  24
   2 4
```

What can you multiply 4 by to get 24? That's 6 again, so write another 6 on top of the line.

```
    6.6
4)26.48
  24
   2 4
   2 4
```

The difference between 24 and 24 is 0, so when you move down the 8, all you have is 8. To get 8 from 4, multiply by 2.

```
    6.62
4)26.48
  24
   2 4
   2 4
     08
      8
      0
```

The remaining difference is 0, and there aren't any digits left in the number you're dividing by, so you're done! Each child gets $6.62 from the lemonade stand.

 Work backward when there are numbers in the answer choices and difficult computations in the question. Start in the middle and substitute each answer choice into the question to see if it works.

The other way to solve this problem is to do it backward. If you're a little fuzzy on long division, this is the way to go. To work backward, you start with the answer choices and plug them into the problem to see if they give you the information in the question. In this case, you'll test each answer choice by multiplying it by 4. If 4 times the answer choice is $26.48, then that answer choice is $26.48 divided by 4. You should start working backward with answer choices B or C, since you'll often be able to tell whether you need a bigger or a smaller number. Let's try choice B:

$$\begin{array}{r} \overset{13}{\$6.48} \\ \times 4 \\ \hline \$25.92 \end{array}$$

The question tells you that the four children made more than $25.92, so you know that choice B is too small. You need a bigger number. Choice **C** must be correct, because choice D is obviously too large. Let's check:

$$\begin{array}{r} \overset{2}{\$6.62} \\ \times 4 \\ \hline \$26.48 \end{array}$$

That's exactly right.

Negative Numbers

Negative numbers can be tricky. Be careful when you're adding, subtracting, multiplying, or dividing negative numbers. Not only do you need to come out with the right number, you also need to be sure you have the right sign. If you're adding numbers with the same sign, just add them and keep the sign. If you're adding numbers with different signs, it's easier to think of the process as subtraction. Find the difference between the absolute values of the numbers (*absolute value* means just the number part, without the sign), and use the sign from the number with the larger absolute value.

 Remember these handy rules for working with positive and negative numbers:

- positive + positive = positive

- negative + negative = negative

- positive + negative or negative + positive: subtract absolute value and use the sign of the number with the larger absolute value

- positive × positive = positive

- positive × negative = negative

- negative × positive = negative

- negative × negative = positive

- positive ÷ positive = positive

- positive ÷ negative = negative

- negative ÷ positive = negative

- negative ÷ negative = positive

Did you notice that division works by the same rules as multiplication?

Which of the following expressions results in a positive number?

A $(-2) + (-4)$

B $(-2) - (-4)$

C $(-6) + (-1)$

D $(-6) - (-1)$

You don't even need to do all the math to find out that the answer is choice **B**. Any negative number plus another negative number will still be negative, so you can eliminate choices A and C right away. To figure out which of the other two answer choices is correct, remember that subtracting a negative number is the same as adding a positive number. The sum of a negative number and a positive number takes the sign of whichever number has the larger absolute value, so comparing the two numbers will tell you what sign their sum will have. $(-2) - (-4)$ is the same as $(-2) + 4$. Because 4 is bigger than 2, you know the sum is positive. In fact, it's 2: $(-2) - (-4) = (-2) + 4 = 4 - 2 = 2$. You can use the same technique to find that choice D is negative. $(-6) - (-1) = (-6) + 1 = 1 - 6 = -5$, since 6 is bigger than 1.

Which of the following is equal to $(-12) \div (-4)$?

A $1 + 4 - 2$

B 12×4

C $4 \div 12$

D $1 \times 1 \times 1$

Dividing a negative number by a negative number will leave you with a positive number. In this case, $\dfrac{-12}{-4} = \dfrac{12}{4} = 3$. Which of the answer choices will also leave you with 3? Well, you can eliminate choices B and C right away—choice B is much too large (it's 48), and choice C is too small $\left(\dfrac{1}{3}\right)$. Choice D is equal to 1, so that's not right either. Choice **A**, though, is equal to 3, so it is correct.

Steven started hiking in a valley 30 feet below sea level. He climbed to the top of a mountain 423 feet above sea level. How many feet did Steven climb?

A 323

B 393

C 423

D 453

Steven climbed a number of feet equal to the difference between the height where he started and the height where he ended. He started below sea level, so represent that as a negative height, –30 feet. He then climbed to positive 423 feet. The difference between the two is 423 – (–30) = 423 + 30 = 453 feet, choice D. Choice B is the difference between 423 and 30, not the difference between 423 and –30. The result of leaving out a negative sign is usually one of the wrong answer choices, so always be careful with your negatives.

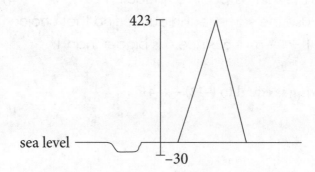

ABSOLUTE VALUE

The *absolute value* of a number is how far away from zero it is on the number line. You can also think of absolute value as the number without its sign. Absolute value is always positive or equal to zero. It can't be negative.

The distance between 0 and 4 is 4, so the absolute value of 4 is 4.

Any positive number is the absolute value of two numbers: itself and its opposite.

The distance between 0 and –4 is also 4, so the absolute value of –4 is 4.

Absolute value is usually written with two parallel lines, like this: $|-4| = 4$.

$|5| + |-5|$

A   –5

B   0

C   5

D   10

This question has two steps. First, find the absolute values of 5 and –5. Then, add them together. The absolute value of 5 is 5, and the absolute value of –5 is also 5, so $|5| + |-5| = 5 + 5 = 10$. Answer choice **D** is correct.

 Since distances can't be negative, in questions dealing with distances, you can eliminate any negative answer choices right away.

What is the distance between −6 and 2 on the number line below?

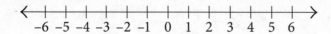

A   −8

B   −4

C   4

D   8

The distance between −6 and 2 is 8, choice **D**. You can either use the number line to count how many numbers you need to move to get from −6 to 2, or you can subtract one number from the other, then take the absolute value. It doesn't matter which number you put first—taking the absolute value will make your answer positive.

$$\left|-6-2\right| = \left|-8\right| = 8$$
$$\left|2-(-6)\right| = \left|2+6\right| = \left|8\right| = 8$$

FRACTIONS

A fraction is part of a whole. The *numerator* is the number on the top of a fraction, and the *denominator* is the number on the bottom: $\dfrac{\text{numerator}}{\text{denominator}}$. You can think of the denominator as the number of equal pieces the whole is broken into and the numerator as the number of those pieces you have.

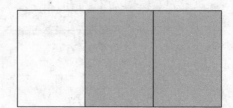

This is $\dfrac{2}{3}$ of a chocolate bar. There are three pieces, and two of them are shaded.

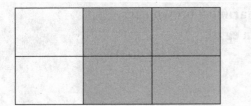 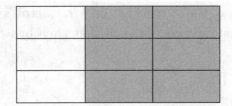

You could also think of $\frac{2}{3}$ as $\frac{4}{6}$ or $\frac{6}{9}$, as shown in the figures above. These fractions are all *equivalent* (they all represent the same amount). You can convert a fraction into an equivalent fraction by multiplying the numerator and the denominator by the same number. For instance, $\frac{2}{3} = \frac{2 \times 2}{3 \times 2} = \frac{4}{6}$.

 Factoring a number means breaking it into pieces. Multiplying the factors together will give you the original number.

You will frequently need to simplify fractions so that the answer you've found is in the same form as the correct answer choice. To simplify a fraction, factor the numerator and denominator, then cancel out any factors that appear in both the numerator and the denominator. For instance, $\frac{9}{18} = \frac{3 \times 3}{2 \times 3 \times 3} = \frac{1}{2}$. When you can't cancel out any more factors, the fraction is in lowest terms.

Another way to simplify a fraction is to find the largest number that divides into both numbers without a remainder. This number is known as the *greatest common factor* (GCF). Divide the numerator and denominator by the greatest common factor to find the simplified fraction. For example, take the fraction $\frac{9}{18}$. The greatest common factor of 9 and 18 is 9, so $\frac{9}{18}$ can be simplified by dividing the numerator and denominator each by 9:

$$\frac{9}{18} = \frac{9 \div 9}{18 \div 9} = \frac{1}{2}.$$

Five of the 30 chickens on Mr. Carroll's farm lay brown eggs. What fraction of the chickens lays brown eggs?

A $\dfrac{1}{6}$

B $\dfrac{1}{5}$

C $\dfrac{1}{3}$

D $\dfrac{5}{3}$

Five brown-egg-laying chickens out of a total of 30 is $\dfrac{5}{30} = \dfrac{\cancel{5}}{\cancel{5} \times 2 \times 3} = \dfrac{1}{2 \times 3} = \dfrac{1}{6}$ of the chickens. Choice **A** is correct.

Another way to simplify this fraction is to use the greatest common factor of 5 and 30, which is 5. Divide the numerator and denominator each by 5 to simplify the fraction:

$$\frac{5}{30} = \frac{5 \div 5}{30 \div 5} = \frac{1}{6}$$

Adding and Subtracting Fractions

To add or subtract fractions, you need to give them a common denominator, then add or subtract the numerators. For instance, $\dfrac{1}{2} + \dfrac{1}{3} = \dfrac{1 \times 3}{2 \times 3} + \dfrac{1 \times 2}{3 \times 2} = \dfrac{3}{6} + \dfrac{2}{6} = \dfrac{3 + 2}{6} = \dfrac{5}{6}$. The least common denominator is the smallest number that each denominator can divide evenly without a remainder. You can find the least common denominator (LCD) by factoring both fractions' denominators, then combining the factors. Don't repeat factors common to both numbers.

$$\frac{14}{15} - \frac{5}{6} =$$

A $\quad \frac{1}{15}$

B $\quad \frac{1}{10}$

C $\quad \frac{9}{15}$

D $\quad \frac{9}{9}$

First, find the lowest common denominator. Because $15 = 3 \times 5$ and $6 = 2 \times 3$, the lowest common denominator is $2 \times 3 \times 5 = 30$. The number 30 is the smallest number that both 15 and 6 divide without leaving a remainder. Convert each fraction into an equivalent fraction with a denominator of 30:

$$\frac{14}{15} + \frac{2}{2} = \frac{28}{30} \text{ and } \frac{5}{6} \times \frac{5}{5} = \frac{25}{30}.$$

Then, subtract the numerators and place the result over this common denominator:

$$\frac{28}{30} - \frac{25}{30} = \frac{3}{30}.$$

This isn't one of the answer choices, so simplify it by factoring the denominator or dividing by the greatest common factor, 3:

$$\frac{3}{30} = \frac{3}{2 \times 3 \times 5} = \frac{1}{2 \times 5} = \frac{1}{10} \text{ or } \frac{3 \div 3}{30 \div 3} = \frac{1}{10}.$$

That's choice B, the correct answer. Don't fall into the trap of selecting choice D. This is the result of subtracting the numerators and denominators without changing to a common denominator.

Sometimes you'll see a fraction larger than 1. It might be written as an *improper fraction*, with a numerator larger than its denominator, or as a *mixed number*, a whole number plus a fraction. Improper fractions are usually easier to work with, but answer choices or information in CAHSEE questions might also be given as mixed numbers, so you should be able to move back and forth between them.

Sam has $3\frac{1}{4}$ pounds of tomatoes. June has $1\frac{3}{8}$ pounds of tomatoes. How many more pounds of tomatoes does Sam have than June?

A $1\frac{7}{8}$

B $2\frac{1}{8}$

C $2\frac{7}{8}$

D $4\frac{5}{8}$

First, turn each mixed number into an improper fraction by multiplying the whole number by the denominator, then adding this result to the numerator. Then, give the fractions a common denominator so you can subtract them:

$$3\frac{1}{4} = \frac{3 \times 4}{4} + \frac{1}{4} = \frac{12}{4} + \frac{1}{4} = \frac{13}{4}$$

$$1\frac{3}{8} = \frac{1 \times 8}{8} + \frac{3}{8} = \frac{8}{8} + \frac{3}{8} = \frac{11}{8}$$

The least common denominator is 8, so multiply $\frac{13}{4}$ by $\frac{2}{2}$ to get $\frac{26}{8}$.

Now you can find the difference between the fractions: $\frac{26}{8} - \frac{11}{8} = \frac{15}{8}$

Since each answer choice is in mixed number form, convert this back to a mixed number by finding the number of times 8 goes into the numerator. If you divide 15 by 8, you will be left with 1 or $\frac{8}{8}$, plus a remainder of 7 over 8, or $\frac{7}{8}$. Look at the example below:

$$\frac{15}{8} = \frac{8+7}{8} = \frac{8}{8} + \frac{7}{8} = 1\frac{7}{8}$$

Sam has $1\frac{7}{8}$ more pounds of tomatoes than June, so choice **A** is correct. Choices B and C are the result of computational errors. Choice D is the result of adding the values in the problem, so be sure to look for key words when solving each problem.

Multiplying and Dividing Fractions

Multiplying fractions is simpler than adding or subtracting them. To multiply a fraction by a fraction, just multiply the numerators, then multiply the denominators. There is no need to find a common denominator. You've seen this in action when converting fractions to equivalent fractions; it works the same way when the numerators and denominators are different.

Multiplying by a fraction that's less than 1 will give you a smaller number than you started with, and dividing by a fraction that's less than 1 will give you a larger number. Knowing this can help you figure out what to do in word problems or let you know when you've made a mistake. Use common sense to make sure your chosen answer is reasonable.

Jody has $\frac{2}{3}$ of a bottle of soda. If she gives $\frac{1}{3}$ of what she has to her sister, what fraction of a bottle of soda will Jody's sister have?

A $\frac{1}{9}$

B $\frac{2}{9}$

C $\frac{1}{3}$

D $\frac{3}{3}$

To solve this problem, find $\frac{1}{3}$ of the $\frac{2}{3}$ in the bottle. The key word *of* tells you to multiply these values together: $\frac{2}{3} \times \frac{1}{3} = \frac{2 \times 1}{3 \times 3} = \frac{2}{9}$. So Jody's sister will have $\frac{2}{9}$ of a bottle of soda. Choice **B** is correct. Choice C is the incorrect result of subtracting the two fractions. Choice D is the incorrect result of adding the two fractions.

 You can write and draw as much as you'd like in your test booklet. Sketching a picture of what is happening in a problem can help you avoid wrong answer choices, so go ahead and use that space!

If you're not quite sure what to do with the fractions when you see a problem like this, or if you want to double-check your answer, try drawing a picture of the situation. Jody has $\frac{2}{3}$ of a bottle of soda, so draw a rectangle divided into thirds and shade two of them.

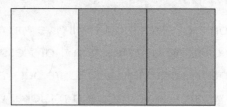

She gives $\frac{1}{3}$ of what she has to her sister, so divide the shaded part into three equal pieces and shade one of them darker. This is the part that Jody's sister has. Can you tell what part of the whole bottle it is? (To make it clearer, you can divide the whole rectangle the way you divided the shaded part.)

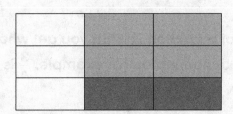

Two out of a total of nine pieces are shaded, so Jody's sister has $\frac{2}{9}$ of a bottle of soda.

To multiply a fraction by a whole number, just multiply the numerator by the whole number and leave the denominator alone. For instance, $\frac{1}{2} \times 3 = \frac{3}{2}$. You can also think of this as converting the whole number into a fraction with a denominator of 1, then multiplying the two fractions: $\frac{1}{2} \times \frac{3}{1} = \frac{3}{2}$.

Pete has four servings of applesauce. Each serving is $\frac{2}{3}$ of a cup of applesauce. How much applesauce does Pete have?

A $\frac{1}{6}$

B $\frac{1}{4}$

C $2\frac{2}{3}$

D $4\frac{2}{3}$

Because $\frac{2}{3} \times 4 = \frac{2}{3} \times \frac{4}{1} = \frac{2 \times 4}{3 \times 1} = \frac{8}{3} = 2\frac{2}{3}$, Pete has $2\frac{2}{3}$ cups of applesauce. Choice **C** is correct.

If you get confused, you can still answer the question without doing any math. Each serving is $\frac{2}{3}$ of a cup, and Pete has 4 servings. Does he have more than $\frac{2}{3}$ of a cup or less than $\frac{2}{3}$ of a cup? He must have more, so you can eliminate choices A and B right away. Because $\frac{2}{3}$ of a cup is less than 1 cup, Pete must have fewer than 4 cups altogether. That lets you eliminate choice D as well. Only choice C could possibly be correct.

The *reciprocal* of a fraction is what you get when you swap the numerator and denominator. For example, $\frac{3}{4}$ is the reciprocal of $\frac{4}{3}$.

Dividing by a fraction is the same as multiplying by its reciprocal. Dividing by a whole number (x) is like multiplying by the fraction 1 over the whole number.

$$\frac{1}{2} \div \frac{1}{4} =$$

A $\frac{1}{8}$

B $\frac{1}{6}$

C $\frac{1}{2}$

D   2

$$\frac{1}{2} \div \frac{1}{4} = \frac{1}{2} \times \frac{4}{1} = \frac{1 \times 4}{2 \times 1} = \frac{4}{2} = \frac{2}{1} = 2$$

We can calculate as follows: $\frac{1}{2} \div \frac{1}{4} = \frac{1}{2} \times \frac{4}{1} = \frac{1 \times 4}{2 \times 1} = \frac{4}{2} = \frac{2}{1} = 2$. So choice **D** is correct. Choice A is the result of multiplying the values without taking the reciprocal of the second number. Choice B is the result of multiplying the numerators and adding the denominators.

Let's look at another example.

$\frac{1}{2} \div 4 =$

A $\frac{1}{8}$

B $\frac{1}{6}$

C $\frac{1}{2}$

D 2

We can calculate as follows: $\frac{1}{2} \div 4 = \frac{1}{2} \times \frac{1}{4} = \frac{1 \times 1}{2 \times 4} = \frac{1}{8}$. So choice **A** is correct. Choice D is the result of multiplying the values without taking the reciprocal of the second number.

Be sure you understand the difference between these last two questions. People can be sloppy when they talk, but there's a big difference between dividing something *in* half (dividing it by two) and dividing something *by* one-half!

Fractions and Decimals

Sometimes you will need to turn a fraction into a decimal or a decimal into a fraction. To convert a fraction into a decimal, just divide the numerator by the denominator. To convert a decimal into a fraction, turn it into a fraction with a denominator of one, then simplify until there is no decimal point in the fraction. Reduce the fraction by dividing the numerator and denominator by the greatest common factor.

For instance, $0.25 = \frac{0.25}{1} \times \frac{100}{100} = \frac{25}{100} = \frac{25}{25 \times 4} = \frac{1}{4}$. You might find it helpful to memorize some of the most common fraction-decimal conversions, but you don't need to. You can always calculate the conversion out the long way to be sure you have the right answer.

Common fraction-decimal conversions:

$$\frac{1}{2} = 0.5 \qquad\qquad \frac{1}{4} = 0.25 \qquad\qquad \frac{1}{8} = 0.125$$

$$\frac{1}{3} = 0.3\overline{3} \qquad\qquad \frac{1}{5} = 0.2 \qquad\qquad \frac{1}{10} = 0.1$$

What is the result of subtracting $\frac{1}{4}$ of 2.4 from $\frac{1}{2}$ of 7.2?

A 0

B 1

C 2

D 3

To solve this question, you need to get both numbers into the same form. You can use either fractions or decimals, so pick the form you feel most comfortable with and are least likely to make mistakes in.

Fraction method:

$$\frac{1}{4} \times 2.4 = \frac{2.4}{4} = \frac{24}{40} = \frac{\cancel{2} \times \cancel{2} \times \cancel{2} \times 3}{\cancel{2} \times \cancel{2} \times 2 \times 5} = \frac{3}{5}$$

$$\frac{1}{2} \times 7.2 = \frac{7.2}{2} = \frac{72}{20} = \frac{\cancel{2} \times \cancel{2} \times 2 \times 3 \times 3}{\cancel{2} \times \cancel{2} \times 5} = \frac{2 \times 3 \times 3}{5} = \frac{18}{5}$$

$$\frac{18}{5} - \frac{3}{5} = \frac{15}{5} = 3$$

Decimal method:

$$0.25 \times 2.4 = 0.6$$

$$0.5 \times 7.2 = 3.6$$

$$3.6 - 0.6 = 3$$

Either way, the answer is choice **D**.

PERCENTS

Percents are everywhere! Stores use percents during sales and on coupons; doctors use percents to show how common a disease is or how well a new drug works; businesspeople use percents to show changes in profits; reporters use percents to describe nearly anything. You'll need to know what information given in percent form means to understand all these descriptions, and you'll need to be able to perform some basic percent calculations to make the most of your finances. Let's see what those basics are.

The easiest way to think of a percent is as a special fraction. *Percent* means "per hundred" or "divided by 100," and that's what a percent is: a number compared to 100. A percent can be written as a percent (65%), a fraction $\left(\frac{65}{100}\right)$, or a decimal (0.65). Any one of these forms might be the easiest one to work with to solve a particular problem, so you should be comfortable working with all three.

To find fractions or percents from word problems, you'll need to identify the part and the whole. The part (the numerator) is usually indicated by the word *is* or *are*. The whole (the denominator) is usually indicated by the word *of*.

 You can use any two of the three unknown parts of the equation
$$\frac{\text{percent}}{100} = \frac{\text{part}}{\text{whole}}$$ **to find the remaining one.**

A bag holds 6 red candies, 9 green candies, and 10 yellow candies. What percent of the candies are red?

A   6%

B   15%

C   18%

D   24%

In this problem, the part is the number of red candies ("are red"), and the whole is the total number of candies ("of the candies"). There are 6 + 9 + 10 = 25 total candies, and 6 of them are red. Therefore, $\frac{6}{25} = \frac{6 \times 4}{25 \times 4} = \frac{24}{100}$ of the candies are red. That's 24%, choice **D**. Choice A is the *number* of red candies, not their *percent* of all candies. This kind of wrong answer choice is common in percent problems, so be sure to check whether the question asks for a number or a percent.

You could also use decimals to solve this problem. Just divide 6 by 25 to get 0.24, then convert that into a percent by moving the decimal point two places to the right and adding a percent sign: 24%.

 Change a percent to a decimal by moving the decimal point two places to the left and dropping the percent sign (dividing by 100%). Change a decimal to a percent by moving the decimal point two places to the right and adding a percent sign (multiplying by 100%).

Approximately 40% of a school's 180 ninth-grade students are taking P.E. this semester. About how many ninth-grade students are taking P.E.?

A   40

B   60

C   70

D   80

The expression 40% of 180 can be written as $\frac{40}{100} \times 180$ or 0.40×180. Or you can use the equation $\frac{percent}{100} = \frac{part}{whole}$. The percent is 40%, the whole is 180, and the part taking P.E. is what you're trying to find. The proportion becomes $\frac{40}{100} = \frac{x}{180}$. Cross multiply to get $100x = 40 \times 180$. Therefore, $100x = 7{,}200$. Divide each side of this equation by 100 to get $x = 72$ (the result of simplifying $\frac{40}{100} = 180$ or 0.40×180). That's about 70, or choice **C**. Choice A is the percent of students taking P.E., not the actual number.

A real estate agent will earn a 0.5% commission for every house she sells. In one month, the real estate agent sells 3 houses, each for $700,000 dollars. What is her commission for that month?

A $3,500

B $10,500

C $350,000

D $1,050,000

Be careful when you're working with very small or very large percents: for example, 0.5% is not 0.5; it's 0.005. To find the real estate agent's commission, multiply 0.005 by the sale price of the houses. Then multiply by 3, because she sold 3 houses. Each house costs $700,000, so the real estate agent earns $0.005 \times 3 \times \$700{,}000 = \$10{,}500$, or choice **B**. Choice A is the commission on one house. Choice C is the commission on one house if the percent is not changed to a decimal. Choice D is the commission on all three houses if the percent is not changed to a decimal.

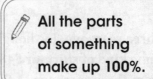

All the parts of something make up 100%.

Nathan has 50 stamps in his collection. Mark has 200 stamps in his collection. What is the number of stamps in Mark's collection expressed as a percentage of the number of stamps in Nathan's collection?

A   25%

B   150%

C   300%

D   400%

This problem is a little unusual. Notice that it's asking for the *larger* number as a percentage of the smaller. That means the percentage will be greater than 100%. In fact, it's $\frac{200}{50} = 4 = 400\%$, or choice **D**. Choice A is the result of using the number of stamps in Nathan's collection as the numerator and the number of stamps in Mark's collection as the denominator.

Percent Change

Changes in prices and other quantities are often expressed as percentages so that they can more easily be compared to the original values.

$$\text{percent change} = \frac{\text{difference between new number and original number}}{\text{original number}}$$

When a change in a number is expressed as a percent, it's always as a percent of the original value, not the new value. When the price of a coat drops from \$100 to \$75, its price has decreased by $\frac{100 - 75}{100} = \frac{25}{100} = 25\%$.

Three years ago, Joe bought a shirt for \$40. This year, he bought another of the same kind of shirt for \$48. What was the percent increase in the price of the shirt from three years ago to this year?

A   17%

B   20%

C   25%

D   40%

The difference in the prices (the increase) is $48 – $40 = $8, and the original price is $40. The percent increase is $\frac{8}{40} = \frac{1}{5}$ = 20%, which is choice **B**. Be sure to use the *original* value when you're finding percent change. Wrong answer choice A is the result of comparing the difference in price ($8) with the new price ($48).

Some common kinds of increases found on the CAHSEE are markups, charges, taxes, fees, and profits. Some common decreases are discounts, percents off, refunds, and losses.

 Use estimation to make sure your answer is in the right ballpark. One or two answer choices may be far enough off that you can eliminate them before you even get to the math.

Stephanie is buying a television. The television has a regular price of $360, but Stephanie has a coupon for 15% off. There is an 8% tax on the discounted price of the television. About how much will Stephanie need to pay for the television, including tax, if she uses her coupon?

A $25
B $330
C $335
D $450

Stephanie's coupon for 15% off means that she'll be paying 100% – 15% = 85% of the regular price of the television, or $360 × 0.85 = $306. (You could also find the discounted price by multiplying 0.15 by $360 to get the discount, then subtracting that from $360, but subtracting the percents first is usually faster.) She'll also be adding an 8% tax, so she'll wind up paying 108% of the discounted price of the television, or $306 × 1.08 = $330.48. That's just about $330, choice **B**. (You could also find the price with tax by multiplying $306 by 0.08, then adding that to $306. Adding 100% to the percent increase is usually faster.)

If you'd rather avoid the percents, notice that you can eliminate two of the answer choices right off the bat. Choice A is way too low—even if you're not sure how much 15% off is, you know it can't be that much! Choice D is almost $100 more than the regular price, so it doesn't make sense for it to be the price with a discount coupon. Even if you have trouble combining percents, common sense will let you eliminate half of the answer choices and give you a much better chance of guessing correctly.

Interest

Interest is one very common application of percents. You can earn interest by putting your money in a savings account, or you can pay interest on a loan.

Steve put $300 into a certificate of deposit with a 4% annual interest rate. How much interest will he earn in one year?

A $3
B $4
C $12
D $40

Each year, Steve's CD will earn 4% of what he put into it. We can calculate that 4% of $300 is 0.04 × $300 = $12, so choice **C** is correct.

If the interest is only being calculated based on the *principal* (the original amount), as in the example above, it is called *simple interest*. If the interest earned stays in the account and earns more interest, it is called *compound interest*.

Carrie put $1,000 into a money market account with a 10% annual interest rate. She will leave the interest she earns in the account. How much money will there be in Carrie's account after 3 years?

A $300

B $1,100

C $1,300

D $1,331

Because the interest Carrie earns each year will be added to the account, her account balance will rise, and she will earn more interest each year than she earned the year before. After the first year, she will have 110% of what she started with; after the second year, she will have 110% of what she had at the end of the first year; and after the third year, she will have 110% of that. All together, that means Carrie will have $1,000 × 1.1 × 1.1 × 1.1 = $1,331 at the end of the third year.

Calculating compound interest all at once is definitely the easiest way to do it, but if you want to see the details, you can make a chart of what's happening each year.

Year	Money at Beginning of Year	Interest Earned	Total Money at End of Year
1	$1,000	$1,000 × 0.1 = $100	$1,100
2	$1,100	$1,100 × 0.1 = $110	$1,210
3	$1,210	$1,210 × 0.1 = $121	$1,331

EXPONENTS AND ROOTS

When you see an expression like 2^3, the normal-sized number is the *base* and the little number is the *exponent*. The exponent tells you how many times to multiply the base by itself. For instance, 2^3 is 2 used as a factor 3 times: $2 \times 2 \times 2$. Exponents help to save space (it's a pain to write out eleven 2s when you could just say 2^{11}) and make some kinds of calculations easier.

Expressions with exponents may be referred to as *powers of* the base. Taking something to the second power is also called squaring it, and taking it to the third power is cubing it. You might see 5^2 called "five squared," "five to the power of two," or "five to the second power." These expressions all mean the same thing.

$3^4 =$

A   7

B   12

C   34

D   81

We can calculate that 3^4 is $3 \times 3 \times 3 \times 3$, or 81. That's choice **D**. Choice A is the result of simply adding the base number to the exponent. Be careful; choice B is the result of multiplying the base by the exponent, $3 \times 4 = 12$, a common error when working with exponents.

Most of the time, you should keep expressions with exponents in that form while you're working with them, instead of multiplying them out. Exponents with the same base are easy to multiply, divide, or raise to another power.

When you multiply numbers with the same base, add the exponents and keep the base: $2^3 \times 2^4 = 2^7$.

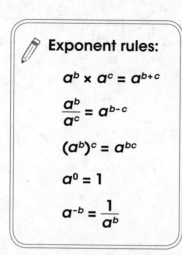

Exponent rules:

$a^b \times a^c = a^{b+c}$

$\dfrac{a^b}{a^c} = a^{b-c}$

$(a^b)^c = a^{bc}$

$a^0 = 1$

$a^{-b} = \dfrac{1}{a^b}$

When you divide numbers with the same base, subtract the exponent of the denominator from the exponent of the numerator and keep the base: $2^3 \div 2^4 = 2^{-1}$.

$$\frac{5^{12} \times 5^{11}}{5^6 \times 5^{10}} =$$

A 5^6

B 5^7

C 5^{12}

D 5^{22}

First, to multiply, add the exponents of the like bases in the numerator and then the denominator. Then, to divide, subtract the exponents of the like bases. The calculation looks like this: $\frac{5^{12} \times 5^{11}}{5^6 \times 5^{10}} = \frac{5^{12+11}}{5^{6+10}} = \frac{5^{23}}{5^{16}} = 5^{23-16} = 5^7$. So choice **B** is correct. Each of the other answer choices is the result of errors in computation or of misunderstanding the rules for exponents.

When you raise a number with an exponent to a power, multiply the exponents and keep the base: $(2^3)^4 = 2^{12}$.

 Any number with an exponent of 0 equals 1. (Exception: 0^0 is undefined. If you find yourself trying to figure out what 0^0 is on the CAHSEE, you know you've done something wrong. They won't ask about it.)

A number with no exponent is the same as a number with an exponent of 1. That is, $2 = 2^1$.

$$\frac{(7^2)^5}{(7^3)^0}$$

A 7^4

B 7^7

C 7^{10}

D 7^{13}

To raise a power to another power, keep the base and multiply the exponents:

$$\frac{(7^2)^5}{(7^3)^0} = \frac{7^{2\times5}}{7^{3\times0}} = \frac{7^{10}}{7^0}$$

To divide powers of the same base, keep the base and subtract the exponents:

$$\frac{7^{10}}{7^0} = 7^{10-0} = 7^{10}$$

Or use the fact that $7^0 = 1$, because anything to the power of zero equals 1, and then use the fact that a fraction with a denominator of 1 is the same as the numerator alone:

$$\frac{7^{10}}{7^0} = \frac{7^{10}}{1} = 7^{10}$$

However you decide to simplify this expression, you'll come out with the same result: choice **C** is correct. Choice A is the result of adding the exponents, instead of multiplying them, in the first step.

Negative exponents tell you how many times to divide by the base: $2^{-3} = \frac{1}{2 \times 2 \times 2}$. An expression with a negative exponent is the reciprocal of the expression with the corresponding positive exponent: $2^{-3} = \frac{1}{2^3}$.

$11^3 \times 11^{-3} =$

A   1

B 11^{-9}

C 11^{-6}

D 11^6

Either rewriting the expression with the negative exponent as a fraction or applying the rules of exponents will get you to the correct answer:

$$11^3 \times 11^{-3} = 11^3 \times \frac{1}{11^3} = \frac{11^3}{11^3} = 1$$

$$11^3 \times 11^{-3} = 11^{3 + (-3)} = 11^{3 - 3} = 11^0 = 1$$

Choice **A** is correct. Choice B is the result of multiplying the exponents. You may have selected choice C or choice D if you added the exponents. There are usually several ways to simplify an exponent problem, so feel free to try different approaches until you find one you're comfortable with.

Squaring a negative number (or raising it to any other even exponent) is the same as multiplying it by a negative number (itself or an even number of itself), so the result is always positive. On the other hand, raising a negative number to any odd exponent always results in a negative number. For instance, $(-3)^2 = (-3) \times (-3) = 9$, but $(-3)^3 = (-3) \times (-3) \times (-3) = -27$.

What is the square of –9?

A   –81

B   –3

C   3

D   81

The square of –9 is $(-9)^2 = (-9) \times (-9) = 81$, which is choice **D**. Choice A is the opposite of the correct answer. When you see word problems that include exponents, be particularly alert for the difference between *square* and *square root*—they're easy to mix up, and the wrong one will usually be one of the wrong answer choices, as in choices B and C.

Square Roots

Finding the square root of a number is the inverse of squaring it. If you square the square root of a number, you get the original number back. For instance, $\sqrt{9^2} = 9$ and $(\sqrt{9})^2 = 9$. Although you can square either a positive or a negative number, when a question asks about a square root, it always means the positive number.

$\sqrt{5^2} - \sqrt{2^2}$

A   3

B   9

C 21

D 25

This isn't nearly as hard as it looks! A square root cancels out a square, so $\sqrt{5^2} - \sqrt{2^2}$ just equals 5 – 2, which is 3. Choice **A** is correct.

The CAHSEE writers don't expect you to be able to find any old square root, but you should recognize the *perfect squares*. A perfect square is a number that is the square of an integer (a whole number), which you can also think of as that integer times itself, as in 3 x 3 = 9 and 7 x 7 = 49. The first few perfect squares are 1, 4, 9, 16, 25, 36, 49, 64, 81, 100, 121, 144, 169, 196, and 225. These are the squares of the integers 1 through 15, and they should look pretty familiar.

What two whole numbers is $\sqrt{30}$ between?

A   5 and 6

B   6 and 7

C   7 and 8

D   8 and 9

There's no reason you should know the square root of 30 off the top of your head, so think about the numbers you *do* know the square roots of. You should know that 25 = 5^2 and 36 = 6^2. Because 30 is between 25 and 36, the square root of 30 must be between 5 and 6.

Which of the following is equal to two times the square root of 900?

A $\sqrt{4} \times \sqrt{300}$

B $\sqrt{9} \times \sqrt{200}$

C $\sqrt{36} \times \sqrt{100}$

D $\sqrt{18} \times \sqrt{200}$

To figure out the square root of 900, you should factor 900 into perfect squares. Two times the square root of 900 is $2 \times \sqrt{900} = 2 \times \sqrt{9 \times 100} = 2 \times \sqrt{9} \times \sqrt{100} = 2 \times 3 \times 10 = 60$. Simplify each of the answer choices to see which one is also equal to 60.

> ✎ **Square root rules:**
>
> $$\sqrt{a^2} = (\sqrt{a})^2 = a$$
>
> $$\sqrt{ab} = \sqrt{a} \times \sqrt{b}$$
>
> $$\sqrt{\frac{a}{b}} = \frac{\sqrt{a}}{\sqrt{b}}$$
>
> **(for $a \geq 0$ and $b > 0$)**

A $\sqrt{4} \times \sqrt{300} = \sqrt{4} \times \sqrt{3} \times \sqrt{100} = 2 \times \sqrt{3} \times 10 = 20\sqrt{3}$

You can't simplify the square root of 3, so you know this isn't equal to 60.

B $\sqrt{9} \times \sqrt{200} = \sqrt{9} \times \sqrt{2} \times \sqrt{100} = 3 \times \sqrt{2} \times 10 = 30\sqrt{2}$

You can't simplify the square root of 2, either.

C $\sqrt{36} \times \sqrt{100} = 6 \times 10 = 60$

Perfect! The answer is **C**. You can stop here, because you know only one answer can be correct, but you can also double-check choice D.

D $\sqrt{36} \times \sqrt{200} = \sqrt{36} \times \sqrt{2} \times \sqrt{100} = 6 \times \sqrt{2} \times 10 = 60\sqrt{2}$

SCIENTIFIC NOTATION

Scientific notation is a way to write very large or very small numbers so that they are easier to work with. A number written in scientific notation consists of a multiplier times some power of 10. The multiplier's absolute value is always between 1 and 10 (it can equal 1, but it must be less than 10), and the exponent is always an integer. To express a number in scientific notation, count the number of places you need to move the decimal point to get a number with an absolute value between 1 and 10. That's your exponent. If you moved the decimal point to the left, the exponent is positive. If you moved it to the right, the exponent is negative. For instance, the number 7,000,000 is written in scientific notation as 7×10^6.

 Positive exponents indicate very large numbers, and negative exponents indicate very small numbers.

A single bacterium is about 0.000002 meters in diameter. What is this diameter in scientific notation?

A 2×10^{-6}

B 2×10^{-5}

C 2×10^5

D 2×10^6

You have to move the decimal point 6 places to the right to turn 0.000002 into 2, so 0.000002 is the same as 2×10^{-6}. That's choice **A**.

Which of these numbers is the largest?

A 1.8×10^{-11}

B 2.3×10^9

C 5.6×10^5

D 8.2×10^{-3}

To find the largest number, just look at the exponents. All the bases are positive, and 9 is the largest exponent, so choice **B** is the largest number. If you're not sure, you can write each number in standard notation to compare them. Choice A is 0.000000000018, choice B is 2,300,000,000, choice C is 560,000, and choice D is 0.0082.

Adding and subtracting numbers written in scientific notation can be confusing. It's usually easier to translate them into standard notation before you begin.

What is the sum of 3.4×10^4 and 1.2×10^2?

A 1.234×10^4

B 3.412×10^4

C 4.6×10^4

D 4.6×10^6

In standard notation, these numbers are 34,000 and 120. Their sum is 34,120. That's 3.412×10^4, or choice **B**. You might have selected choice C, if you simply added the first number of each expression and kept the exponent of 4. Choice D is the result of adding the first number of each expression and also adding the exponents.

Multiplying and dividing, on the other hand, are usually easier in scientific notation, because you just have to cancel out the powers of 10 and then you can work with much simpler numbers.

A tax refund resulted in 3.3×10^6 dollars being equally distributed among 1.1×10^5 taxpayers. How many dollars did each taxpayer receive?

A $30

B $300

C $3,000

D $30,000

Divide the number of dollars by the number of taxpayers receiving the refund. Use the rules for exponents discussed in the previous section. In this case, when dividing like bases, subtract the exponents: $\frac{3.3 \times 10^6}{1.1 \times 10^5} = \frac{3.3 \times 10}{1.1}$ $= \frac{3.3}{1.1} \times 10 = 3 \times 10 = 30$, so each taxpayer received $30, choice **A**. Choices B, C, and D are each the result of confusing the placement of the decimal point in the answer.

SUMMARY

You learned a lot in this chapter. Let's review the most important points.

- Add, subtract, divide, and multiply decimals and fractions.
    o Practice in test-like conditions—do your arithmetic by hand.
    o Be careful with negative numbers.
    o Factor numbers to simplify fractions.
    o Backsolve to avoid complicated calculations.
- Find the absolute value of a number (its distance from 0 on the number line).
- Use percentages.
    o Common percentage topics on the CAHSEE include percent change and interest.
    o Use estimation to eliminate wrong answer choices.
    o CAHSEE questions may present percentage problems that involve percents, fractions, or decimals.
- Simplify exponents and square roots.
    o Memorize the rules to solve these problems more quickly.
    o Recognize the perfect squares.
- Understand scientific notation.
    o Positive exponents indicate large numbers.
    o Negative exponents indicate small numbers.

Number Sense Quiz

Read the following questions and answer questions 1 through 20.

1. What is the number 0.0005064 written in scientific notation?

   A 5.064×10^{-4}

   B 5.64×10^{-420}

   C 5.064×10^{-3}

   D 5.064×10^{4}

2. Which of the following is equivalent to 7.301×10^{5}?

   A 0.000007301

   B 0.00007301

   C 730,100

   D 730,100,000

3. Simplify $\frac{4}{5} - \left(\frac{1}{2} + \frac{1}{10}\right)$

   A $\frac{1}{10}$

   B $\frac{1}{5}$

   C $\frac{2}{5}$

   D $\frac{3}{5}$

4. Simplify $\left(\frac{2}{5}\right)^{3}$

   A $\frac{2}{125}$

   B $\frac{8}{125}$

   C $\frac{6}{15}$

   D $\frac{6}{5}$

5. In the senior class, 5 out of every 8 students have taken Spanish. What percentage of the seniors have taken Spanish?

   A 5%

   B 40%

   C 58%

   D 62.5%

6. Which of the following is equivalent to $\frac{9}{20}$?

   A 0.45

   B 0.920

   C 4.5

   D 9.2

7. A cellular phone, originally priced at $49.00, is on sale for 30% off the original price. What is the sale price of the phone?

   A $14.70

   B $19.00

   C $34.30

   D $63.70

8. Sportech Sporting Goods had $6,000 income for the month of January. Its operating costs were $2,050 the same month. What was Sportech's percent of profit for January, to the nearest percent?

   A 21%

   B 34%

   C 60%

   D 66%

9. Piles of Pennies Bank offers 5% simple interest on its savings accounts. What would a $450.00 deposit be worth in this account after 3 years?

   A $22.50

   B $67.50

   C $472.50

   D $517.50

10. Juan's salary rose from $23.00 per hour to $27.00 per hour. What was the percent increase, rounded to the nearest percent?

    A 4%

    B 15%

    C 17%

    D 40%

11. The weight of a brand of digital music player dropped from 18 ounces to 3 ounces. What was the percent decrease, rounded to the nearest percent?

    A 3%

    B 15%

    C 83%

    D 500%

12. Simplify $7^5 \times 7^{-3}$.

    A 7^{-8}

    B 7^{-2}

    C 7^2

    D 7^8

13. The square root of 52 lies between which two integers?

    A 2 and 5

    B 7 and 8

    C 51 and 53

    D 49 and 64

14. Simplify $(2^3)^2$.

   A   12
   B   32
   C   64
   D   512

15. Simplify $\dfrac{4^{-8}}{4^{-2}}$.

   A 4^{-10}
   B 1^{-6}
   C 4^{-6}
   D 4^6

16. Simplify 3^{-2}.

   A -9
   B -6
   C $-\dfrac{1}{9}$
   D $\dfrac{1}{9}$

17. Simplify $(-3)^3$.

   A -27
   B -9
   C 9
   D 27

18. Simplify $\dfrac{5}{6} \div \dfrac{1}{3}$.

   A $\dfrac{5}{18}$
   B $\dfrac{6}{15}$
   C $\dfrac{5}{3}$
   D $\dfrac{5}{2}$

19. What percent of 150 is 4.5?

   A   0.03%
   B   3%
   C   6%
   D   30%

20. Which number has the greatest value?

   A $-|37|$
   B $|-35|$
   C $|15|$
   D   28

Answers and Explanations

1. A

To express 0.0005064 as a number between 1 and 10, you must move the decimal point four places to the right. Therefore, the power of 10 is −4. The number written in scientific notation is 5.064×10^{-4}, choice A. Choice B is the result of leaving out the 0 between the 5 and 6. Choice C is the result of not counting enough decimal places when converting. Choice D is the result of forgetting to make the exponent negative when moving the decimal point to the right.

2. C

To find the equivalent value, multiply 7.301×10^5. We know that $10^5 = 100{,}000$. This is the same as taking 10 and moving the decimal point five places to the right. The value written in standard form is 730,100, choice C. Choice A is the result of putting 5 zeros before the number and moving the decimal point to the space before the zeros. Choice B is the result of moving the decimal point the correct number of places but in the wrong direction. Choice D is the result of putting 5 zeros after the number and moving the decimal point to the space after them.

3. B

To simplify this expression, first find a common denominator for the fractions. The least common multiple of 5, 2, and 10 is 10. Convert each fraction to an equivalent fraction with a denominator of 10. So $\frac{4}{5} \times \frac{2}{2} = \frac{8}{10}$, and $\frac{1}{2} \times \frac{5}{5} = \frac{5}{10}$.

Now follow the order of operations and add the fractions in parentheses first: $\frac{5}{10} + \frac{1}{10} = \frac{6}{10}$. Subtract this quantity from $\frac{8}{10}$: $\frac{8}{10} - \frac{6}{10} = \frac{2}{10} = \frac{1}{5}$ in lowest terms. Choice B is the correct answer. Choice C is the result of working through the problem in order from left to right, instead of performing the operation within the parentheses first. Choice D may have been selected if the sum of $\frac{1}{2} + \frac{1}{10}$ mistakenly yielded a result of $\frac{1}{5}$.

4. B

A fraction raised to a power is the same as taking both the numerator and the denominator to this power: $\left(\frac{2}{5}\right)^3 = \frac{2^3}{5^3} = \frac{2 \times 2 \times 2}{5 \times 5 \times 5} = \frac{8}{125}$. Choice B is the correct answer. Choice A is the result of applying the exponent to the denominator only. Choice C is the result of multiplying each number of the fraction by 3 to get the numerator and denominator of the answer. Choice D is the result of multiplying 2 by 3 in the numerator and keeping the denominator of 5.

5. D

Five of every eight seniors is represented as the fraction $\frac{5}{8}$. Convert this fraction into a percent. One way to do this is to let n represent the percentage and solve the proportion $\frac{\text{part}}{\text{whole}} = \frac{\text{percent}}{100}$. The proportion is: $\frac{5}{8} = \frac{n}{100}$.

Cross multiply to get: $5 \times 100 = 8n$

Divide each side by 8: $\frac{500}{8} = \frac{8n}{8}$

The percentage is: $62.5\% = n$

Another method to solving the problem involves dividing 5 by 8. This yields the decimal 0.625. You will need to move the decimal two places to the right to determine the correct percent: 62.5%.

Choice A is the number of students out of every eight who take Spanish, not the percentage who take Spanish. Choice C may have been selected if the values of 5 and 8 were added to arrive at the percentage.

6. A

The fraction $\frac{9}{20}$ can be converted to a decimal equivalent by dividing 9 by 20 to get 0.45. Choices B and D are the result of using the values of the numerator and denominator to convert to decimal form. Choice C is the result of an error in the placement of the decimal point.

7. C

The phone is discounted by 30%. You can solve this problem in two ways. First, subtract 30% from 100% to get 70%, which you will then multiply by $49.00. The answer is $34.30, and the correct answer is choice C. Another way to solve this problem involves finding 30% of $49.00 and subtracting this discount from the original price. Thirty percent of $49.00 is 0.30 × $49.00 = $14.70. The sale price is $49.00 – $14.70 = $34.30. Choice A is the amount of discount, not the sale price charged. Choice D may have been selected if the discount was incorrectly added to the original price of the phone.

8. D

The percent of profit is the ratio of profit to income, converted to a percentage. The profit is the income minus the operating costs, or 6,000 – 2,050 = 3,950. The percent of profit can be found by converting the ratio of profit to income into a percentage. You can use a proportion to find the percent, represented as the variable n: The proportion is: $\frac{3,950}{6,000} = \frac{n}{100}$.

Cross multiply to get: $\qquad 6,000n = 395,000$

Divide both sides by 6,000: $\qquad \frac{6,000n}{6,000} = \frac{395,000}{6,000}$.

The percentage is: $\qquad n = 65.83\overline{3}$

The percentage, rounded to the nearest percent, is 66%, choice D. Choice B is the percent that the operating costs were of the total income for the month.

9. D

The formula for calculating simple interest is $I = PRT$, where I is the interest earned, P is the principal invested, R is the interest rate, and T is the time in years.

Write the formula:	$I = PRT$
Substitute in the given values:	$I = 450 \times 0.05 \times 3$
Multiply to get the interest earned:	$I = 67.50$

The value of the deposit after three years will be the deposit plus the interest earned, or $450 + 67.50 = \$517.50$. Choice A is incorrect, because it is the amount of simple interest earned each year. Choice B is the total amount of interest earned over the three years, but not the total balance in the account. Choice C is the result of adding the interest earned for one year only, instead of the total interest over three years.

10. C

The percent of increase is found by converting the ratio of $\dfrac{\text{change in pay}}{\text{original pay}}$ to a percent. The change in pay is $\$27 - \$23 = \$4$. Set up a proportion to find the percentage increase, represented as the variable n:

The proportion is:	$\dfrac{4}{23} = \dfrac{n}{100}$
Cross multiply to get:	$23n = 400$
Divide both sides by 23:	$\dfrac{23n}{23} = \dfrac{400}{23}$
The percentage is:	$n = 17.3913\ldots$

The percentage, rounded to the nearest percent, is 17%. Choice A is the amount of increase in dollars, not the percent increase. Choice B is the result of using $27 for the original rate of pay instead of $23.

11. C

The percent of decrease is found by taking the ratio of $\dfrac{\text{change in weight}}{\text{original weight}}$ and then converting this ratio to a percent. The change in weight is 18 – 3 = 15. Set up a proportion to find the percentage decrease, represented as the variable n:

The proportion is: $\qquad\qquad \dfrac{15}{18} = \dfrac{n}{100}$

Cross multiply to get: $\qquad 18n = 1{,}500$

Divide both sides by 18: $\qquad \dfrac{18n}{18} = \dfrac{1{,}500}{18}$

The percentage is: $\qquad\qquad n = 83.333\ldots$

The percentage, rounded to the nearest percent, is 83%. Choice B is the result of using the decrease in ounces as the percent decrease. Choice D is the result of using 3 ounces, instead of 18 ounces, as the original weight in the proportion.

12. C

When you multiply two powers with the same base, keep the base number and add the exponents. In this problem, the common base is 7, and the exponents are 5 and –3. Add the exponents to get 5 + –3 = 2. The correct expression is 7^2, choice C. Choice A is the result of adding the absolute values of the exponents and making the result negative. Choice B is the result of subtracting the absolute values of the exponents and making the result negative. Choice D is the result of adding the absolute values of the exponents and making the result positive.

13. B

To find the answer to this question, first find the perfect squares that the integer 52 lies between. These are 49 and 64. Because $\sqrt{49} = 7$ and $\sqrt{64} = 8$, the square root of 52, $\sqrt{52}$, lies between the integers 7 and 8. You may have selected choice C or choice D if you did not consider the square root of 52, just the number 52.

14. C

To find the value of a power raised to a power, keep the base number, in this case 2, and multiply the exponents. Because $3 \times 2 = 6$, the expression $(2^3)^2$ is equivalent to $2^6 = 2 \times 2 \times 2 \times 2 \times 2 \times 2 = 64$, choice C. Choice A is the result of multiplying 2 by 3 to get 6 and then multiplying that result by 2. Choice B is the result of adding the exponents. Choice D is the result of raising the exponent of 3 to a power of 2 to make the expression 2^9.

15. C

When you divide two powers with the same base, keep the base number and subtract the exponent of the denominator from the exponent of the numerator. In this problem, the common base is 4, and the exponents are -8 and -2. Subtract the exponents to get $-8 - (-2) = -8 + 2 = -6$. The correct expression is 4^{-6}. Choice A is the result of incorrectly subtracting -2 from -8. In choice B, the base numbers were incorrectly divided. In choice D, the exponent has the incorrect sign.

16. D

When you are given a base number to a negative exponent, you take the reciprocal of the base number and make the exponent positive. The expression 3^{-2} is equivalent to $\left(\frac{1}{3}\right)^2 = \frac{1^2}{3^2} = \frac{1}{9}$, choice D. In choice A, the value of 9 was incorrectly changed to its negative, and the reciprocal was not taken. In choice B, the reciprocal was also not taken, and the exponent was not applied correctly; 3 was multiplied by 2 instead of being raised to an exponent of 2. In choice C, the negative sign is incorrectly applied; a negative exponent does not make the value of the expression negative.

17. A

The expression $(-3)^3$ is equivalent to $-3 \times -3 \times -3$. Multiply these negative integers left to right. Because a negative times a negative is equal to a positive, $-3 \times -3 = 9$, and the expression becomes 9×-3. A positive times a negative is a negative, so $9 \times -3 = -27$. In choices B and C, the base value was raised to an exponent of 2 instead of 3. Choice D is the result of not applying the negative sign.

18. D

To divide fractions, change the problem so that the dividend, the first term, is multiplied by the reciprocal of the divisor, the second term. This expression becomes $\frac{5}{6} \div \frac{1}{3} = \frac{5}{6} \times \frac{3}{1} = \frac{15}{6} = \frac{5}{2}$, in lowest terms. Choice A is the result of not taking the reciprocal of the divisor. Choice B is the result of taking the reciprocal of the first term, or dividend.

19. B

A percent is a ratio of part to whole. In this problem, the part is 4.5, and the whole is 150. Let the variable n represent the percent, set up a proportion, and solve:

The proportion is: $\frac{4.5}{150} = \frac{n}{100}$

Cross multiply to get: $150n = 450$

Divide both sides by 150: $\frac{150n}{150} = \frac{450}{150}$

The percent is: $n = 3\%$

Answer choice B is correct. Choice A and choice D are the results of an error in the placement of the decimal point or the use of an incorrect proportion.

20. B

Choices A, B, and C all have absolute value symbols. The absolute value of a number is always the positive equivalent of the value inside the absolute value symbols. The greatest value is 35, choice B, which is the correct answer. In choice A, $|37| = 37$; the minus sign is outside the symbols, so the final value is -37. For choice B, $|-35| = 35$. For choice C, $|15| = 15$. Choice D is 28.

Statistics, Data Analysis, and Probability

STATISTICS

Statistical measures of central tendency are a way to think about a large set of data more simply. They reduce a long list to simple representative numbers. Different statistical measures give you a different idea of what a set of data looks like, so mean, median, or mode all might be useful ways to describe the data, depending on what you're doing with the information. For the CAHSEE, you'll need to know how to calculate each of these three measures.

 Mean can also be called *arithmetic mean* or *average*.

$$\text{mean} = \frac{\text{sum of terms}}{\text{number of terms}}$$

The *mean* of a set of terms is the sum of all the terms divided by the number of terms. The mean is the most useful measure of central tendency when the distribution of terms is fairly even. Outliers (values that are much larger or smaller than most of the other values) have a much larger effect on the mean than on other measures of central tendency.

Jack earned grades of 80, 95, 75, and 60 on his first four spelling tests. What is the mean of Jack's grades?

A   75

B   77.5

C   85

D   90.5

Add up all four grades, then divide by 4: $\dfrac{80 + 95 + 75 + 60}{4} = \dfrac{310}{4} = 77.5$, or choice **B**.

The *median* of a set of terms is the number in the middle when the terms are arranged from least to greatest. If an even number of terms exists, then the median is the average (mean) of the two terms closest to the middle. There are always exactly as many numbers above the median as there are below the median. When some values are much larger or smaller than most of the numbers, the median gives you a better idea what most of the population is like than the mean would.

 Rewrite the numbers in order to make it easier to find the median.

Caroline has been counting the number of dandelions in the yards in her neighborhood. The number of dandelions in each of the nine yards on her street is 2, 5, 12, 4, 3, 0, 0, 6, and 2. What is the median number of dandelions in these yards?

A   0

B   2

C   3

D   4

Arrange the numbers in order so that you can find the middle one: 0, 0, 2, 2, 3, 4, 5, 6, 12. The number in the middle is 3, so choice **C** is correct.

The *mode* is the number that appears most often. If every number appears once, there is no mode; if more than one number appears the most times, then there are several modes. The mode is a good measure of central tendency if most of the population has similar values.

In a grocery store checkout line, two people bought 4 items each, three people bought 5 items each, two people bought 6 items each, one person bought 7 items, and three people bought 8 items each. What are the modes of the number of items bought?

A 4 and 5

B 4 and 6

C 5 and 7

D 5 and 8

The mode is the most common number. Here, two numbers are equally common—three people bought 5 items each and three people bought 8 items each. 5 and 8 are the modes, so choice **D** is correct.

Most CAHSEE questions about statistics will just ask you calculate a mean, median, or mode, but some may require you to think about a situation more abstractly.

The ten members of a Boy Scout troop collected cans of food for a week. The average number of cans each scout collected was 8. Which of the following questions can be answered from this information?

A How many cans did the scout who collected the most cans have?

B How many cans were collected each day?

C What was the total number of cans collected by the troop?

D What percentage of the cans contained green beans?

Because you don't know how many cans each scout collected, only the average number, you can't say how many cans the scout who collected the most had. The question also doesn't say anything about how many cans were collected each day of the week—they could all have been collected on the first day, evenly distributed over the week, or spread out in some other way. The question also doesn't say anything about what type of food the cans contained. However, it does include the number of scouts and the average number of cans each scout collected. Because the average number of cans is the total number of cans divided by the number of scouts, the total number of cans is the average number of cans times the number of scouts ($8 \times 10 = 80$). You can find the total number of cans collected, choice **C**.

DATA ANALYSIS

Another way to make a large set of data more understandable is to represent it as a graph rather than as a long list of information. On the CAHSEE, you may see pictograms, bar graphs, circle graphs, and Venn diagrams. Each type of graph is best at displaying certain types of data.

The first thing you should do when you see a question with a chart or graph is to check the title, the labels on the *x*- and *y*-axes, the scale, and the key if there is one. Make sure you know what the chart shows before you dive into solving the problem. Pay particular attention to the units of measurement so that you know where to look for what kind of information.

Pictograms are a lot like tables. These very simple graphs use a picture to represent some number of objects. The most important thing to remember about pictograms is that one picture doesn't necessarily mean one object—you should always check the key to see what the picture means.

T-Ball Team Members	
Teddy Bears	○ ○ ○ ○
Rockets	○ ○ ○ ○ ○
Tigers	○ ○ ○ ○ ○ ○
Astronauts	○ ○ ○ ○

Key
○ = 3 team members

What is the mode of the number of team members on these four T-ball teams?

A 4

B 12

C 14

D 18

The mode is the number that appears most frequently. Two of these teams have 4 circles. Each circle represents 3 team members, so the most common number of team members is 4 × 3 = 12. That's choice **B**.

Scatter plots make the most sense when you don't know the relationship between the two things you're graphing. In fact, a scatter plot can help you figure out what that relationship is. Once you have graphed each point, you can see whether they seem to fall into a line or not. If the points make a line with a positive slope, then there is a positive correlation between the *x*-values and the *y*-values. In other words, as *x* increases, *y* also increases. A line with a negative slope is a negative correlation: as *x* increases, *y* decreases.

The more closely the points stick to the line, the stronger the correlation. If the points are scattered all over the graph and don't seem to cluster around a line, then no correlation exists between the *x*-values and the *y*-values.

Which of the following graphs shows a positive correlation between the number of hours spent studying and the grade on a test?

A
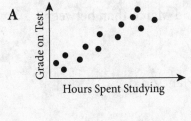

C
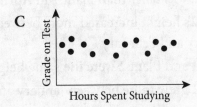

B
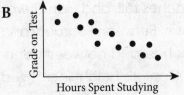

D
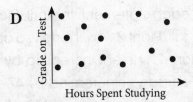

A line drawn among the points in the first graph would have a positive slope, so the graph in choice **A** shows a positive correlation. Choice B shows a negative correlation, choice C shows all the students getting about the same grade no matter how long they studied, and choice D shows a random distribution of points.

Line graphs are best when you're dealing with a continuous form of data—that is, when a *y*-value exists for every *x*-value, not just for certain points. Line graphs are particularly good for showing a value or values changing over time.

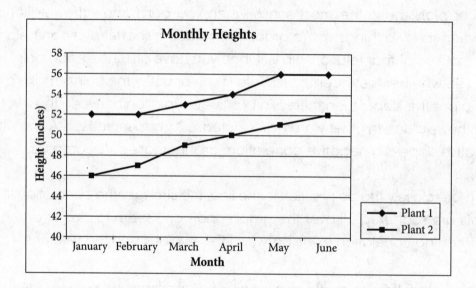

Which of the following statements is true?

A Plant 2 was taller than Plant 1 in April.

B Plant 2's height increased more between February and March than between January and February.

C Plant 1 and Plant 2 were the same height in June.

D Plant 1 grew more between January and June than Plant 2 did.

Consider each statement. In April, Plant 2 was 50 inches tall, and Plant 1 was 54 inches tall. Plant 2 was shorter, so choice A isn't true. Between February and March, Plant 2's height increased by 49 – 47 = 2 inches, and between January and February, it increased by 47 – 46 = 1 inch. Plant 2's height increased more between February and March than between January and February, so choice **B** is true. In June, Plant 1 was 56 inches tall and Plant 2 was only 52 inches tall, so choice C isn't true. Between January and June, Plant 1 grew 56 – 52 = 4 inches and Plant 2 grew 52 – 46 = 6 inches, so choice D isn't true either. Choice B is the only true statement and the correct answer.

Bar graphs make it easy to compare different values. They're also a good choice if you're graphing things you can't put in numerical order. Like pictograms, they can be labeled with names instead of numbers.

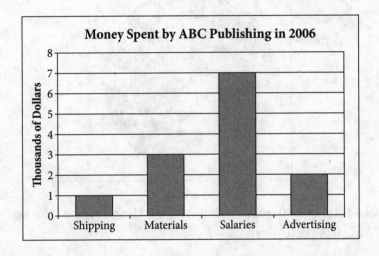

What is the difference between the largest and smallest amounts spent shown in the graph above?

A $1,000

B $3,000

C $6,000

D $7,000

The largest amount spent is salaries, at $7,000. The smallest is shipping, at $1,000. The difference between them is $7,000 – $1,000 = $6,000, or choice **C**.

Circle graphs, which you may also know as pie charts, are a good way to represent parts of a whole. They're usually marked in percentages. Some questions will ask about the percentages themselves, but most will also give you a total and have you calculate the actual numbers.

If you need to review percents, see pages 23–28 in the Percents section of Chapter 1, "Number Sense."

The graph below shows the posters sold by an art store in one month.

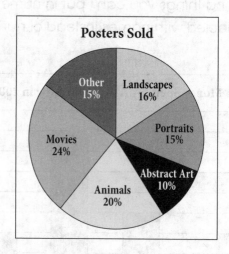

The store sold a total of 300 posters that month. How many of the posters sold were in the "Animals" category?

A 20

B 30

C 40

D 60

Of the 300 posters sold, 20% were in the "Animals" category. To determine how many posters that is, remember that the key word *of* generally means "to multiply." Convert the percent to a decimal and multiply. That's 0.20(300) = 60 posters, or choice **D**.

Venn diagrams are a bit different from other graphs. They describe relationships among independent characteristics of the members of a group instead of the value of one or two characteristics. Each labeled region contains the members that have that characteristic; members with multiple characteristics go in the overlapping portion of the regions. Because of their structure,

Venn diagrams are hardly ever used for numerical information, like prices or weights, but are used instead for named categories, like colors.

The diagram below shows what types of pets are owned by the students in Mrs. Jay's homeroom class.

Student Pets

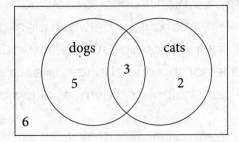

How many students own cats?

A   2

B   3

C   5

D   6

The circle on the right indicates students who own cats. Two students own cats but not dogs, and 3 students own both cats and dogs. The total number of students who own cats is 2 + 3 = 5, or choice **C**. The value of 5 represents those students who own a dog only. The value of 6 represents those students who own neither a dog nor a cat.

Susan is trying to figure out whether there is a correlation between the height of her tomato plants and the number of tomatoes on them. She has measured the height of 10 tomato plants and counted the number of tomatoes on each. Which of the following would be the most useful way for Susan to display the data she has collected?

A   Bar graph

B   Circle graph

C   Scatter plot graph

D   Line graph

A correlation is a relationship between two different characteristics. Because Susan is looking for a relationship between the plants' height and the number of tomatoes, she needs to use a display that shows both kinds of information. The only answer choice that could include both plant height and number of tomatoes is the scatter plot in choice **C**. Choice A, a bar graph, is a good choice to compare the plants' heights but not the number of tomatoes. Choice B is a circle graph, which is good to show parts of a whole but would completely fail to show the relationship between plant height and number of tomatoes. Choice D is similar to choice A in that it would show plant height, but line graphs are better for showing changes over time, not for showing the relationship between plant height and number of tomatoes.

PROBABILITY

Probability is a measure of the likelihood of an event happening.

 If an answer choice represents a probability less than 0 or greater than 1, you can eliminate it right away. Nothing less than 0 or greater than 1 can be a probability.

The probability of any event is between 0 and 1. If something is completely impossible, then it has a probability of 0. If it is certain to happen, then it has a probability of 1. All other probabilities are between 0 and 1. The chances of all the different things that could happen in a situation must add up to 1—after all, *something* has to happen.

Probabilities can be expressed as decimals, fractions, or percentages. If they are expressed as a percentage, it's a percentage of 1 and must be between 0% and 100%.

If the chance of rain tomorrow is 35%, what is the chance that it will not rain tomorrow?

A   0%

B   15%

C   35%

D   65%

The chance that something will happen and the chance that it won't happen always add up to 100%. The chance that it will not rain is 100% – 35% = 65%, or choice **D**.

Most CAHSEE questions about probability involve selecting certain possibilities from a list of equally likely situations. When all outcomes are equally likely, probability can be defined as the ratio between the number of desired outcomes and the number of possible outcomes.

$$\text{probability} = \frac{\text{number of desired outcomes}}{\text{number of possible outcomes}}$$

An ordinary deck of cards has 13 hearts, 13 clubs, 13 spades, and 13 diamonds. What is the probability that a randomly selected card will be a spade?

A $\frac{1}{13}$

B $\frac{1}{4}$

C $\frac{4}{13}$

D   13

The desired outcome is that the card will be a spade. There are 13 spades in the deck, so there are 13 ways to get this outcome. There are a total of 13 + 13 + 13 + 13 = 52 cards in the deck, so there are 52 total possible outcomes. The chance that a randomly selected card will be a spade is $\frac{13}{52} = \frac{1}{4}$, choice **B**.

Often, it is necessary to determine the number of possible outcomes in situations. There is a fundamental counting principle that is used for this determination. The counting principle tells you to take the number of choices for each category and multiply them together to find the total number of outcomes.

The ice cream store has 2 types of cones, 7 ice cream flavors, and 3 different toppings. How many different ice cream cones can be made consisting of 1 cone, 1 ice cream flavor, and 1 topping?

A   2

B   7

C   12

D   42

To find the total number of outcomes—in this case, the number of different ice cream cones—multiply the number of cones, 2, by the number of different flavors, 7, then by the number of different toppings, 3: $2 \times 7 \times 3 = 42$ possible ice cream cones, choice **D**. Choice A is the number of different cones only, choice B is the number of flavors only, and choice C is the result of adding the numbers instead of multiplying.

Sometimes, you need to know what all the possible outcomes are, not just how many there are. In these cases, it's useful to make a list, chart, or diagram so that you can more easily count the possibilities that have particular characteristics.

 On the CAHSEE, you can assume that all coins are fair (equally likely to land on heads or tails) unless the question tells you otherwise. Similarly, assume that all dice are equally likely to land on each side and all spinners are equally likely to point in any direction.

Paula flips a coin 3 times. What are the chances that it will land heads-up exactly once?

A $\dfrac{1}{8}$

B $\dfrac{3}{8}$

C $\dfrac{1}{3}$

D 3

The first coin flip can be either heads or tails. No matter what it is, the second coin flip can then be heads or tails, as can the third. A tree diagram can help keep track of all the possible results. H stands for heads and T for tails.

Each column of the tree represents 1 flip of the coin. Three columns represent 3 flips of the coin.

You could also show the results in a list. Following the branches of the tree above from left to right yields the list of all possible outcomes:

HHH
HHT
HTH
HTT
THH
THT
TTH
TTT

There are 8 possible outcomes of three coin flips. Three of them (HTT, THT, and TTH) have exactly 1 heads, so the probability that exactly one flip will be heads is $\frac{3}{8}$, choice **B**.

Five students are trying out for parts in a play. The play has three parts: a king, a thief, and a cow. Baxter, Stacy, and Fred tried out for the king. Pat and Alvin tried out for the thief. Baxter, Fred, and Pat tried out for the cow. All three parts must have a student in them, no student can play more than one part, and students can only be assigned to parts they tried out for. Which of the following organized charts shows all of the possible ways that the students could be assigned to parts?

A

KING	THIEF	COW
Baxter	Pat	Fred
Baxter	Alvin	Pat
Stacy	Pat	Baxter
Stacy	Alvin	Fred
Fred	Pat	Baxter
Fred	Alvin	Pat

C

KING	THIEF	COW
Baxter	Pat	Fred
Baxter	Alvin	Fred
Baxter	Alvin	Pat
Stacy	Pat	Baxter
Stacy	Pat	Fred
Stacy	Alvin	Baxter
Stacy	Alvin	Fred
Stacy	Alvin	Pat
Fred	Pat	Baxter
Fred	Alvin	Baxter
Fred	Alvin	Pat

B

KING	THIEF	COW
Stacy	Pat	Baxter
Stacy	Alvin	Baxter
Stacy	Alvin	Pat
Fred	Pat	Baxter
Fred	Alvin	Baxter
Fred	Alvin	Pat

D

KING	THIEF	COW
Baxter	Pat	Baxter
Baxter	Pat	Fred
Baxter	Pat	Pat
Baxter	Alvin	Baxter
Baxter	Alvin	Fred
Baxter	Alvin	Pat
Stacy	Pat	Baxter
Stacy	Pat	Fred
Stacy	Pat	Pat
Stacy	Alvin	Baxter
Stacy	Alvin	Fred
Stacy	Alvin	Pat
Fred	Pat	Baxter
Fred	Pat	Fred
Fred	Pat	Pat
Fred	Alvin	Baxter
Fred	Alvin	Fred
Fred	Alvin	Pat

The best way to find all the possible combinations is to consider them one part at a time. You could make a tree diagram or, as these answer choices show, an organized list in chart form. If Baxter gets the king part, then either Pat or Alvin could be the thief. If Pat is the thief, then the only student left for the cow is Fred, because Pat and Baxter already have parts. If Baxter is the king and Alvin is the thief, then either Fred or Pat could be the cow. Write down the possibilities as you find them, to be sure you don't leave any out.

Choice **C** is correct. It lists all the possible combinations of students. Choice A and choice B leave out some possibilities, and choice D includes combinations that have one student playing two parts.

The chart below shows all possible results of rolling two 6-sided number cubes. What is the probability of rolling a sum of 8 on two number cubes?

1, 1	1, 2	1, 3	1, 4	1, 5	1, 6
2, 1	2, 2	2, 3	2, 4	2, 5	2, 6
3, 1	3, 2	3, 3	3, 4	3, 5	3, 6
4, 1	4, 2	4, 3	4, 4	4, 5	4, 6
5, 1	5, 2	5, 3	5, 4	5, 5	5, 6
6, 1	6, 2	6, 3	6, 4	6, 5	6, 6

A $\dfrac{5}{36}$

B $\dfrac{1}{6}$

C $\dfrac{2}{9}$

D $\dfrac{1}{4}$

Look at the chart on the following page. The chart shows 36 possible results on two number cubes. The combinations that represent a sum of 8 are in bold. Five of them have a sum of 8, so the probability of rolling a sum of 8 on two number cubes is $\dfrac{5}{36}$, choice **A**.

1, 1	1, 2	1, 3	1, 4	1, 5	1, 6
2, 1	2, 2	2, 3	2, 4	2, 5	**2, 6**
3, 1	3, 2	3, 3	3, 4	**3, 5**	3, 6
4, 1	4, 2	4, 3	**4, 4**	4, 5	4, 6
5, 1	5, 2	**5, 3**	5, 4	5, 5	5, 6
6, 1	**6, 2**	6, 3	6, 4	6, 5	6, 6

 Estimation comes in handy on probability questions, especially if more than one event is involved. When a desired outcome is more complicated, it is less likely, so the probability of two events happening is less than the probability of either event alone.

Rolling two number cubes is an example of a set of *independent* events. The result of the first number cube roll doesn't affect the result of the second number cube roll. The probability of two independent events can be calculated by multiplying the probability of the first event by the probability of the second event. (Remember, probabilities are always between 0 and 1, so the result of multiplying will be smaller—less likely—than the individual probabilities.)

What is the probability of getting heads twice when you flip a coin twice in a row?

A   0.25

B   0.5

C   0.75

D   1

The coin can either land heads-up or tails-up, so the probability of getting heads on one coin flip is $\frac{1}{2}$, or 0.5. The probability of getting heads on two coin flips is $0.5 \times 0.5 = 0.25$, or choice **A**.

You could also make a simple chart or tree diagram to see all the possible results:

HH
HT
TH
TT

Two heads is one of four possible outcomes, so the probability of getting two heads is $\frac{1}{4} = 0.25$.

If the result of the first event does change the probability of the second event, the second event is *dependent* on the first. You still calculate the probability of both happening by multiplying, but remember to adjust the second probability before you do.

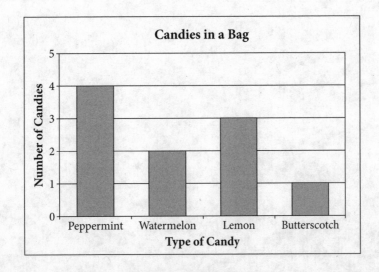

Russ is randomly pulling candies out of the bag. What is the probability that Russ will draw two peppermints out of the bag, if he does not return the candy to the bag after the first draw?

A $\frac{2}{15}$

B $\frac{4}{25}$

C $\frac{1}{5}$

D $\frac{3}{10}$

The chance of drawing a peppermint on the first try is $\frac{4}{10}$, because there are 4 peppermints and 10 total candies. After the first peppermint has been removed, though, there are only 3 peppermints and 9 total candies left in the bag, so the chance of drawing a second peppermint is $\frac{3}{9}$. The chance of drawing two peppermints is $\frac{4}{10} \times \frac{3}{9} = \frac{12}{90} = \frac{2}{15}$, or choice **A**.

SUMMARY

After reading this chapter, you should be able to do the following:

- Describe a set of terms statistically.
    - Calculate the mean by using the formula
    $$\text{mean} = \frac{\text{sum of terms}}{\text{number of terms}}.$$
    - Identify the median as the middle term when the terms are in order.
    - Identify the mode as the term that appears most often.
- Understand pictograms, line graphs, bar graphs, circle graphs, Venn diagrams, and scatterplots.
    - Find information from each type of graph.
    - Know which type of data each graph can help describe.
- Calculate the probability of an event from a list of possible events.
    - Use the formula $\text{probability} = \frac{\text{number of desired outcomes}}{\text{number of possible outcomes}}.$
    - Use the counting principle to find the number of possible outcomes.
    - Make a chart, organized list, or tree diagram to list all possible events.
    - Identify dependent and independent events.
    - Multiply probabilities to find the probability of several events happening.

Statististics, Data Analysis, and Probability Quiz

1. When selecting from the letters in the word MATHEMATICS, what is the probability of <u>not</u> selecting an M or a T?

   A $\frac{4}{11}$

   B $\frac{4}{7}$

   C $\frac{7}{11}$

   D $\frac{7}{4}$

2. The circle graph below shows how Tonya spent her money while on a trip.

   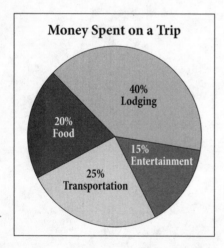

   Money Spent on a Trip

   40% Lodging
   20% Food
   15% Entertainment
   25% Transportation

   If she spent a total of $200 on the trip, how much did she spend on both food and lodging?

   A $60
   B $120
   C $130
   D $240

3. While on the track team, Cheryl ran the following number of laps.

Day 1	12 laps
Day 2	12 laps
Day 3	16 laps
Day 4	18 laps
Day 5	19 laps

   What is the median number of laps Cheryl ran?

   A   7
   B   12
   C   15.4
   D   16

4. The list below shows the high temperatures recorded at a city over a period of 7 days.

   60, 62, 65, 75, 61, 59, 65

   What temperature is the mode?

   A   62
   B   63.86
   C   65
   D   75

5. The chart below shows the amount of rainfall in inches over a period of 5 months. What is the mean rainfall?

Month	Number of Inches
Nov.	17
Dec.	20
Jan.	15
Feb.	25
Mar.	18

A 15 inches

B 17 inches

C 18 inches

D 19 inches

6. The graph below shows the number of books read each day by a certain class. Which table correctly matches this graph?

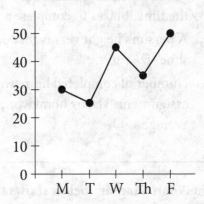

Number of Books Read

A

Day	Number of Books
M	50
T	35
W	45
Th	25
F	30

C

Day	Number of Books
M	40
T	35
W	55
Th	45
F	60

B

Day	Number of Books
M	30
T	25
W	45
Th	35
F	50

D

Day	Number of Books
M	30
T	40
W	50
Th	25
F	35

7. Which of the following is MOST likely to represent a negative correlation?

   A   Time a person runs versus distance that runner travels

   B   Number of people working versus the time it takes to complete a task

   C   A person's height versus that person's shoe size

   D   Number of completed homework assignments versus homework grade average

8. The Venn Diagram below shows the number of students in the band and the chorus at a school.

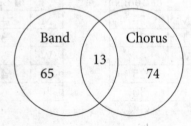

   How many students are in the chorus?

   A   13

   B   65

   C   74

   D   87

9. Kathleen has 4 green, 5 red, and 6 blue marbles in a jar. If she selects one without looking, what is the approximate probability the marble is red?

   A   0.27

   B   0.33

   C   0.40

   D   0.50

10. The graph below compares the number of flights of two different airlines. How many more flights did Smooth Skies have than Comfort Airlines?

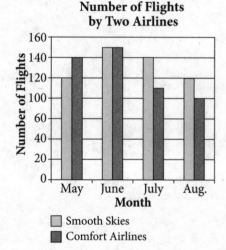

   A   30

   B   40

   C   120

   D   140

11. The line graph below shows the total number of cars that passed through a toll booth during a 40-minute period. If the traffic trend continues at the same rate, how many cars will pass through the booth in one hour?

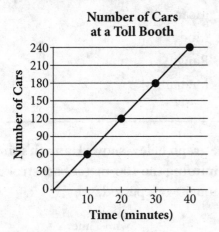

Number of Cars at a Toll Booth

A   60

B   120

C   300

D   360

12. If the probability of having a girl is $\frac{1}{2}$, what is the probability that a family with three children will have three girls?

A $\frac{1}{8}$

B $\frac{1}{6}$

C $\frac{1}{2}$

D $\frac{3}{2}$

13. Jason is playing a board game with letter tiles where one letter is used at a time. Jason holds the 6 tiles P, X, T, R, S, and A. On his next turn, he uses the tile S. If he is equally likely to use any of his remaining tiles and does not draw any new tiles, what is the probability that he will use the tile R on the following turn?

A $\frac{1}{30}$

B $\frac{11}{30}$

C $\frac{1}{6}$

D $\frac{1}{5}$

14. Which of the following best describes the relationship of the data in the scatter plot below?

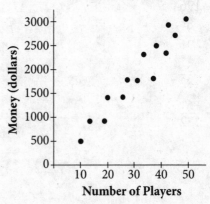

MP3 Player Sales

A   Negative correlation

B   Exponential correlation

C   Positive correlation

D   No correlation

15. Serena can select a team shirt in blue, red, or green. The letters on the team shirt can be black or white, and each shirt comes in small, medium, or large. How many different team shirts does Serena have to choose from?

A   3

B   8

C   18

D   36

16. While on a class picnic, Jorge randomly selects a drink from a cooler with 3 colas, 6 lemonades, and 5 bottles of water. Later in the day, he randomly selects another drink from the same cooler. Nobody else took any drinks from that cooler. What is the probability that both drinks Jorge selected were colas?

A $\dfrac{6}{196}$

B $\dfrac{9}{196}$

C $\dfrac{5}{182}$

D $\dfrac{6}{182}$

17. Stevie is doing a survey of the students in his high school. He would like to find the most common rate of hourly pay earned by students in part-time jobs. Which measure should Stevie use after collecting this data?

A   Mean

B   Mode

C   Range

D   Median

18. The graph below shows Hannah's times swimming the 100-meter backstroke over a 5-week period.

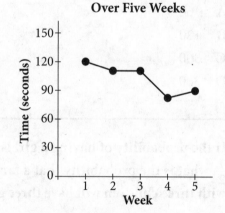

Between which 2 weeks did Hannah's time decrease the most?

A   Week 1 and week 2

B   Week 2 and week 3

C   Week 3 and week 4

D   Week 4 and week 5

19. The scatter plot below shows the amount of time students spent preparing for a test and the test scores they received. Based on the graph, which statement is most likely to be supported by the data?

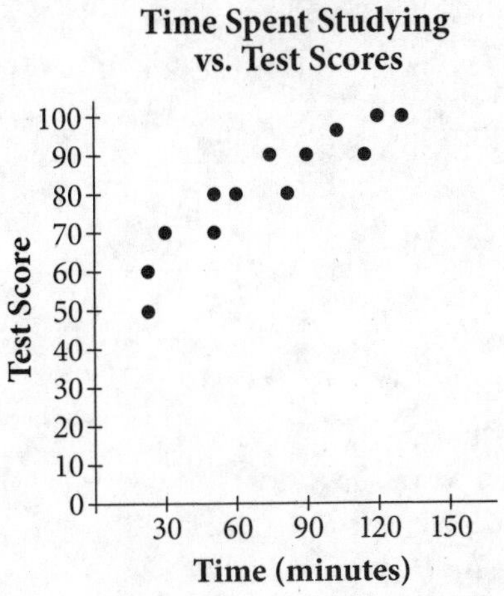

Time Spent Studying vs. Test Scores

A The test scores increase as the amount of time spent preparing for the test increases.

B The test scores decrease as the amount of time spent preparing for the test increases.

C The test scores remain unchanged as the amount of time spent preparing for the test increases.

D There is no relationship between the test scores and the amount of time spent preparing for the test.

20. The chart below shows the number of different books on a shelf in a library. If one book is selected at random, what is the probability the book is a science book?

Category	Number of Books
Math	12
Science	15
History	9
Literature	14

A 15%

B 24%

C 30%

D 50%

Answers and Explanations

1. C

The probability of an event's (E) <u>not</u> occurring is

$$P \text{ (not E)} = 1 - \frac{\text{number of ways the event can occur}}{\text{total number of possible outcomes}}.$$

Because there are 2 Ms and 2 Ts, the event can occur 4 ways out of a total of 11 letters. Therefore, the probability of <u>not</u> selecting an M or a T is equal to P with (not M or T) $= 1 - \frac{4}{11} = \frac{11}{11} - \frac{4}{11} = \frac{7}{11}$. Choice A is the probability of selecting an M or a T. If you chose B, you set up a ratio comparing the ways to select an M or a T and the ways of not selecting an M or a T. Choice D is the reciprocal of incorrect choice B.

2. B

To find the amount spent on food and lodging, first find the percent for each in the circle graph and add these amounts together: 40% + 20% = 60%. Next, find 60% of the total spent on the trip, $200. The key word *of* means "to multiply." Convert the percentage into a decimal equivalent: 60% of $200 = 0.60. Then multiply: 0.60 × 200 = 120. She spent $120 on both food and lodging on her trip. Choice A would be the amount spent on food and lodging if the total spent on the trip was $100. Choice C is the amount spent on lodging and transportation. Choice D would be the amount spent on food and lodging if the total spent on the trip was $400.

3. D

The median of a list of values is the middle number after the numbers are arranged in order. Because this is an increasing list of numbers, they are already in order. The middle number in the list is 16, so 16 is the median number of laps. Choice A is the difference between the largest and the smallest value in the list. Choice B is the mode of the data. Choice C is the mean, or average, of the data.

4. C

The mode of a set of data is the number that appears most often in the list. Because 65 appears twice and each other numbers appears only once, 65 is the mode of this set of data. Choice A is the median of the data, the number in the middle when the values are arranged in order. Choice B is the mean, or average, of the data. Choice D is the largest value in the data set.

5. D

The mean rainfall is found by adding the number of inches of rainfall for each month and then dividing by the total number of months. The sum of the inches of rainfall is $17 + 20 + 15 + 25 + 18 = 95$ inches. Divide this amount by 5 months: $95 \div 5 = 19$ inches. Choice A is the smallest value in the data set. Choice C is the median of the data, that is, the number in the middle when the values are arranged in order.

6. B

Read the line graph by matching the point directly above each day with the scale on the vertical axis. On Monday, the students read 30 books; on Tuesday, they read 25 books; on Wednesday, they read 45 books; on Thursday, they read 35 books; and on Friday, they read 50 books. The table in choice B is the only one that matches this data in the correct order. Choice A is the list of values but in reverse order. If you chose choice C, you may have misread the scale of the y-axis, which indicates the number of books.

7. B

A negative correlation is a relationship between two sets of data where as the values in one set increase, the values in the other set decrease. This would be true in choice B. As the number of people helping with a task increases, the time it takes to complete the task would most likely decrease. Each of the other choices would most likely represent positive correlations, where as the values in one set increase, the values in the other set also increase. For choice A, it is logical that as the time a person runs increases, so does the distance traveled. It is generally true that the taller the person, the larger their shoe size, so choice C would be a positive correlation. For choice D, as the number of homework assignments completed rises, logically so does the homework grade average.

8. D

This Venn diagram is made up of two intersecting circles. The numbers in the parts of the circles that do not overlap are the number of students who participate in only that activity. The number in the overlapping section is the number of students who participate in both activities. The total number of students in the chorus is the sum of the students in the chorus only (74) plus the number of students in both the band and chorus (13): 74 + 13 = 87. Choice A is the number of students in both band and chorus. Choice B is the number of students in band only. Choice C is the number of students in chorus only.

9. B

The probability of an event (E) occurring is

$$P(E) = 1 - \frac{\text{number of ways the event can occur}}{\text{total number of possible outcomes}}.$$

There are 5 red marbles out of a total of 4 + 5 + 6 = 15 marbles. Therefore, the probability is $P(\text{red}) = \frac{5}{15} = \frac{1}{3}$. Expressed as a decimal, this is $1 \div 3 \approx 0.33$. Choice A is the probability that the marble chosen is green. Choice C is the probability that the marble chosen is blue. Choice D is the number of red marbles, written incorrectly as a decimal.

10. A

To find how many more flights Smooth Skies had than Comfort Airlines, find the total number of flights over the four months for both airlines and subtract one total from another. The total for Smooth Skies is 120 + 150 + 140 + 120 = 530 flights. The total for Comfort Airlines is 140 + 150 + 110 + 100 = 500. The difference of the two totals is 530 – 500 = 30 flights. If your answer was B, you may have read one or more data points incorrectly. Choices C and D are just data values on the graph; perhaps you just looked at data values for one of the companies for the month of May.

11. D

By reading the line graph, 60 cars passed in 10 minutes, 120 cars in 20 minutes, 180 cars in 30 minutes, and 240 cars in 40 minutes. This is an increase of 60 cars every 10 minutes. Thus, in 50 minutes, the total should be 240 + 60 = 300 cars; in 60 minutes (1 hour), the total should be 300 + 60 = 360 cars. Choice A is the number of cars that passed after 10 minutes. Choice B is the number of additional cars that passed between 40 minutes (the end of the graph data) and 60 minutes. Choice C is the number of cars that passed after 50 minutes.

12. A

The probability that an event (E) will occur is

$$P(E) = \frac{\text{number of ways the event can occur}}{\text{total number of possible outcomes}}.$$

If more than one independent event is occurring, multiply the probabilities of each event to find the probability that they will happen consecutively. Because the probability of having a girl is $\frac{1}{2}$, then the probability of having three girls is $\frac{1}{2} \times \frac{1}{2} \times \frac{1}{2} = \frac{1}{8}$. If your answer was B, you incorrectly added the denominators and kept the numerator, or perhaps you multiplied 2 × 3 instead of 2 × 2 × 2. Answer choice C is the probability of having a girl, not the probability of having three girls. If you chose choice D, you added the probabilities instead of multiplying. Remember that answer choice D could not make sense, because a probability cannot be greater than 1.

13. D

The probability that an event (E) will occur is

$$P(E) = \frac{\text{number of ways the event can occur}}{\text{total number of possible outcomes}}.$$

Because Jason used 1 tile on the first turn, he only has 5 tiles left. There is only one R, so the probability he will use an R next is $P(R) = \frac{1}{5}$. Choice A is the combined probability of using an S and then an R. This problem only asks for the probability of using an R when the S is already gone. Choice C would be the probability of using an R if the S had never been used.

14. C

As the number of students attending the school play increases, the amount of ticket sales also increases. Because both data sets increase, this is a positive correlation. If A were the correct choice, the graph would have had a downward slant, or trend. Choice B would show a curved trend. If D were the correct choice, the data would be randomly scattered on the graph and would not approximate a straight line.

15. C

Using the fundamental counting principle, multiply the number of choices in each category to find the total number of possibilities. There are 3 choices of colors, 2 choices for the letters, and 3 choices of size. Thus, the total number of different shirts is $3 \times 2 \times 3 = 18$. Answer choice A is just the number of colors there are to choose from. If you chose B, you added the choices instead of multiplying.

16. D

The probability of an event (E) happening is

$$P(E) = \frac{\text{number of ways the event can occur}}{\text{total number of possible outcomes}}.$$

If more than one event is happening consecutively, multiply the probabilities together. The probability that the first drink is a cola is $\frac{3}{14}$, because there are 3 colas in the cooler and a total of 14 drinks. The probability that the next drink chosen is also a cola must take into account the fact that the first cola is gone. The probability that the second drink is a cola is $\frac{2}{13}$, because there are only 2 colas and a total of 13 drinks left in the cooler. Multiply the probabilities together: $\frac{3}{13} \times \frac{2}{13} = \frac{6}{182}$. If you chose answer choice A, you mistakenly left the denominator of the second probability at 14 instead of changing it to 13. Answer choice B is the probability of selecting a cola, replacing it, and randomly selecting a cola again. If your answer was C, you may have mistakenly added the numerators instead of multiplying.

17. B

In this question, Stevie is looking for the most common rate of pay, or the pay that occurs most often. The value that occurs most often is the mode of the data, so he should find the mode. Choice A, the mean, is the average rate of hourly pay, not necessarily the most common. Choice C, the range, is the difference between the highest pay and the lowest pay. Choice D, the median, is the middle value when all of the rates of pay are put in numerical order.

18. C

The best time for a swimming event is the lowest time. The place on the graph that shows the greatest decrease in swimming time is the place on the line with the steepest drop. In week 3, her time was approximately 110 seconds. In week 4, her time was approximately 80 seconds. This is a drop of about 30 seconds and is the greatest decrease during this 5-week period. Choice A is the first decrease, but the improvement is only 10 seconds, which is lower than the drop of 30 seconds. Choice B is the period in which there was no change in performance. Choice D is the period in which there was an increase, not a decrease.

19. A

In the scatter plot, test scores increase as the time spent studying increases. For example, a person who studied 30 minutes received 60 on the test, a person who studied for 90 minutes received a 90 on the test, and a person who studied 120 minutes received a 95 on the test. This is the general trend of the graph. If choice B were true, the graph would show a downward slant or trend. If choice C were true, the graph would approximate a horizontal line. If choice D were true, the points would be randomly scattered and would not approximate a straight line.

20. C

The probability that an event (E) will occur is

$$P(E) = \frac{\text{number of ways the event can occur}}{\text{total number of possible outcomes}}.$$

Because there are a total of 50 books and 15 of them are science books, the probability is P(science book) = $\frac{15}{50}$. To change the fraction to a percent, first divide: 15 ÷ 50 = 0.30. Then, multiply 0.30 by 100 to get a final answer of 30%. Choice A is the number of science books incorrectly written as a percent. Choice B is the probability of randomly selecting a math book. Choice D is the total number of books incorrectly written as a decimal.

Algebra and Functions

HOW TO APPROACH ALGEBRA PROBLEMS

This chapter will give you a chance to review the basic algebra concepts that you'll see on the test. Remember, algebra problems may look complicated, but there are strategies you can use to make the problems less intimidating and easier to understand.

Kaplan's Four Strategies for Solving Algebra Problems

STRATEGY 1: Read through the question carefully.

STRATEGY 2: Decide whether to do the problem or skip it for now.

STRATEGY 3: Use either the picking-numbers strategy or the backsolving strategy.

STRATEGY 4: Make an educated guess.

STRATEGY 1: READ THROUGH THE QUESTION CAREFULLY

You need to read the question carefully and deliberately before you start solving the problem. If you don't, it's easy to make careless mistakes. Consider the following problem:

Jane is a salesperson for PDQ Carpet Company. In the last 3 years, she earned $36,000, $38,000, and $40,000 dollars annually. What is her approximate average monthly income?

A $3,000

B $15,000

C $30,000

D $38,000

It's crucial that you play close attention to precisely what the question asks. This question contains a classic trap that's very easy to fall into if you don't read carefully. You are asked to solve for Jane's monthly income, not her yearly income. Solving for her yearly income would be a careless error; you would not get the right answer **A**, even though you knew how to do the math.

A second reason to read the entire question carefully before you start solving is that you may save yourself some work. If you start answering too quickly, you may assume a problem is more or less difficult than it actually is.

STRATEGY 2: DECIDE WHETHER TO DO THE PROBLEM OR SKIP IT FOR NOW

- Another reason to read carefully before answering is that you don't have to solve every problem on your first pass. Each time you approach a new math problem, you have the option of doing it now or putting it aside until later.
- If you can solve the problem quickly and efficiently, do it! This is the best option.
- If you think you can solve it but it will take you a long time, circle the number in your test booklet and go back to it later.

STRATEGY 3: USE EITHER THE PICKING-NUMBERS STRATEGY OR THE BACKSOLVING STRATEGY

If you choose to tackle any given problem, consider picking numbers or backsolving. Depending on the problem, look for the method that is fastest for you.

Patricia is *a* years old, and her brother Mark is 5 years older than she. In terms of *a*, how old will Mark be in 3 years?

A $3(a + 5)$

B $a + 5 - 3$

C $a + 3$

D $a + 5 + 3$

You could solve the problem using algebra. If Patricia is *a* years old, then Mark is $a + 5$ years old. In three years, he will be $a + 5 + 3$ years old. Thus answer choice **D** is the correct choice.

You could also solve the problem by picking numbers. Let's say Patricia is 12 years old. That makes Mark, who is 5 years older, 17. In three years, he'll be 20. Now substitute Patricia's age, 12, for the unknown *a* in all the answer choices and see which equation gives us the result we're looking for—20. Once you try all the answer choices, only **D** works.

Try backsolving when the answer choices are numbers.

What is the value of *x* in the equation $6x - 7 = 11$?

A 12

B 8

C 4

D 3

You can solve this problem with algebra by solving for *x*. First, add 7 to both sides. This gives you $6x = 18$. Then divide both sides by 6. This gives you $x = 3$.

You can also solve this problem by backsolving. First, plug answer choice A into the equation: $12 \times 6 - 7 = 65$. This cannot be the correct choice, because the equation should yield 11. Because 65 is much bigger than 11, you can tell that larger numbers probably won't work in this equation. Try skipping answer choice B and moving on to answer choice C. Plugging in 4 gives $4 \times 6 - 7 = 17$. This is not the correct choice, but you can tell that by choosing smaller numbers, you are getting closer to the answer (17 is much closer to 11 than 65). Now try backsolving for answer choice D: $3 \times 6 - 7 = 11$. Answer choice **D**, 3, is correct.

STRATEGY 4: MAKE AN EDUCATED GUESS

Don't leave answers blank on the CAHSEE. Because there's no penalty for wrong answers, there is no harm in guessing when you don't know the answer. However, you should guess strategically whenever possible to maximize your chance of getting the answer right. Remember, each answer choice you eliminate increases your odds of choosing the correct answer. Look at the question below to begin to understand how to make an educated guess.

What is the greatest prime factor of 26 and 273?

A   13
B   4
C   2
D   5

If you read this problem and cannot remember how to find a factor, let alone a prime factor, or if you are running out of time and want to save your time for other questions, you should be able to eliminate at least one answer choice pretty easily. Do you see which one?

Because all multiples of 5 end in either 5 or 0, the number 5 cannot be a factor of 26. So choice D must be wrong. You could also easily eliminate choices B and C, because multiples of 4 and 2 must be even numbers. **A**, 13, is the correct answer.

As you can see, there is often more than one way to do a particular problem. The best method is whichever one will help you arrive at the correct answer accurately and quickly.

SIMPLIFYING EXPRESSIONS

An *expression* is a mathematical statement, like 2 + 3 or 3*xy*, made of numbers or variables connected by operations. Complicated expressions are difficult to work with, so many CAHSEE questions will require you to simplify them by performing the given operations.

When you're simplifying a complicated expression, you must do the arithmetic in the correct order to get the correct answer. First, simplify anything inside parentheses. Absolute value signs and fraction bars also function as parentheses.

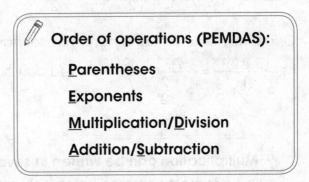

Order of operations (PEMDAS):

Parentheses

Exponents

Multiplication/Division

Addition/Subtraction

You should simplify any part of an expression inside absolute value signs as though it were in parentheses. If there are multiple sets of parentheses, absolute value signs, or fractions, start from the inside and work out.

Then, evaluate any values with exponents. Next, multiply and divide from left to right. Finally, add and subtract from left to right. A fraction bar acts like a grouping symbol; you'll simplify the numerator and the denominator separately, then divide them as the last step. The acronym PEMDAS or the phrase "Please Excuse My Dear Aunt Sally" can help you remember the order of operations: Parentheses, Exponents, Multiplication and Division (from left to right), and Addition and Subtraction (from left to right).

Which of the following is equivalent to the expression $\dfrac{(5+2)^2}{6+\frac{1}{2}\times 2}$ **?**

A $2\dfrac{3}{13}$

B $3\dfrac{10}{13}$

C $4\dfrac{1}{7}$

D 7

Follow the order of operations. Start by simplifying the part of the expression that is inside parentheses: $5 + 2 = 7$. Next, evaluate the exponent: $7^2 = 49$. That's as simple as the numerator can get, so move on to the denominator.

According to the order of operations, you should always multiply before you add, so start there: $6 + \frac{1}{2} \times 2 = 6 + \frac{2}{2} = 6 + 1 = 7$.

Once the numerator and denominator have been simplified, the expression is $\frac{(5 + 2)^2}{6 + \frac{1}{2} \times 2} = \frac{7^2}{6 + \frac{2}{2}} = \frac{49}{7}$. Now you can divide: $\frac{49}{7} = 7$, choice **D**.

 Multiplication can be written in several different ways. The form $a \times b$ is most common when only numbers are involved, but $a \cdot b$, ab, and $a(b)$ are frequently used with variables.

A *variable* is a letter used to represent a number. If you are asked to evaluate an expression with variables and you're given the values of variables, just substitute in the values wherever you see the variables, then simplify the expression.

If $r = 4$ and $s = 7$, what is the value of $\frac{6r + 4s}{rs - 5r}$?

A $2\frac{1}{10}$

B $6\frac{1}{2}$

C $8\frac{2}{7}$

D 17

Substitute in the values of r and s: $\frac{6r + 4s}{rs - 5r} = \frac{6(4) + 4(7)}{(4)(7) - 5(4)} = \frac{24 + 28}{28 - 20} = \frac{52}{8} = 6\frac{4}{8} = 6\frac{1}{2}$. **B** is correct. Some questions ask you to simplify an expression with one or more variables but don't give you any values for the variables. You can still simplify these expressions by treating the variables like numbers.

$$\frac{8a + 7a}{3a} =$$

A   5

B   15

C   5a

D   15a

First, add the terms in the numerator. Because $8a$ is 8 times a and $7a$ is 7 times a, when you add these terms, you get $(8 + 7)$ times a, or $15a$. To put it another way, $8 + 7 = 15$, so $8a + 7a = 15a$. Or to express it yet another way, $8a$ is $a + a + a + a + a + a + a + a$, and $7a$ is $a + a + a + a + a + a + a$, so $8a + 7a = a + a + a + a + a + a + a + a + a + a + a + a + a + a + a = 15a$.

$$\frac{8a + 7a}{3a} = \frac{15a}{3a}$$

Next, divide the numerator by the denominator. The easiest way to do so is to factor the numerator and denominator, then cancel out the terms that appear in both places. You don't have to know what a variable stands for to cancel it out: $\frac{x}{x} = 1$ no matter what x is. (The exception is when $x = 0$, but you won't need to worry about that on the CAHSEE. Like 0^0, dividing by 0 is undefined. This test won't ask you to do it, so if you find yourself trying, something's wrong.)

$$\frac{15a}{3a} = \frac{3 \times 5 \times a}{3 \times a} = 5$$

That leaves you with 5, choice **A**.

Pick numbers when:

- **there are variables in the answer choices; or**
- **the question describes a relationship between numbers without giving any specific numbers.**

Pick numbers that are:

- **appropriate (follow any rules given in the question); and**
- **easy to work with (small, easily divisible by other numbers in the question, or, for percents, 100).**

If you find variables confusing, you can avoid them by *picking numbers*. Say $a = 2$. Then $\frac{8a + 7a}{3a} = \frac{8(2) + 7(2)}{3(2)} = \frac{16 + 14}{6} = \frac{30}{6} = 5$. That's choice **A**. Choice C is $5(2) = 10$, and choice D is $15(2) = 30$. If you picked $a = 1$, then choices A and C would come out to be the same number, because $5(1) = 5$. If you accidentally pick a number that makes two answer choices the same on the test, don't worry. Just try those answer choices again with a different number.

One thing to watch out for is that you can only add or subtract *like terms*, terms that have the same variable or the same exponent. For example, $2x$, $7x$, and $-3x$ are like terms, because they all have x in them. You can add them to get $2x + 7x + (-3x) = 6x$. However, $4x^2$ and $4x^3$ are not like terms. As x^2 has a different exponent from x^3, you can't combine terms containing x^2 with terms containing x^3.

Simplify $8 - 2t + 3s + 2t + 5s$.

A $16s$

B $8 + 8s$

C $8 - 4t + 8s$

D $8 + 4t + 8s$

To simplify this expression, group all the like terms together so you can see which ones to add and subtract:

$$8 - 2t + 3s + 2t + 5s = 8 - 2t + 2t + 3s + 5s = 8 + 8s$$

That's choice **B**. Remember that addition is commutative, so the terms in the answer could be written in a different order and still be correct.

If you're multiplying or dividing expressions with *coefficients* (numbers before variables), multiply or divide the coefficients and the variables separately. For instance, $4x(5x) = 4 \cdot x \cdot 5 \cdot x = 4 \cdot 5 \cdot x \cdot x = 20x^2$.

$4a + 5a(6a + 2a) - (5a^2 + 2a \times a) =$

A $4a - 33a^2$

B $4a + 33a^2$

C $44a - 7a^2$

D $44a + 7a^2$

Again, start inside the parentheses, following PEMDAS:

$$4a + 5a(6a + 2a) - (5a^2 + 2a \cdot a) =$$
$$4a + 5a(8a) - (5a^2 + 2a^2) = 4a + 5a(8a) - (7a^2)$$

Because no values with exponents need to be simplified, multiplication is next:

$$4a + 5a(8a) - (7a^2) = 4a + 40a^2 - 7a^2$$

Last, add and subtract the like terms from left to right:

$$4a + 40a^2 - 7a^2 = 4a + 33a^2$$

You can't simplify any further, because $4a$ and $33a^2$ are unlike terms, so you're done. Choice **B** is correct.

The *distributive property*, $a(b + c) = ab + ac$ or $a(b - c) = ab - ac$, is particularly useful when you're trying to simplify a complicated expression that includes variables. By the order of operations, you should add the terms inside parentheses first, but if they aren't like terms, you can't do that. The distributive property lets you skip the addition and subtraction step and keep going. To use the distributive property, multiply each term inside the parentheses by the term outside the parentheses.

Exponents can also be distributed. They follow the rule $(ab)^c = a^c b^c$. In practice, this usually looks something like $(3x)^2 = 3^2 x^2 = 9x^2$.

Be particularly careful distributing multiplication or exponents when negative numbers are involved. You have to distribute the negative sign along with the coefficient. If you can simplify the expression inside the parentheses, this is easy to see, but it's much less obvious if you need to distribute. For example, $-2(4 + 3) = -2(7) = -14$, and $-2(4 + 3) = (-2)(4) + (-2)(3) = -8 - 6 = -14$. However, $-2(4 + a) = -8 - 2a$, not $-8 + 2a$.

$7(x + y) + 3x \cdot 2x - x(7 + x) - (2x)^2 =$

A $x^2 + 7y$

B $5x^2 + 7y$

C $10x^2 - 7x + 7y$

D $15x^2$

Nothing in the parentheses in this expression can be simplified, so go on to the next step, exponents: $(2x)^2$ is $2^2 \cdot x^2$, or $4x^2$. Multiplication is next, so distribute across the parentheses and perform the other multiplication (watch out for that negative!):

$$7(x + y) + 3x \cdot 2x - x(7 + x) - 4x^2 = 7x + 7y + 6x^2 - 7x - x^2 - 4x^2$$

And, last, add and subtract the like terms:

$$7x + 7y + 6x^2 - 7x - x^2 - 4x^2 = (7x - 7x) + (6x^2 - x^2 - 4x^2) + 7y = x^2 + 7y$$

Choice **A** is correct.

Many questions will test your knowledge of the rules of exponents. These work just the same with variables as they do with numbers.

$$\frac{gh}{g^3h} \cdot \frac{g^3h}{gh^{-1}} =$$

A $\dfrac{g}{h}$

B $\dfrac{h}{g}$

C g

D h

> ✏️ **Exponent rules:**
>
> $a^b \times a^c = a^{b+c}$
>
> $\dfrac{a^b}{a^c} = a^{b-c}$
>
> $(a^b)^c = a^{bc}$
>
> $a^0 = 1$
>
> $a^{-b} = \dfrac{1}{a^b}$

Because this question only uses multiplication and division, you can simplify it in any order you want.

One easy way is to simplify each fraction as much as possible, then multiply. First, cancel out anything that appears in the numerator and denominator of each fraction:

$$\frac{gh}{g^3h^2} = \frac{\cancel{g} \cdot \cancel{h}}{\cancel{g} \cdot g \cdot g \cdot \cancel{h} \cdot h} = \frac{1}{g \cdot g \cdot h}$$

$$\frac{g^2h}{gh^{-1}} = \frac{g \cdot g \cdot h}{g \cdot \dfrac{1}{h}} = \frac{\cancel{g} \cdot g \cdot h \cdot h}{\cancel{g}} = g \cdot h \cdot h$$

Now multiply the simplified fractions.

$$\frac{1}{g \cdot g \cdot h} \cdot g \cdot h \cdot h = \frac{\cancel{g} \cdot \cancel{h} \cdot h}{g \cdot \cancel{g} \cdot \cancel{h}} = \frac{h}{g}$$

That's choice **B**.

You could also use the rules of exponents:

$$\frac{gh}{g^3h^2} \cdot \frac{g^2h}{gh^{-1}} = g^{(1-3)}h^{(1-2)} \cdot g^{(2-1)}h^{[1-(-1)]} =$$

$$g^{-2}h^{-1} \cdot g^1h^2 = g^{(-2+1)}h^{(-1+2)} = g^{-1}h^1 = \frac{h}{g}$$

Don't worry if you see an ugly, complicated-looking expression. Once you start simplifying, it'll make a lot more sense.

$\sqrt{9x^4} + (2x)^2 - 3x \cdot 2x =$

A $\quad x^2$

B $\quad 2x^2$

C $\quad 7x^2 - 6x$

D $\quad 5x^4 - 6x$

> ✏ **Square root rules:**
>
> $$\sqrt{a^2} = (\sqrt{a})^2 = a$$
>
> $$\sqrt{ab} = \sqrt{a} \times \sqrt{b}$$
>
> $$\sqrt{\frac{a}{b}} = \frac{\sqrt{a}}{\sqrt{b}}$$
>
> **(for $a \geq 0$ and $b > 0$)**

Because $\sqrt{9x^4} = \sqrt{9} \cdot \sqrt{x^4} = 3 \cdot x^2$, the whole expression becomes $\sqrt{9x^4} + (2x)^2 - 3x \cdot 2x = 3x^2 + 4x^2 - 3x \cdot 2x = 3x^2 + 4x^2 - 6x^2 = x^2$. Choice **A** is correct.

> **Picking numbers lets you work with easy numbers instead of complicated variables.**

Or if you're not sure how to simplify that square root, pick numbers. Say x is 2:

$$\sqrt{9x^4} + (2x)^2 - 3x \cdot 2x = \sqrt{9(2^4)} + (2 \cdot 2)^2 - 3(2) \cdot 2(2) =$$

$$\sqrt{9(16)} + 4^2 - 6 \cdot 2 \cdot 2 = \sqrt{144} + 16 - 24 = 12 + 16 - 24 = 4$$

Plug $x = 2$ into each answer choice to see which is also equal to 4.

A $2^2 = 4$

Perfect! Check the other answer choices as well to be sure this is the only one that works. That's a way to confirm that you did the math right.

B $2(2^2) = 2(4) = 8$
C $7(2^2) - 6(2) = 7(4) - 6(2) = 28 - 12 = 16$
D $5(2^4) - 6(2) = 5(16) - 6(2) = 80 - 12 = 68$

SOLVING EQUATIONS AND INEQUALITIES

Equations

An *equation* is two expressions that represent the same quantity, connected by an equal sign. Many CAHSEE questions will require you to write, solve, or manipulate equations, so you'll want to have these skills down cold.

Usually, one side of an equation contains a variable you're trying to *solve for*, or find the value of. To solve for a variable, get that variable alone on one side of the equation. To isolate the variable, do the opposite of whatever the equation says, until eventually the variable in question will be alone on one side of the equation.

 The most important thing you absolutely positively must remember about solving equations: you MUST do the same thing to both sides.

The whole time you're working with an equation, you must keep the sides equal. Whether you're adding, subtracting, multiplying, dividing, finding the square root, or taking a number to the hundredth power, you must always do the same thing to both sides so that they continue to be equal.

What is the value of x when $4x + 5 = 25$?

A   4

B   5

C   105

D   120

Start isolating the variable by getting all the parts of the equation that have the variable in them on one side and all the parts that are just numbers on the other side. In this case, you'll need to subtract 5 from both sides to get all the numbers on the right-hand side of the equation:

$$4x + 5 = 25$$
$$4x + 5 - 5 = 25 - 5$$
$$4x = 20$$

Then, divide both sides by 4 to get x alone:

$$\frac{4x}{4} = \frac{02}{4}$$
$$x = 5$$

That's choice **B**.

If $\dfrac{4 - 6q}{2} = -13$, what is q?

A   −5

B   −4

C   4

D   5

Start by multiplying both sides by 2 to get rid of the fraction. This will make the left side of the equation much easier to work with.

$$\frac{4 - 6q}{2} = -13$$

$$\frac{4 - 6q}{2}(2) = -13(2)$$

$$4 - 6q = -26$$

Next, subtract 4 from both sides to get all the terms that are just numbers on one side of the equation:

$$4 - 6q - 4 = -26 - 4$$

$$-6q = -30$$

Divide by –6 to isolate q:

$$\frac{-6q}{-6} = \frac{-30}{-6}$$

$$q = 5$$

That's choice **D**.

> ✏️ **Backsolving lets you avoid algebra.**

If you want to double-check your answer, if you forget a rule, or if you just think all this algebra takes a long time, backsolving is a great alternative. Just plug the answer choices into the original equation and see which one works. It's usually a good idea to start in the middle of the options, so start with C.

Choice C gives you $\frac{4 - 6(4)}{2} = \frac{4 - 24}{2} = \frac{-20}{2} = -10$. That's not the original equation, so choice C is incorrect. It looks as though q needs to be larger than 4 to make $\frac{4 - 6q}{2}$ less than –10. (If you're not sure whether you need a larger number or a smaller number, just try the one that's easier to work with. You can always check the other answer choices later if you need to.)

Choice **D** gives you $\frac{4 - 6(5)}{2} = \frac{4 - 30}{2} = \frac{-26}{2} = -13$. That's perfect.

Again, read every question carefully. You may not always be asked to solve for the obvious thing.

If $d(5 + 3d) = 3d^2 + 1$, what is the value of $5d$?

A −4

B $\dfrac{1}{5}$

C 1

D 5

Distribute the left-hand side of the equation:

$$d(5 + 3d) = 3d^2 + 1$$
$$5d + 3d^2 = 3d^2 + 1$$

Because $3d^2$ appears on both sides of the equation, you can subtract it to get rid of it:

$$5d + 3d^2 - 3d^2 = 3d^2 + 1 - 3d^2$$
$$5d = 1$$

You're done! That's all this question asks for, and the correct answer is **C**. It's tempting to solve for d and choose incorrect answer choice B, so be sure to double-check what the question asks for before you fill in your answer.

Inequalities

An *inequality* is a way of comparing two expressions that are not equal. The symbols <, >, ≤, and ≥ tell you that the expression on the left is less than, greater than, less than or equal to, or greater than or equal to the expression on the right.

 $a < b$ is the same as $b > a$. Answer choices might be written differently than your solution, so look for the one that means the same thing.

Negative numbers can be a little confusing to put in order, but you can't go wrong as long as you remember that the greater number is the one further to the right on a number line.

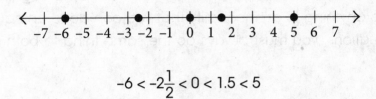

$$-6 < -2\frac{1}{2} < 0 < 1.5 < 5$$

A range of possible values is represented by a line segment on a number line. If the possible values include the endpoint of the line segment, it's marked by a filled-in circle like those above. If the possible values don't include the endpoint, it's marked by an open circle. That's the difference between ≤ (less than or equal to; does include the endpoint) and < (less than; doesn't include the endpoint).

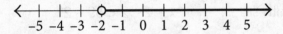

This could be written as $x > -2$ or $-2 < x$. Either way, x could be any number greater than –2 but could not be equal to –2.

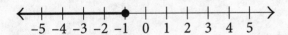

This could be written as $x \leq 1$ or $1 \geq x$, and x could be 1 or any number less than 1.

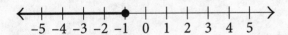

Ranges can be limited at both ends. If you know that $x > -2$ and $x \leq 1$, you can combine those inequalities and write $-2 < x \leq 1$.

> ✏️ **If $a < b$, then $-a > -b$.**

Solving an inequality is just like solving an equation, with one extra thing to keep in mind: if you multiply or divide by a negative number, you must reverse the inequality symbol. As long as you remember to change the direction of the inequality symbol when you multiply or divide by a negative number, you can do anything to an inequality that you can do to an equation. Just as with equations, you must always do the same thing to both sides of an inequality.

Simplify $3x + 2 < 65$.

A $x < 3$

B $x < 14$

C $x < 19$

D $x < 21$

Write out the inequality: $\qquad$ $3x + 2 < 65$

Subtract 2 from both sides: $\qquad$ $3x + 2 - 2 < 65 - 2$

Simplify: $\qquad$ $3x < 63$

Divide both sides by 3: $\qquad$ $\dfrac{3x}{3} < \dfrac{63}{3}$

Simplify: $\qquad$ $x < 21$

Choice **D** is correct.

Solve for *x*.

$$15 \leq \frac{-5x}{2}$$

A $x \leq -6$

B $x \geq -6$

C $x \leq 6$

D $x \geq 6$

Write out the inequality: $\qquad 15 \leq \frac{-5x}{2}$

Multiply both sides by 2: $\qquad 15(2) \leq \frac{-5x}{2}(2)$

Simplify: $\qquad 30 \leq -5x$

Divide both sides by –5 (remember to change the direction of the inequality symbol, because you are dividing by a negative number): $\frac{30}{-5} \geq \frac{-5x}{-5}$

Simplify: $\quad -6 \geq x$

The expression "–6 is greater than or equal to *x*" is the same as "*x* is less than or equal to –6," so choice **A** is correct.

Remember to double-check exactly what a question is asking for before filling in your answer. Be sure you've answered the right question.

If $5y + 7 > 32$, which of the following could be the value of y ?

A 2

B 3

C 5

D 7

Write out the inequality:	$5y + 7 > 32$
Subtract 7 from both sides:	$5y + 7 - 7 > 32 - 7$
Simplify:	$5y > 25$
Divide both sides by 5:	$\dfrac{-5y}{5} > \dfrac{25}{5}$
Simplify:	$y > 5$

This means that y is greater than 5, so choice **D** is the only possible value of y. Note that y must be greater than 5, not equal to 5, so choice C is not correct.

TRANSLATING VERBAL STATEMENTS TO MATHEMATICAL EXPRESSIONS

Expressions and equations can be written with words instead of with numbers and variables.

 CAHSEE word problems can range from simple descriptions of an equation to complex situations involving rates and time.

Word problems aren't asking you for anything you don't know how to find. They're just phrasing the question a little differently. Think about the situation to understand what the question is asking for, then translate it into an equation or expression.

Which of the following equations contains the same information as the statement "The sum of 15 and x is equal to 5 times x divided by 3"?

A $15x = \dfrac{5 + x}{3}$

B $\dfrac{15x}{3} = \dfrac{5x}{3}$

C $\dfrac{15 + x}{3} = 5x$

D $15 + x = \dfrac{5x}{3}$

"The sum of 15 and x" is what you get when you add 15 and x. You can write it as $15 + x$. This quantity "is equal to" something else, so include an equal sign to get $15 + x =$. Then we read "5 times x," which is $5x$, and $5x$ "divided by 3" is $\dfrac{5x}{3}$. The whole sentence translates to $15 + x = \dfrac{5x}{3}$, which is choice **D**.

Choice A would be "The product of 15 and x is equal to the sum of 5 and x divided by 3." Choice B would be "The product of 15 and x divided by 3 is equal to the product of 5 and x divided by 3." Choice C would be "The sum of 15 and x divided by 3 is equal to the product of 5 and x."

Some common ways to write mathematical operators in English are shown in the table below. Look for these key words to figure out how to turn a long English description into an expression, equation, or inequality.

	Translation Table
=	equals, is, was, will be, has, costs, gets
<	less than, fewer than, under
>	more than, greater than, over
≤	less than or equal to, at most, up to and including, maximum, no more than
≥	greater than or equal to, at least, minimum, no less than
×	multiplied by, times, of, product, each
÷	divided by, per, out of, each
+	plus, added to, sum of, combined, total, more than, and, exceed
−	minus, subtracted from, less than, decreased by, reduced by, difference between

Some words can mean more than one thing, depending on how they appear in the question. Pay attention to the situation to be sure you're translating them correctly.

Calvin bought some school supplies. He bought one binder for $2.50, four notebooks for $1.50 each, five pencils for $0.25 each, and an eraser for $0.30. Which of these expressions represents the amount Calvin paid for all the school supplies, in dollars?

A $1 + 2.50 + 4 + 1.50 + 5 + 0.25 + 0.30$

B $2.50 + 1.50 + 0.25 + 0.30$

C $2.50 + \dfrac{1.50}{4} + \dfrac{0.25}{5} + 0.30$

D $2.50 + 4(1.50) + 5(0.25) + 0.30$

Here, *each* tells you that the price given is the price of one notebook or pencil. To find the total amount Calvin spent on notebooks and pencils, multiply the given number purchased by the price of each item. Add up the prices of all the items Calvin bought to get the total amount he paid.

One binder for $2.50 is 2.50.
Four notebooks for $1.50 each is 4(1.50).
Five pencils for $0.25 each is 5(0.25).
An eraser for $0.30 is 0.30.

The amount Calvin paid for all the school supplies is 2.50 + 4(1.50) + 5(0.25) + 0.30, or choice **D**.

Use variables to represent unknown quantities. Most questions with variables in the answer choices will tell you what variables to use.

A sign at an amusement park says, "You must be at least 48 inches tall to get on this ride." Which of the following inequalities represents the information on this sign, if h is the height in inches of a person who can get on the ride?

A $h > 48$

B $h < 48$

C $h \geq 48$

D $h \leq 48$

If the person is at least 48 inches tall, that person is either 48 inches tall or taller than 48 inches. The height, h, must be greater than or equal to 48 inches, so choice **C** is correct.

Some questions will require you to turn more than one sentence into an equation. Translate one statement at a time to answer these questions with the least risk of making a mistake.

A bag contains r red and g green gumballs. There are 85 red and green gumballs in the bag, and there are 25 more red gumballs than green gumballs. Which of the following systems of equations correctly describes the number of gumballs of each color in the bag?

A $r + g = 85$

  $r = g + 25$

B $r + g = 85$

  $g = r + 25$

C $r + g = 85$

  $r = g - 25$

D $r - g = 85$

  $r = 25 - g$

Because there are 85 red and green gumballs, the sum of the number of red gumballs and the number of green gumballs is 85. That means that $r + g = 85$. Because there are 25 more red gumballs than green gumballs, $r = g + 25$. These two equations are found in choice **A**.

Parentheses aren't written in words the way operations are, so you need to understand the situation described in a word problem to figure out whether you need them.

Felicia is buying tickets to an art museum. Tickets are normally $t each, but Felicia has a coupon that lets her save $2 per ticket. How much will Felicia pay, in dollars, for 4 tickets when she uses her coupon?

A $2t - 4$
B $4(t - 2)$
C $4t - 2$
D $4(2t)$

Each ticket will cost $t - 2$ dollars with the coupon. Because Felicia is buying 4 tickets, multiply the whole cost of 1 ticket by 4 to get $4(t - 2)$. That's choice **B**.

Choice C would be correct if the coupon was $2 off for the whole purchase, but because it applies to each ticket, the subtraction must go within parentheses.

 Picking numbers can make a word problem easier to understand.

If you're not sure how to translate a word problem or you want to check your answer, try picking numbers. If tickets usually cost $5, then the price with the coupon is $5 – $2 = $3. Therefore, 4 tickets will costs 4($3) = $12. Plug $t = 5$ into each answer choice to see which one equals 12.

A $2(5) - 4 = 10 - 4 = 6$
B $4(5 - 2) = 4(3) = 12$
C $4(5) - 2 = 20 - 2 = 18$
D $4[2(5)] = 4(10) = 40$

Only choice **B** works, so it must be correct.

Many questions will require you not only to come up with an equation or inequality, but also to solve it. Use your translating skills to turn the English description into math, then solve for whatever you need to find.

Samantha bought a 15-pound bag of dog food for her three dogs. If each dog eats the same amount of food, how many pounds of food will each dog eat?

A   3
B   5
C   12
D   15

For each of the three dogs to eat the same amount of food, the 15-pound bag must be divided evenly among them. That means that each dog will eat $\frac{15}{3} = 5$ pounds of food, choice **B**.

 Backsolving is a great way to double-check word problems.

You can also find the answer to this problem (or any word problem with numbers in the answer choices) by backsolving, plugging each answer choice into the question. Backsolving is a great alternative if translating the problem into math leaves you with a complicated equation. In some cases, it can even be faster than solving the problem algebraically.

Each answer choice represents the number of pounds of food that each dog eats, so all three dogs together will eat 3 times that. Plug in each answer choice to see which one times 3 is 15. Start in the middle so you can see whether you need a bigger or smaller number.

C $12 \times 3 = 36$

That's much too large, so try a smaller number.

B $5 \times 3 = 15$

Perfect!

Twice Jamil's weekly salary is less than half of Carla's weekly salary. Carla's weekly salary is $600. Which of the following inequalities correctly describes Jamil's weekly salary in dollars, J?

A $J < 150$

B $J < 300$

C $J < 600$

D $J < 1,200$

Translate the sentence into an inequality. Twice Jamil's weekly salary is $2J$, and half of Carla's weekly salary is $\frac{1}{2}(600)$. Once you know both sides of the inequality and have connected them with the correct symbol, you just need to solve for J.

Write the inequality: $2J < \frac{1}{2}(600)$

Simplify: $2J < 300$

Divide both sides by 2: $\frac{2J}{2} < \frac{300}{2}$

Simplify: $J < 150$

That's choice **A**. Jamil's weekly salary is less than $150.

Alex can knit 6 socks in a month. Joanne can knit 4 socks in a month. How many socks can they both knit in 5 months?

A   10

B   20

C   30

D   50

Once again, whenever you solve a word problem, make sure you've found the answer to the actual question. Here, it's easy to find the number of socks Alex and Joanne can knit in a month and forget to multiply that by 5 to get the answer to the question. In one month, Alex and Joanne can knit 6 + 4 = 10 socks, so in 5 months they can knit 10 × 5 = 50 socks, or choice **D**.

RATES

A *rate* compares two things that are measured in different units (miles per hour, words per page, gallons of paint per square foot of wall, etc.). When you see the word *per*, you've probably got a rate on your hands. A rate can be any "something per something."

When one thing increases at a constant rate as something else increases, the relationship between them is called *direct variation*. Direct variation can be written as $y = kx$, where k is a constant and x and y are the things that vary.

Danielle has painted $\frac{1}{3}$ of her room in 2 hours. If she continues painting at the same rate, how long will it take her to paint the rest of her room?

A $\frac{2}{3}$ hours

B $\frac{3}{2}$ hours

C 4 hours

D 6 hours

The rate here is rooms painted per hour. As the fraction of the room being painted goes up, the time it takes to paint it will also go up. Danielle still needs to paint $1 - \frac{1}{3} = \frac{2}{3}$ of her room. That's twice as much as she's already painted, so painting the rest of the room will take twice as long as painting the first third: 2 × 2 hours = 4 hours. Choice **C** is correct. A common error is to choose answer choice D, which is the total time to do the job, not the time it takes to paint the rest of the room. Be sure you know what the question asks for before you fill in your answer.

Estimating answers is a great strategy for solving rates problems. Here, you know it took Danielle 2 hours to paint $\frac{1}{3}$ of her room. That means it'll take her at least that long to paint the rest of it, so choices A and B are clearly too small. Because multiplying when you should have divided and dividing when you should have multiplied are very common errors on this type of problem, those results tend to turn up in the wrong answer choices. Making a simple estimate of the answer can help you eliminate answers that are clearly too big or too small and save you from these mistakes.

If the answer choices are too close together to estimate and the numbers aren't as easy to work with as in that last problem, you'll need to solve the problem a different way. One simple way to answer most rate problems is to set up a proportion, an equation with a ratio on each side. Make sure you keep the units on each side in the same place—whatever is in the numerator on the left should also be in the numerator on the right. To solve a proportion, cross multiply.

A printing press can print 7,500 newspapers in 30 minutes. How long would the printing press take to print 100 newspapers?

A $\frac{2}{5}$ of a minute

B 2 minutes

C 3 minutes

D 5 minutes

Set up a proportion of newspapers over minutes. Include a variable such as *t* for the time the printing press will take to print 100 newspapers.

Set up the proportion: $\dfrac{7,500 \text{ newspapers}}{30 \text{ minutes}} = \dfrac{100 \text{ newspapers}}{t \text{ minutes}}$

Cross multiply: $7,500t = 100(30)$

Divide both sides by 7,500: $t = \dfrac{3,000}{7,500}$

Simplify: $t = .4 \text{ or } \dfrac{2}{5}$

It will take $\frac{2}{5}$ of a minute for the press to print 100 newspapers. That's choice **A**. The most common rate is speed or velocity. This can be written as rate $= \dfrac{\text{distance}}{\text{time}}$. You can rewrite the equation as rate × time = distance or time $= \dfrac{\text{distance}}{\text{rate}}$ to solve for different parts of the equation, or you can set these problems up as proportions.

Michael can ride his bicycle at 15 miles per hour. Which of the following equations could you use to figure out the number of hours (t) it would take him to travel 20 miles at this rate?

A $15 = \dfrac{t}{20}$

B $15 = \dfrac{20}{t}$

C $20 = \dfrac{15}{t}$

D $15(20) = t$

Use the equation rate = $\dfrac{\text{distance}}{\text{time}}$. The rate, 15 miles per hour, must equal the distance Michael travels (20 miles) divided by the time it takes him to do it (*t*). Choice **B** shows exactly this situation.

You could also use a combination of estimation and picking numbers to answer this question. If Michael's traveling at 15 miles per hour, you know it will take him a little more than an hour to travel 20 miles. Which of the answer choices is true when *t* is a little more than 1?

Choice A doesn't work. If *t* is a little more than 1, then $\dfrac{t}{20}$ is a small fraction and can't possibly equal 15.

Choice B does work: 20 divided by something a little bigger than 1 could be 15.

Choice C doesn't work: 15 divided by anything bigger than 1 will be less than 15, so $\dfrac{15}{t}$ can't equal 20 if *t* is more than 1.

Choice D doesn't work at all: 15(20) is huge, much larger than 1.

The only plausible answer is choice **B**.

> ✏️ **Keep the units in the mathematical expressions when you're working with rates. They can help you see how to set up a problem and are a useful warning if you make one of the more common mistakes.**

A high-speed train travels at a speed of 200 km/hr for 2.5 hours. How far does the train travel in this time?

A   80 km

B   200 km

C   500 km

D   1,000 km

Distance traveled is rate times time, so the train has traveled 200 km/hr × 2.5 hours = 500 km, and **C** is the correct answer. Writing out the units like this can help you spot the most common mistakes in rates problems. If you'd accidentally divided instead of multiplying, you'd have wound up with km/hr². That's certainly not what the answer choices have, and it's not a distance, so you'd know something was wrong and be able to fix it before answering the question incorrectly.

To set this up as a proportion, turn the rate into a distance and a time. The train travels at 200 km/hr, so it goes 200 km in 1 hour. Call the distance the train travels in 2.5 hours d.

Set up the proportion: $\dfrac{200 \text{ km}}{1 \text{ hr}} = \dfrac{d \text{ km}}{2.5 \text{ hrs}}$

Cross multiply: $200(2.5) = d$

Simplify: $500 = d$

That's choice **C**.

GRAPHING FUNCTIONS

A *coordinate plane* is formed by the intersection of two number lines, the *x*-axis and the *y*-axis. The center of the coordinate plane, where the *x*- and *y*-axes intersect, is known as the *origin*. Just as every real number has a position on the number line, every point has a position on the coordinate plane.

An *ordered pair* is a set of two numbers that tells you where on the coordinate plane a point is located. Having an ordered pair is like having a point's address—you know exactly where to find it. The first number in an ordered pair is the *x*-coordinate, which tells you where along the *x*-axis the point is located. If the *x*-coordinate is negative, count to the left from the origin. If the number is positive, you should count to the right. The second number is the *y*-coordinate, which tells you where along the *y*-axis the point is. A negative *y*-coordinate tells you to count down from the origin. A positive *y*-coordinate tells you to count up. Every point is described in terms of its distance from the origin, so the origin itself is the point (0, 0).

What is the location of point A in the coordinate plane below?

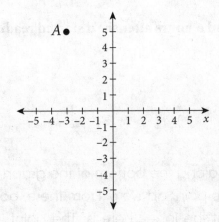

A (−5, 3)

B (−3, 5)

C (3, 5)

D (5, −3)

Point *A* is 3 units to the left on the *x*-axis and 5 units up on the *y*-axis, so it is at (−3, 5). Choice **B** is correct.

Reading Information From Graphs

Graphs of real-world information, like prices, heights, or distances, usually just show the top right quadrant of the coordinate plane, where both *x* and *y* are positive. These graphs will include labels to show you what each axis is measuring. To get information from a graph, read carefully so you know exactly what you're looking for. Don't be distracted by extra information.

The graph below shows the total number of pages of a book that Charlene read one day.

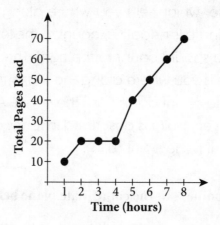

How many pages had Charlene read 6 hours after she'd started reading the book?

A 40

B 50

C 60

D 70

Hours are on the *x*-axis, so look along the bottom of the graph until you see 6. Then look up until you find the point above 6. From there, go left until you reach the *y*-axis, then see what the label there is. The point in question is (6, 50). Six hours after she started reading, Charlene had read 50 pages, so choice **B** is correct.

The table below shows the prices of different-sized chocolate bars.

Weight (oz.)	Price
4	$0.50
8	$1.00
10	$1.25
12	$1.50
16	$2.00

Which of the following graphs shows the information in the table?

A
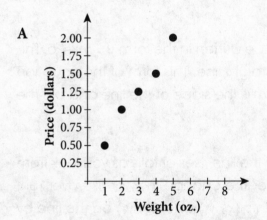

C
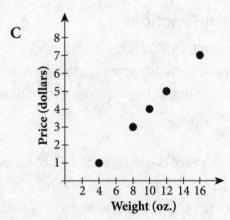

B
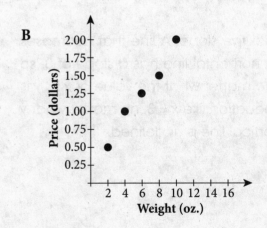

D
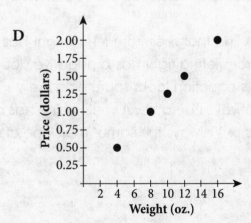

Pay attention to the numbers on the sides of the graph. All four answer choices have weight in oz. on the x-axis and price in dollars on the y-axis, but they have different scales. The first chocolate bar in the table weighs 4 ounces and costs $0.50. Which of the graphs includes the point (4, 0.50)? Choices B and D do, but choices A and C don't, so A and C can be eliminated. To tell whether choice B or D is correct, pick another chocolate bar from the table. The next one is 8 ounces for $1.00—does that appear on B or D? It appears in choice D, so **D** is correct. Choice B has the 8 oz. chocolate bar priced at $1.25, which doesn't match the table.

Linear Functions

A *linear function* is an equation that can be written in the form $y = mx + b$. The graph of any equation in this form is a straight line. This form of the equation is called the *slope-intercept form* where m is the slope of the line and b is the y-intercept.

The *slope* of a line describes how steeply the line rises or falls as you look from left to right. Slope is the change in y over the change in x, or rise over run. You can find the slope from any two points (x_1, y_1) and (x_2, y_2) on the line by plugging them into the equation $m = \dfrac{y_2 - y_1}{x_2 - x_1}$.

A line that rises from left to right has a positive slope. A line that decreases from left to right has a negative slope. A horizontal line has a slope of 0, so its equation looks something like $y = 2$; no matter what the value of x is, y is always the same. A vertical line has an equation like $x = 3$; no matter what y is, x is always the same. The slope of a vertical line is undefined.

Points You May Want to Remember

- For a horizontal line, the equation is $y = b$, where b is the y-intercept.

- For a horizontal line, the "rise" will always be 0, so the slope will always be 0.

- For a vertical line, the equation is $x = a$, where a is the x-intercept.

- For a vertical line, the "run" is always 0, so the slope will always be undefined.

What is the slope of a line that passes through the points (3, 3) and (6, –15)?

A   –6

B   –5

C   3

D   4

Plug the points into the equation $m = \dfrac{y_2 - y_1}{x_2 - x_1}$ to get $\dfrac{-15 - 3}{6 - 3} = \dfrac{-18}{3} = -6$.

The slope of this line is –6, or choice **A**. It goes down quite steeply as it goes to the right.

The *y-intercept* is the value of y when $x = 0$, or when the line crosses, or intercepts, the y-axis.

What is the *y*-intercept of the line on the graph below?

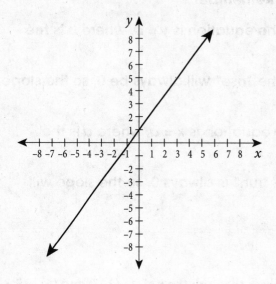

A   –2

B   –1

C   1

D   2

This line passes through the point (0, 1), so its *y*-intercept is 1, which is choice **C**.

CAHSEE questions might ask you to find the slope or *y*-intercept of a line from an equation, a graph, or two points on the line. You might also be asked to find the entire equation of a line from a graph or from points on the line.

What is the equation of the line in the graph below?

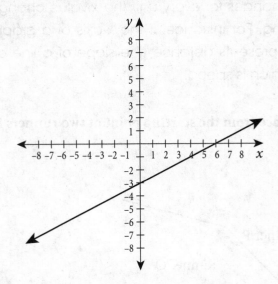

A $\quad y = \dfrac{1}{3}x - 2$

B $\quad y = \dfrac{1}{2}x - 3$

C $\quad y = 2x - 3$

D $\quad y = 3x - 2$

The easiest part of the equation to find from a graph is the *y*-intercept. This line crosses the *y*-axis at *y* = –3, so in the equation *y* = *mx* + *b*, *b* is –3. You can eliminate choices A and D right away. The slope is a little less obvious, but you can see that the line goes up more slowly than it goes to the right. Therefore, the slope is less than 1, so choice **B** must be correct. If you want to prove it to yourself, pick any two points from the graph to calculate the slope. Good points are (0, –3) and (6, 0), because they're very clear on the graph and are easy to work with: $\dfrac{0 - (-3)}{6 - 0} = \dfrac{3}{6} = \dfrac{1}{2}$

The slope of the graph, *m* in the equation *y* = *mx* + *b*, is $\dfrac{1}{2}$. Choice **B** is correct.

Because the slope of a line is the change in *y* over the change in *x*, it shows how many units the *y*-value changes for every unit the *x*-value changes, or the rate at which *y* is changing. For instance, if the *x*-axis of a graph represents time and the *y*-axis represents distance, the slope of a line on the graph is distance over time, which is speed.

The graph below shows the distance from the starting point of two runners in a 1,600-meter race.

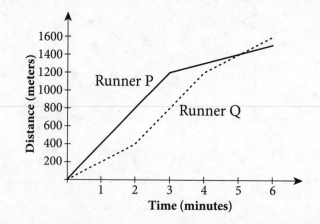

At which of the following times was runner P running faster than runner Q?

A   Between the start of the race and minute 1

B   Between minute 2 and minute 3

C   Between minute 3 and minute 4

D   Between minute 5 and minute 6

The graph shows time on the *x*-axis and distance on the *y*-axis. Speed is $\frac{distance}{time}$, which is the slope. When runner P is running faster than runner Q, the slope of runner P's line will be steeper than the slope of runner Q's line. That's the case between the start of the race and minute 1, so choice **A** is correct.

The slopes are equal between minutes 2 and 3, and runner Q is running faster than runner P from minutes 3 to 4 and from minutes 5 to 6. Even though runner P has run farther than runner Q at minutes 2, 3, and 4, runner Q is not running faster at those times.

Stan walked directly away from his house at a constant rate of 2 miles per hour for half an hour. Then he jogged in the same direction at 6 miles per hour for one hour before turning around and walking home at a rate of 2 miles per hour. Which of the following graphs could represent Stan's trip?

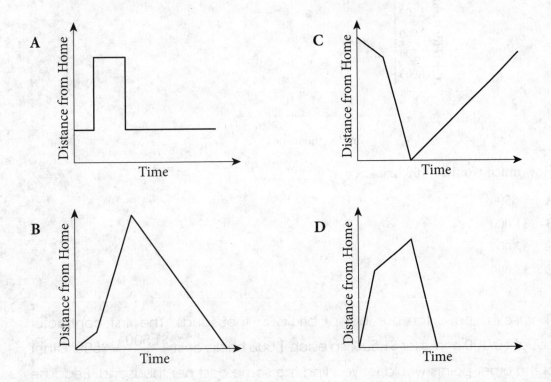

As Stan walks away from home, his distance from home (on the *y*-axis) is increasing, so the slope of the first part of the graph must be positive. You can eliminate choice C, because the slope of the first part of its graph is negative, and choice A, because the slope of the first part of its graph is 0. When Stan starts jogging, he is moving faster, so the line must get steeper. The second part of the graph in choice B is steeper than the first part, while the second part of the graph in choice D is shallower than the first part. Choice **B** must be correct.

The graph below shows the cost of 3 contractors' purchases of bricks.

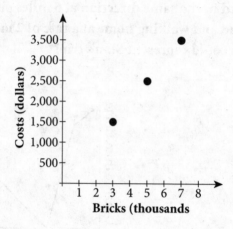

How much would 1,000 bricks cost?

A $500

B $1,000

C $2,000

D $5,000

The *x*-axis shows the number of bricks in thousands. The first contractor bought 3,000 bricks for $1,500, so each 1,000 bricks cost $\frac{\$1,500}{3}$ = $500. Either of the other points would let you find the same cost per thousand. Because the three points lie on a straight line, you know that the cost per thousand bricks is constant—when the slope of a line stays the same, the rate stays the same.

Nonlinear Functions

On the CAHSEE, you may see *quadratic functions* of the form $y = ax^2$, where *a* is a constant. Every quadratic equation looks something like this:

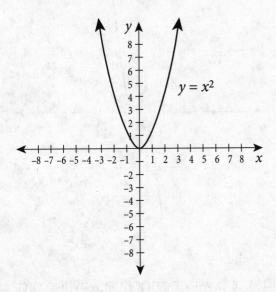

If *a* is positive, the parabola will open upward, as in the figure above. If *a* is negative, the parabola will open downward. Different values of *a* will make the parabola wider or skinnier.

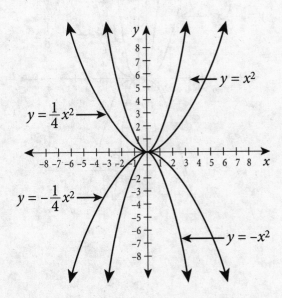

Cubic functions on the CAHSEE take the form $y = ax^3$. They look something like this:

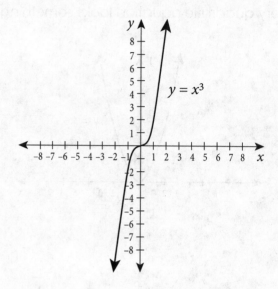

Again, different values of a will change the way the graph looks:

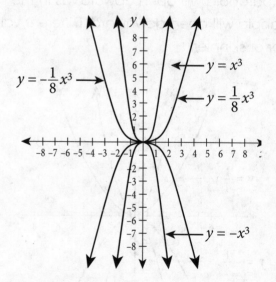

You should be familiar with the general shape of quadratic and cubic functions. Sometimes, you might need to plug a few values of x into the equation to see what the corresponding values of y are, but you'll usually just need to have a general idea what the shape of the graph in question ought to be. Graphs like $y = x^2$ and $y = x^3$ appear frequently, so you should recognize them when you see them.

Which of the following graphs shows the equation $y = 5x^3$?

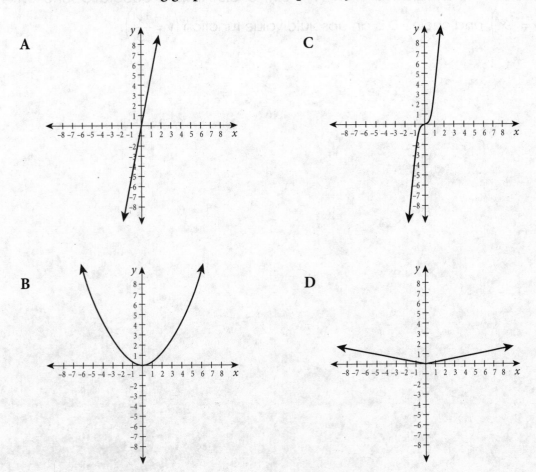

Any cubic function will have a characteristic shape—above the x-axis on one side, below the x-axis on the other, and curved. The only graph here with this shape is choice **C**. If you don't remember what a cubic function looks like, plug a few values of x into the equation $y = 5x^3$ and see which graph they appear on.

If $x = 1$, then $y = 5(1)^3 = 5(1) = 5$. The point (1, 5) appears in choices A and C but not in choices B or D, so you can eliminate B and D.

If $x = 2$, then $y = 5(2)^3 = 5(8) = 40$. That's higher than these graphs show, but you can tell that the point in choice A with an x-value of 2 is more like (2, 10) than (2, 40). Only choice **C** works.

Choice A is a linear function ($y = 5x$), choice B is a quadratic function $\left(y = \frac{1}{5}x^2\right)$, and choice D is an absolute value function $\left(y = \frac{|x|}{5}\right)$.

SUMMARY

After reading this chapter, you should be able to do the following:

- Use Kaplan strategies to solve CAHSEE questions.
  - o Picking numbers and backsolving will let you avoid some of the trickiest math.
  - o Pick numbers when there are variables in the answer choices.
  - o Pick numbers that are appropriate and easy to work with.
  - o Backsolve when there are numbers in the answer choices.
- Simplify expressions.
  - o Use PEMDAS to remember the order of operations: parentheses, exponents, multiplication and division, addition and subtraction.
  - o Memorizing the rules of exponents and square roots will help you solve many CAHSEE questions.
  - o If you have trouble remembering a rule, picking numbers can help you remember it or let you solve the problem without it.
- Work with variables.
  - o Variables stand for unknown numbers.
  - o Add or subtract like terms only.
  - o Multiply and divide variables and coefficients separately.
- Solve equations and inequalities.
  - o Solve for a variable by isolating it on one side of an equation or inequality.
  - o Always perform the same operations to both sides of an equation or inequality.
  - o Remember to change the direction of the inequality symbol if you multiply or divide by a negative number.
  - o Backsolving lets you avoid complicated algebra.

- Solve word problems.
  - The first step in solving word problems is translating them from English to math.
  - Backsolving can let you avoid a complicated translation.
  - Picking numbers can make an abstract word problem easier to understand.
  - Set up proportions to solve problems about rates.
- Understand graphs.
  - Read graphs carefully. Be sure you know what each axis shows.
  - Use the equations $y = mx + b$ and $m = \dfrac{y_2 - y_1}{x_2 - x_1}$ to work with lines.
  - Know the shapes of the equations $y = x^2$ and $y = x^3$.

Algebra and Functions Quiz

Algebra and Functions Quiz

1. Which of the following equations represents the statement, "Twenty less than five times a number, *x*, is equal to forty"?

A $20 - 5x = 40$

B $5x + 20 = 40$

C $5x - 20 = 40$

D $5x - 40 = 20$

2. If $m = 5$ and $n = 0.2$, then $4m - mn =$

A 3

B 10

C 19

D 44

3. A phone company charges $50 for installation and $25 per month for phone service. Which of the following graphs correctly shows the total amount of money spent on phone service over a 12-month period?

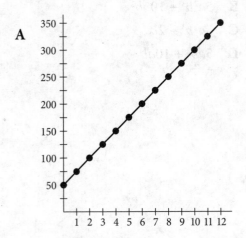

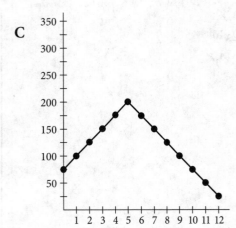

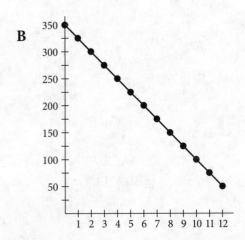

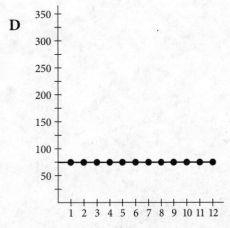

4. Simplify the expression shown below.

$$(3x^2y^5)(4xy^3)$$

A $7x^2y^8$

B $7x^3y^8$

C $12x^2y^{15}$

D $12x^3y^8$

5. Which of the following is equivalent to $5ab(ab^2 + 2b)$?

A $10a^2b^4$

B $5a^2b^3 + 10ab^2$

C $5a^2b^3 + 2b$

D $5ab^2 + 10ab$

6. Which of the following is the graph of $y = -x^2$?

A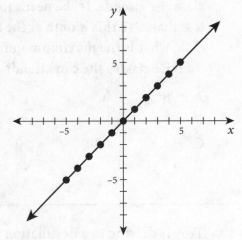

C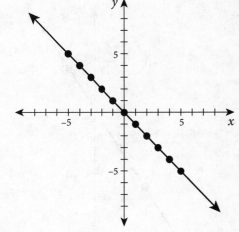

B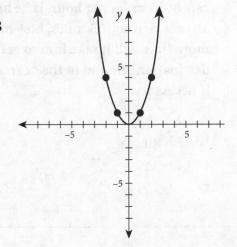

D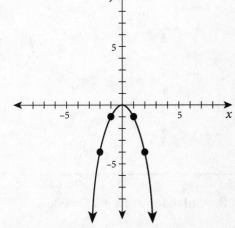

7. What is the slope of the line shown in the graph below?

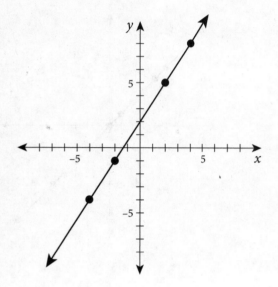

   A $-\dfrac{3}{2}$

   B $-\dfrac{2}{3}$

   C $\dfrac{2}{3}$

   D $\dfrac{3}{2}$

8. Solve for x: $6x + 15 = 63$.

   A   7

   B   8

   C   10.5

   D   13

9. Danielle pays a \$15 monthly fee for her health club plus \$3 for each exercise class she attends. If she needs to spend less than \$42 this month at the health club, what is the maximum number of exercise classes she can attend?

   A   8

   B   9

   C   14

   D   19

10. Troy is driving to a destination 268 miles away. He will travel at an average rate of 55 miles per hour. If he has already driven 103 miles, how much more time will it take him to get to his destination? Round to the nearest hour, if necessary.

   A   2 hours

   B   3 hours

   C   4 hours

   D   5 hours

11. Solve for x: $7x - 12 > 9$.

   A $x < -\dfrac{3}{7}$

   B $x < 3$

   C $x > -\dfrac{3}{7}$

   D $x > 3$

12. Petra can type 105 words in 3 minutes. At this rate, how many words can she type in 10 minutes?

   A   3.5
   B   35
   C   350
   D   450

13. The graph below shows the amount of money spent on gasoline for a certain number of miles driven. If the price of gasoline was the same each time, what is the price per gallon?

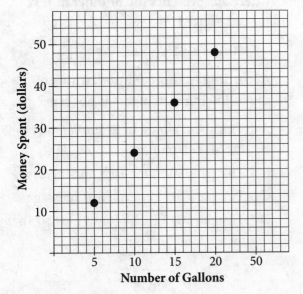

   A $0.42
   B $1.20
   C $2.40
   D $12.00

14. What is the equation of the graph shown below?

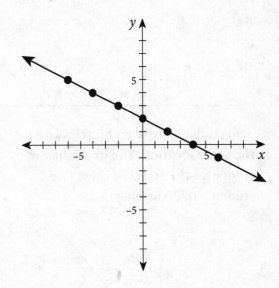

   A $y = -2x + 2$
   B $y = 2x - 2$
   C $y = \frac{1}{2}x + 2$
   D $y = -\frac{1}{2}x + 2$

15. $\sqrt{25x^{16}y^2} =$

   A $5xy$
   B $5x^4y$
   C $5x^8y$
   D $5x^4y^2$

16. $38 - 3(10 + 2) =$

   A   1
   B   2
   C   10
   D   420

17. What is the value of $-3x^2$ when $x = -3$?

    A -9

    B 9

    C -27

    D 27

18. Two students leave on bicycles from the same location. The graph below compares the travel of these two students in 30 minutes.

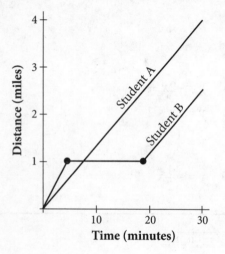

    Based on the graph, which of the following is true about the two students?

    A   Student B biked farther than Student A.

    B   Student A biked at a rate of 4 miles per hour.

    C   Both students biked the same distance.

    D   Both students left the starting point at the same time.

19. Marilyn works h hours each day and makes d dollars per hour. How much will she make if she works 5 days this week?

    A $\dfrac{dh}{5}$

    B $\dfrac{5d}{h}$

    C $5dh$

    D $\dfrac{5h}{d}$

20. Tim's cell phone bill for January can be represented by the equation below, where x represents the number of text messages used.

    $$\$0.10x + \$15 = \$25$$

    According to this equation, which of the following statements is **not** true?

    A   Tim spent a total of $25 in January for his cell phone.

    B   Tim pays $0.10 for each text message.

    C   Tim pays $15 for each text message.

    D   Tim pays $15 each month plus $0.10 for each text message.

Answers and Explanations

1. C

Translate each part of the statement into numbers and mathematical symbols using key words and expressions. The first part of the statement, "twenty less than," means to subtract 20 from some quantity. The next part of the statement, "five times a number, x," becomes the expression $5x$. Therefore, the first two parts of the statement translate to $5x - 20$. The last part of the statement, "is equal to forty," sets the first part equal to forty. This makes the equation $5x - 20 = 40$, which is choice C. Choice A would represent "Twenty minus five times a number is equal to forty." Choice B would represent "The sum of twenty and five times a number is forty." Choice D would represent "Forty less than five times a number is twenty."

2. C

In this question, first substitute each of the values for m and n. Then evaluate the expression using the correct order of operations. The order of operations can be remembered as **PEMDAS**: **P**arentheses, **E**xponents, **M**ultiplication, **D**ivision, **A**ddition, and **S**ubtraction.

After substituting, the expression $4m - mn$ becomes: $4(5) - (5)(0.2)$

Follow order of operations and multiply: $20 - 1$

Subtract to complete the problem: 19

If your answer was A, you did not follow the correct order of operations, first subtracting 5 from 20 and multiplying by 0.2 last. Multiplication always comes before addition or subtraction. If your answer was B, you multiplied 5 by 0.2 and got 10 instead of the correct value of 1. If you chose D, you thought that 4*m* represented the number 45, not the correct value of 4 times 5.

3. A

Because the phone company charges $50 for installation, the graph should begin at the point (0, 50). The charge each month is $25, so the graph should increase by $25 each month. Therefore, the correct graph will also have the points (1, 75), (2, 100), (3, 125), and so on. The graph that contains each of these points is graph A. Graph B starts at (0, 350) and decreases. This would mean that the total cost decreases over time, which does not make sense. Graph C starts at (0, 75), and the total cost increases for a period and then starts to decrease. Again, this does not make sense. The total cost would never decrease. Graph D starts at (0, 75) and never rises; the problem states that there is a charge every month, so the graph must increase.

4. D

To simplify the expression, multiply the coefficients and add the exponents of the like bases. Because the coefficients, or numbers in front of the variables, are 3 and 4, 3 · 4 = 12. To multiply the variables, add the exponents of the like bases:

$$x^2 \cdot x = x^2 \cdot x^1 = x^3$$

$$y^5 \cdot y^3 = y^8$$

Therefore, the simplified expression becomes $12x^3y^8$, which is choice D. If you chose either choice A or B, you added the coefficients instead of multiplying. If your answer was choice C, you multiplied the exponents instead of adding them.

5. B

Use the distributive property and the laws of exponents to multiply: the expression $5ab(ab^2 + 2b)$ becomes $5ab \cdot ab^2 + 5ab \cdot 2b$.

Simplify each part of the expression by multiplying the coefficients and adding the exponents of the like bases: $5a^1b^1 \cdot a^1b^2 + 5a^1b^1 \cdot 2b^1 = 5a^{(1+1)}b^{(1+2)} + 5 \cdot 2a^1b^{(1+1)} = 5a^2b^3 + 10ab^2$.

If your answer was choice A, you multiplied all of the terms together, without regard to the addition sign. If you chose C, you did not distribute the $5ab$ term to the $2b$ term within the parentheses. In choice D, the $5ab$ term was not correctly distributed to either of the terms in parentheses.

6. D

The graph of the equation $y = -x^2$ is a parabola, or U-shaped graph. Because there is a negative in front of the x^2, the coefficient of x^2 is -1. This will cause the graph to open down. Therefore, the graph of the parabola $y = -x^2$ is choice D. Choice A is the graph of the equation $y = x$. Choice B is the graph of the equation $y = x^2$. Choice C is the graph of the equation $y = -x$.

7. D

The slope is the change in y over the change in x. In formula form, slope $= \frac{\text{rise}}{\text{run}} = \frac{y_1 - y_2}{x_1 - x_2}$. To find the slope of the line, locate two points on the line and substitute the values into the formula. Two points on the line are $(0, 2)$ and $(2, 5)$. Use the first point for (x_1, y_1) and the second point for (x_2, y_2). Substitute these values the formula: $\frac{y_1 - y_2}{x_1 - x_2} = \frac{2 - 5}{0 - 2} = \frac{-3}{-2} = \frac{3}{2}$

The slope of the line is $\frac{3}{2}$. Choice A is the opposite of the slope. If the slope was negative, the line would decrease when reading from left to right. Choice B is the negative reciprocal of the slope. Again, the line would decrease when reading from left to right. If your answer was choice C, you wrote the incorrect ratio, putting the change in x-coordinates in the numerator and the change in y-coordinates in the denominator.

8. B

Solve for *x* using the steps for equation solving to get the variable alone.

First, subtract 15 from each side of the equation: $6x + 15 - 15 = 63 - 15$

The equation becomes: $6x = 48$

Divide each side of the equation by 6: $\dfrac{6x}{6} = \dfrac{48}{6}$

$x = 8$

The correct value of x is 8. If you chose C, you ignored the 15 and just divided 63 by 6. If your answer was D, you added 15 to both sides instead of subtracting it.

9. A

To solve this problem, write an inequality to represent the facts stated in the question. Let *x* represent the number of classes Danielle attends. Because she pays $15 plus $3 per class at her health club, this can be expressed as $15 + 3x$. Danielle needs to spend less than $42 this month, so the inequality is $15 + 3x < 42$. Solve the inequality by getting the variable alone.

First, subtract 15 from each side of the inequality: $15 - 15 + 3x < 42 - 15$

The inequality is now: $3x < 27$

Divide each side of the inequality by 3: $\dfrac{3x}{3} < \dfrac{27}{3}$

The variable is now alone: $x < 9$

The number of classes Danielle can attend must be less than 9, so the correct answer is A, 8 classes. If you chose B, you used the boundary, or endpoint, 9. Because she needs to spend *less than* $42.00, she cannot attend 9 classes. If your answer was choice D, you added 15 to both sides of the equation instead of subtracting it.

10. B

Use the distance formula, distance = rate × time ($d = r \times t$), to solve this problem. The total distance he needs to drive is 268 miles, and he has already driven 103 miles. Therefore, he still needs to drive 268 – 103 = 165 miles. Because the distance is 165 miles and the rate is 55 miles per hour, the equation becomes: 165 = 55 × t. Divide each side of the equation by 55 to get t alone:

$$\frac{165}{55} = \frac{55t}{55}$$

$$3 = t$$

It will take him 3 more hours to get to his destination. If your answer was choice A, you interpreted the problem incorrectly and thought that Troy had 103 miles left to drive. Choice D is the total time, rounded to the nearest hour, that the trip will take Troy, not the time remaining.

11. D

To solve for x, first add 12 to each side of the inequality:

$$7x - 12 > 9$$
$$7x - 12 + 12 > 9 + 12$$

The inequality now becomes:

$$7x > 21$$

Divide each side of the inequality by 7 to get x alone:

$$\frac{7x}{7} > \frac{21}{7}$$

$$x > 3$$

If your answer was A, you subtracted 12 from each side of the equation instead of adding it. Also, you incorrectly switched the inequality symbol. If you chose B, you also switched the inequality symbol. You only switch the symbol when you multiply or divide by a negative number. Choice C would be the result of subtracting 12 from each side of the equation instead of adding it.

12. C

To solve this problem, which involves rate, use a proportion. Line up the corresponding words in the proportion and cross multiply to solve. Because Petra can type 105 words in 3 minutes, set up the ratio $\frac{105 \text{ words}}{3 \text{ minutes}}$. Now, to find the number of words she can type in 10 minutes, use that ratio to set up the proportion: $\frac{105 \text{ words}}{3 \text{ minutes}} = \frac{x \text{ words}}{10 \text{ minutes}}$

Cross multiply to find the value of x: $3x = 1{,}050$

Divide each side of the equation
by 3 to get the variable alone: $\frac{3x}{3} = \frac{1{,}050}{3}$

$$x = 350$$

She can type 350 words in 10 minutes. If your answer was A, you incorrectly divided 105 by 30. Choice B is the number of words that she can type per minute.

13. C

To find the price per gallon, locate a point on the graph. The price per gallon can be found by using the total cost, or the y-value of the point, divided by the number of miles driven, or the x-value of the point. Because the cost for 5 gallons is $12, one point is (5, 12). Divide the cost of $12 by 5 gallons to get $\frac{\$12}{5}$ = $2.40 per gallon. If your answer was A, you divided 5 by 12 instead of dividing 12 by 5. Choice B is the price per gallon if 10 gallons had cost $12.00; you may have read the graph incorrectly. Choice D is the price of 5 gallons of gasoline.

14. D

The slope-intercept form of a linear equation is $y = mx + b$, where m represents the slope of the line and b represents the y-intercept. To find the value of the y-intercept (b), find the place where the line intersects the y-axis (the vertical axis). The line intersects the y-axis at (0, 2), so the y-intercept is 2. The slope of a line is represented by the fraction $m = \frac{\text{change in } y}{\text{change in } x} = \frac{\text{rise}}{\text{run}}$. Therefore, to find the slope (m), start at the y-axis and count up and over until you get to the next point on the line. Lines that slant up to the right have positive slopes, and lines that slant up to the left have negative slopes. In this case, you need to count up one unit and over two units to the left to get to the next point (–2, 3), making the slope $-\frac{1}{2}$. The equation in slope-intercept form is $y = -\frac{1}{2}x + 2$. Choice A would be a graph where you would count up two and over to the left one. The graph of choice B would cross the y-axis at –2, not positive 2, and the graph would increase when read from left to right. Answer choice C has a positive slope, which indicates a graph that increases when read from left to right.

15. C

The symbol over the numbers and variables in the expression is called the radical, or square root symbol. To simplify this expression, find the square root of each coefficient and variable. The square root of the coefficient 25 is 5, because $5 \times 5 = 25$. The square root of x^{16} is x^8, because $x^8 \cdot x^8 = x^{16}$. The square root of y^2 is y because $y \times y = y^2$. Therefore, the simplified expression is $5x^8y$, which is choice C. If you chose A, you ignored the exponents and just evaluated the square root of 25. If your answer was B, you took the square root of the exponent on the x term instead of dividing it by 2.

16. B

In this problem, follow the correct order of operations to simplify. The order of operations can be remembered as PEMDAS: Parentheses, Exponents, Multiplication, Division, Addition, and Subtraction.

Evaluate within the parentheses first:	38 – 3(10 + 2)
	38 – 3(12)
Multiply:	38 – 36
Subtract:	2

If your answer was C, you forgot to distribute the 3 to the 2 term in parentheses and evaluated 38 – (3 × 10) + 2. If your answer was D, you subtracted and added first, then multiplied.

17. C

To solve this problem, first substitute the value of x into the expression. Then evaluate using the correct order of operations. Keep in mind that evaluating $(-3)^2$ means that you are squaring -3: $(-3)(-3) = 9$.

First, substitute $x = -3$ into the expression: $\qquad -3(-3)^2$

Evaluate the exponent: $\qquad\qquad\qquad\qquad -3(9)$

Multiply: $\qquad\qquad\qquad\qquad\qquad\qquad -27$

If you chose A, you made two mistakes. You ignored the coefficient, -3, and also thought that $-3 \times -3 = -9$. If your answer was B, you ignored the coefficient, -3. If you chose D, you did not do the integer multiplication correctly.

18. D

The correct answer is choice **D**. Each student left the same place at time 0. This is indicated in the lower left-hand corner of the graph. This graph compares the distance of two people as they traveled a certain length of time. Both graphs end at the 30-minute mark. Student A traveled farther in 30 minutes, so the answer cannot be choice A. Student A traveled 4 miles in 30 minutes. At this rate, student A would travel 8 miles in 1 hour, so choice B cannot be true. Choice C cannot be true, because the lines for student A and student B are not parallel for the entire length of time. In fact, student A traveled at a constant speed, but student B stopped for 15 minutes, shown by the horizontal portion of the graph.

19. C

The best way to solve this problem is to pick numbers. Solving the problem with numbers will indicate what operations are necessary to find the general case with variables. Assume that Marilyn works 8 hours each day and makes $10 per hour. To calculate the amount of money she would make in one day, multiply $8 \times \$10 = \$80$. Thus, if she works h hours and makes d dollars, she makes dh dollars each day. This question asks for the amount of money she will make if she works for 5 days, so multiply the expression by 5 to get $5dh$.

20. C

Because x represents the number of text messages sent by Tim and this amount is being multiplied by $0.10, Tim is being charged $0.10 for each text message. Therefore, choice B is true. Because $15 is added on the same side of the equation, this is an amount added each month that is not related to the number of text messages he sends. Thus, choice D is true. Because the expression $0.10x + $15 is set equal to $25, $25 is the total amount of the cell phone bill for January. Therefore, choice A is true. The statement that is not true is choice C, that Tim pays $15 for each text message. He pays $0.10 for each text message plus $15 per month for a total of $25 in January.

Measurement and Geometry

UNITS

One very important CAHSEE skill is converting measurements from one unit to another. You'll need to be able to use any conversion factor the test provides for you and have some of the most common conversions memorized. Fortunately, you probably already know most of what you'll need to have memorized for the test.

The two main systems of measurement in use in the United States today are the metric system and the customary system. The metric system, based on powers of 10, is used all over the world, while the customary system is limited to the United States. You'll need to be fluent in both systems to answer all the questions on the CAHSEE.

The basic units in the metric system are meters (length), liters (volume), and grams (mass). Different prefixes produce units larger or smaller than the base units.

milli	centi	deci	base	deca	hecto	kilo
0.001	0.01	0.1	1	10	100	1,000
10^{-3}	10^{-2}	10^{-1}	10^0	10^1	10^2	10^3

(The italicized prefixes aren't used very often. You're not likely to see them on the test.)

The metric system is used in most scientific research because it's easy to express very large or very small numbers in it. Scientific notation (page 35 in Number Sense) is based on powers of ten just like the metric system is.

So a millimeter is $\frac{1}{1,000}$ of a meter, and a kilogram is 1,000 grams. To convert back and forth between the different metric units, just multiply by the appropriate power of 10.

When you're changing the units of a measurement, keep the direction of the change in mind. You need a greater number of smaller units to equal the same amount, so if you're changing to smaller units, you'll end up with more of them. If you're changing to larger units, you don't need as many of the larger units to equal the original amount. The easiest way to make sure you're multiplying by the correct factor is to set up the problem with all the units written out. If they cancel out and leave you with the correct unit, you've set up the problem correctly. If not, you've made a mistake, but you can correct it before you fill in your answer.

Gunther has 50 bottles of food coloring. Each bottle contains 25 milliliters of food coloring. How many liters of food coloring does Gunther have?

A $1\frac{1}{4}$ L

B   2 L

C   5 L

D $12\frac{1}{2}$ L

First, find the number of milliliters of food coloring that Gunther has. We multiply: 50 bottles of 25 mL each is 50 bottles $\times \frac{25\ mL}{1\ bottle} = 1{,}250$ mL. Each milliliter is $\frac{1}{1,000}$ of a liter, so 1,250 mL is 1,250 mL $\times \frac{1\ L}{1{,}000\ mL} = 1.25$ L, or $1\frac{1}{4}$ L, choice **A**. Choice B is the result of dividing 50 bottles by 25 milliliters. Choice D is the result of an error in the placement of the decimal point.

The customary system of measurement is more complicated than the metric system, but it may also be more familiar. Each unit in the customary system of measurement has its own name rather than being built from a prefix and a base unit.

The customary units of length are inches, feet, yards, and miles: 12 inches equal 1 foot, 3 feet equal 1 yard, and 1,760 yards equal 1 mile. Volume in the customary system is measured in liquid ounces, cups, pints, quarts, and gallons: 8 ounces equal 1 cup, 2 cups equal 1 pint, 2 pints equal 1 quart, and 4 quarts equal 1 gallon. Weight is generally measured in ounces and pounds: 16 ounces equal 1 pound.

Alice is 4 feet and 10 inches tall. Her younger brother, Bruce, is 3 feet and 11 inches tall. How tall are Alice and Bruce together?

A 4 feet 11 inches

B 7 feet 11 inches

C 8 feet 9 inches

D 9 feet 1 inch

First, add the feet and inches separately: 4 + 3 = 7 and 10 + 11 = 21, so Alice and Bruce together are 7 feet and 21 inches tall. Because 21 inches is more than a foot, you need to simplify the amount by subtracting 12 inches and regrouping this amount to add it to the number of feet. 21 – 12 = 9, so 21 inches is 1 foot and 9 inches. Alice and Bruce together are 7 feet + 1 foot + 9 inches tall, or 8 feet and 9 inches tall. Choice **C** is correct. Choice A is the result of using the number of feet in Alice's height and the number of inches in Bruce's height. Choice B may have been selected if the amount of feet was added correctly but the number of inches was added incorrectly. Choice D is the result of an error in computation.

If you need to work with a more unusual customary measure, such as acres (area), the conversion factor will be given in the question.

Karen inherited a small farm from her uncle. The farm has an area of 3 square miles. What is the area of the farm in acres? (1 square mile = 640 acres)

A   213 acres

B   640 acres

C   1,280 acres

D   1,920 acres

To answer this question, multiply the number of square miles in the farm by the given conversion factor: 3 square miles $\times \dfrac{640 \text{ acres}}{1 \text{ square mile}} = 1,920$ acres. Choice **D** is correct. Choice A is the result of dividing 640 acres by 3, instead of multiplying. Choice B is not correct because 1 square mile is equal to 640 acres, and the farm has an area three times this size. Choice C is the result of multiplying 640 by 2 acres, instead of by 3.

In addition to the metric and customary units for length, volume, and mass or weight, you should be comfortable using and converting different measures of time and temperature.

You should already know the units of time: there are 60 seconds in a minute, 60 minutes in an hour, 24 hours in a day, and 7 days in a week. The tricky thing about working with time is that it's very easy to lose an hour when you are subtracting times given in hours and minutes, and it's easy to write the *number* of minutes instead of the decimal fraction of an hour that they represent. Remember that 30 minutes is half an hour, or 0.5 hour, and not 0.3 hour. Because this is such an easy mistake to make, the result will usually be one of the wrong answer choices.

How many minutes are between 8:30 A.M. on Monday and 4:15 P.M. on Wednesday?

A   465

B   495

C   2,880

D   3,345

For problems like this one, which involve a long time period, find the longest whole units first. From 8:30 A.M. Monday to 8:30 A.M. Wednesday is 2 days. From 8:30 A.M. Wednesday to noon is 3 hours and 30 minutes, and from noon to 4:15 P.M. is another 4 hours and 15 minutes. That's a total of 2 days, 7 hours, and 45 minutes. The question asks for everything in terms of minutes. We can convert the days to minutes: 2 days is 2 days $\times \dfrac{24 \text{ hours}}{1 \text{ day}} = 48$ hours, which is 48 hours $\times \dfrac{60 \text{ minutes}}{1 \text{ hour}} = 2{,}880$ minutes. And we can convert the hours to minutes: 7 hours is 7 hours $\times \dfrac{60 \text{ minutes}}{1 \text{ hour}} = 420$ minutes. All together, that's $2{,}880 + 420 + 45 = 3{,}345$ minutes, choice **D**. Choice B is the number of minutes in 7 hours, 45 minutes. Choice C is the total number of minutes in 2 days.

Temperature conversions are a little trickier than most, because the two common temperature scales don't start at the same place. To convert from Celsius to Fahrenheit, instead of multiplying by a simple conversion factor, substitute the temperature into the equation $F = \dfrac{9}{5}C + 32$ (don't worry about memorizing this; it will be given on the test if you need it). If the temperature is given in degrees Celsius, substitute it for C and solve for F. For instance, a temperature of 0°C is the same as a Fahrenheit temperature of $F = \dfrac{9}{5}(0) + 32 = 0 + 32 = 32$°F. To convert from Fahrenheit to Celsius, use the same formula, substitute the given temperature for F, and solve for C.

 Estimating is always a good idea on conversion problems. Fahrenheit degrees are smaller than Celsius degrees, so it takes more Fahrenheit degrees than Celsius degrees to express the same temperature.

What is the temperature in degrees Celsius when the temperature in degrees Fahrenheit is 68°F?

$$\left(F = \frac{9}{5}C + 32 \right)$$

A   20.0°C

B   37.8°C

C   55.6°C

D   154.4°C

Be sure to substitute the given temperature into the right place. It's given in degrees Fahrenheit, so it goes in for F. (If you substitute it for C, you'll get wrong answer choice D.)

Substitute into the formula: $68 = \frac{9}{5}C + 32$

Subtract 32 from each side: $36 = \frac{9}{5}C$

Multiply each side by $\frac{5}{9}$: $36 \times \frac{5}{9} = C$

Simplify: $20 = C$

Choice **A** is correct. Choice C is the result of adding 32 to each side of the equation in the second step. As stated above, choice D is the result of substituting 68 for C in the formula. Also, you can eliminate choice D right away by remembering that a temperature in degrees Fahrenheit can be expressed in *fewer* degrees Celsius.

The CAHSEE may ask you to convert units within the same system of measurement (feet to inches or milliliters to liters) or between systems of measurement (inches to centimeters or liters to gallons). Both kinds of conversions work the same way, so don't be intimidated by an unusual request. Acres to square millimeters? No problem! The conversion factors you need will be given in the question.

You can even change multiple units at once. Check that the units cancel out properly to be sure you've multiplied everywhere you needed to multiply and divided everywhere you needed to divide.

Marguerite is planning a trip to Canada. She knows that her rental car will get about 15 kilometers per liter of gasoline. Approximately how many miles per gallon will her rental car get? (1 mile ≈ 1.6 km; 1 gallon ≈ 3.79 L)

A   25 mpg

B   36 mpg

C   63 mpg

D   91 mpg

$$\frac{15 \text{ km}}{1 \text{ L}} \times \frac{1 \text{ mile}}{1.6 \text{ km}} \times \frac{3.79 \text{ L}}{1 \text{ gal}} = \frac{56.85 \text{ miles}}{1.6 \text{ gal}} = 35.53125 \text{ mgp} \approx 36 \text{ mpg},$$ which is choice **B**. Choice D is the result of simply multiplying each of the numbers in the conversion factors by 15.

Notice that kilometers and liters both cancel out, leaving you with only miles and gallons as the only labels that do not cancel out. This method of setting up a problem so that all the unneeded units cancel out is called *dimensional analysis*. It's often used in chemistry and other scientific disciplines.

SCALE DRAWINGS

Blueprints, maps, and models all use a small object to represent a much bigger real object. The relationship between the sides of a real object and a scale drawing of it is a proportion. If you know the length of one side of the object and the length of that side in the drawing, you can find the *scale factor*, or ratio between a measurement of the scale drawing and the corresponding measurement of the real object.

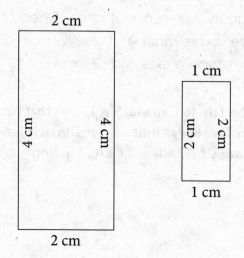

The rectangle on the right is a scale drawing of the rectangle on the left. Each side of the smaller rectangle is half the length of the rectangle on the left, so the scale of the drawing is 1:2. You can see that the sides of the rectangles are in the same proportion by writing the relationship between the short sides and the long sides:

$$\frac{1}{2} = \frac{2}{4}$$

Setting up this kind of proportion is the easiest way to find a side length that's not labeled on the scale drawing. After you set up the proportion, cross multiply and simplify to find the missing side.

 Always check to be sure your answer is reasonable.

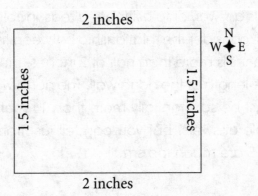

The north wall of the fort shown in this scale drawing is 28 meters long. What is the length of the east wall of the fort?

A   7 meters

B   15 meters

C   18 meters

D   21 meters

You know that the north wall of the fort is 28 meters long and the length of the north wall of the scale drawing is 2 inches. The east wall in the scale drawing is 1.5 inches, so you can set up a proportion to find the length of the east wall of the fort. Call the length of the east wall *l*.

$$\frac{\text{original}}{\text{scale drawing}} = \frac{28 \text{ meters}}{2 \text{ inches}} = \frac{l \text{ meter}}{1.5 \text{ inches}}$$

Make sure each side of the proportion has the original object in the numerator and the scale drawing in the denominator. If they're in different places on different sides of the proportion, you won't get the right answer.

Cross multiply the proportion: 28 meters × 1.5 inches = *l* meters × 2 inches

The equation becomes: 42 = 2*l*

Divide each side of the equation by 2:   21 = *l*

The east wall of the fort is 21 meters long, so choice **D** is correct.

To double-check this answer, or to estimate a reasonable answer before doing the calculations, consider the relationship between the sides of the drawing. Because 1.5 inches is more than half of 2 inches, the east wall of the fort is more than half the length of the north wall. The north wall is 28 meters long, so the east wall must be substantially more than 14 meters. Choices C or D could be reasonable answers, but you can tell just from this simple check that choices A and B are much too small.

DIMENSIONAL ANALYSIS

 This topic includes some of the most difficult questions on the CAHSEE. Don't get discouraged if you get stuck on a particularly complicated one while you're taking the test—circle it, leave it for later, and show off your skills on the rest of the math section before coming back to give it another try.

As you found out in the Units section, you can multiply and divide units just like numbers or variables. You can even square or cube them. The last problem in that section used dimensional analysis, the practice of setting up a problem so that the unnecessary units cancel out to leave you with whatever unit the question asks for, to convert kilometers per liter to miles per gallon. But dimensional analysis can be used for more than just converting units of measure. You already know how to use estimation and proportions to solve problems about rates (see pages 113–116 in the Rates section of Chapter 3, "Algebra and Functions"); dimensional analysis adds another method to your arsenal.

Mark's toy car can travel $\frac{1}{3}$ of a meter in a second. How long would it take the toy car to travel a kilometer at that rate?

A   6 minutes

B   12 minutes

C   50 minutes

D   200 minutes

The question gives the rate in meters per second but asks for minutes per kilometer. You'll need to make two conversions to get the information in the right form:

$$\frac{\frac{1}{3}\ \text{meter}}{1\ \text{second}} \times \frac{60\ \text{seconds}}{1\ \text{minute}} \times \frac{1\ \text{kilometer}}{1,000\ \text{meters}} = \frac{20\ \text{kilometers}}{1,000\ \text{meters}} = \frac{1\ \text{kilometer}}{50\ \text{minutes}}$$

The seconds and meters cancel out, leaving you with kilometers and minutes. You can see that traveling 1 kilometer will take the toy car 50 minutes, choice **C**. You may have selected choice A if you had the units in the wrong places.

You could also set this problem up as a proportion. You know that a kilometer is 1,000 meters, so you can find the number of seconds it will take the car to travel that distance:

$$\frac{\frac{1}{3}\ \text{meter}}{1\ \text{second}} = \frac{1,000\ \text{meters}}{x\ \text{seconds}}$$

$$\frac{1}{3}x = 1,000$$

$$x = 3,000$$

Convert the number of seconds into the number of minutes by setting up another proportion:

$$\frac{3,000\ \text{seconds}}{y\ \text{minutes}} = \frac{60\ \text{seconds}}{1\ \text{minute}}$$

$$3,000 = 60y$$

$$\frac{3,000}{60} = y$$

$$50 = y$$

Setting the problem up as a proportion lets you find exactly the same information, but it can be easier to multiply accidentally instead of dividing or divide instead of multiplying. When you're setting up a proportion, be sure the units are in the same place on each side of the equation to avoid that kind of error.

Dimensional analysis also lets you solve problems that involve multiple units but aren't expressed as a simple rate, like force $\left(\frac{kg \cdot m}{s^2}\right)$ or density $\left(\frac{g}{m^3}\right)$.

 Work problems can be particularly difficult. Thinking about the problem logically can help you avoid some of the most common mistakes. For example, if many people are working together, a job will be done faster than if only one person was working on it.

One person can paint 20 square feet in 30 minutes. How long will it take 3 people to paint 6 panels, each of which is 30 square feet, for the backdrop of a play?

A 1.5 hours

B 3 hours

C 4.5 hours

D 6 hours

This is a complicated one! There's a lot of information to keep track of, so build your equation carefully to make sure you've included everything.

There are 6 panels, each of which is 30 square feet:

$$6 \text{ panels} \times \frac{30 \text{ ft}^2}{1 \text{ panel}}$$

It takes one person 30 minutes to paint 20 square feet, but the question asks for hours:

$$6 \text{ panels} \times \frac{30 \text{ ft}^2}{1 \text{ panel}} \times \frac{30 \text{ minutes}}{20 \text{ ft}^2} \times \frac{1 \text{ hour}}{60 \text{ minutes}}$$

The work is divided among 3 people:

$$6 \text{ panels} \times \frac{30 \text{ ft}^2}{1 \text{ panel}} \times \frac{30 \text{ minutes}}{20 \text{ ft}^2} \times \frac{1 \text{ hour}}{60 \text{ minutes}} \times \frac{1}{3} = 1.5 \text{ hours}$$

All the units except hours cancel out, so choice **A** is correct. Choice B is the result of adding the time for 2 people: 1.5 + 1.5 = 3. Choice C is the result of adding the time for each of the 3 people: 1.5 + 1.5 + 1.5 = 4.5.

You could also solve the problem piece by piece. There are 3 people painting 6 panels, so each person will paint 2 panels. The panels are each 30 ft², so each person is painting 60 ft². They can paint 20 ft² (one-third of the area they're painting) in 30 minutes, so the entire area will take 3 • 30 = 90 minutes, or 1.5 hours. There are usually many different ways to solve dimensional analysis problems, so if one method isn't working, stop and try something else.

PLANE GEOMETRY

CAHSEE geometry questions rely on understanding diagrams and working with common geometric shapes. Most of the shapes on the CAHSEE are *polygons*, two-dimensional figures with line segments as sides, but you'll also see some circles and three-dimensional figures.

Number of Sides	Name of Polygon
3	triangle
4	quadrilateral
5	pentagon
6	hexagon
8	octagon

The two characteristics of a shape that you'll use most often are perimeter and area. The *perimeter* of a shape is the distance around it, which is the sum of the lengths of all its sides. The *area* of a shape is the number of square units that it covers. You'll need to remember the formulas for the areas of the most common shapes, but anything unusual will be given to you in the question.

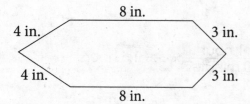

What is the perimeter of this polygon?

A   15 in.

B   16 in.

C   20 in.

D   30 in.

The perimeter is the sum of the lengths of all the sides, so the perimeter of this polygon is 4 + 8 + 3 + 3 + 8 + 4 = 30 in. That's choice **D**. Choice A represents one of the most common mistakes students make when calculating perimeter—when a figure is symmetrical, like this one, it's easy to count up only half of the sides.

Figures that are *congruent* are exactly the same shape and size. They have all the same corresponding side lengths and all the same corresponding angles. Figures that are the same shape but different sizes are *similar*. For example, a scale drawing and the object that it represents are similar, because they are the same shape but different sizes.

 A *vertex* is the point where two straight sides of a figure meet. Polygons are commonly named by listing their vertices in order as you go around the polygon. A line segment between two points is named by listing both endpoints.

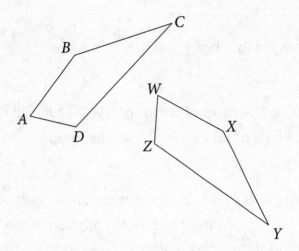

Quadrilaterals *ABCD* and *WXYZ* in the figure above are congruent. Which side of quadrilateral *WXYZ* is the same length as $\overline{AD}$?

A $\overline{WX}$

B $\overline{XY}$

C $\overline{YZ}$

D $\overline{ZW}$

$\overline{AD}$ is the shortest side of quadrilateral *ABCD*. It is the same length as the shortest side of the congruent quadrilateral, $\overline{WZ}$. $\overline{WZ}$ and $\overline{ZW}$ both refer to the same side of the quadrilateral. The order in which the endpoints of a line segment are written does not matter. Choice **D** is correct.

Triangles

A *triangle* is a polygon that has three sides and three angles.

 The formula for the area of a triangle, $A = \frac{1}{2}bh$, will not be printed on the test. You'll need to remember this one.

The area of a triangle is one half of the base times the height. This formula is often written as $A = \frac{1}{2}bh$. The height of a triangle is the distance straight up from the base to the opposite vertex of the triangle. The height can be the length of a side, or it can be inside or outside the triangle. The base and height of a triangle are always *perpendicular*—they intersect at 90°, forming a right angle.

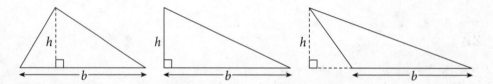

These three triangles all have the same base and the same height. That means they also have the same area.

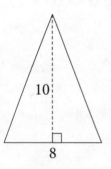

What is the area of this triangle, in square units?

A 28

B 32

C 40

D 80

The area of the triangle is $A = \frac{1}{2}bh$, or $\frac{1}{2}(8)(10) = 4(10) = 40$ square units. That's choice **C**. Choice D shows the common mistake of forgetting to multiply by $\frac{1}{2}$.

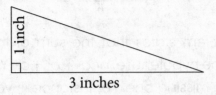

3 inches

Julianne drew the picture above as a plan for a vegetable garden. If the actual garden is 2 yards long for every inch in the picture, what is the area of the vegetable garden?

A   1.5 square yards

B   3 square yards

C   6 square yards

D   12 square yards

The actual garden's base and height are 6 yards and 2 yards, because each side is 2 yards for every inch in the picture. That means the area is $\frac{1}{2}(6)(2) = 6$ square yards, or choice **C**. If you multiplied by $\frac{1}{2}$ more than once, you may have selected choice A or choice B. If you forgot to multiply by $\frac{1}{2}$ in the formula, you may have selected choice D.

 To review finding square roots and solving equations, see pages 98–100 in the Simplifying Expressions and the Solving Equations and Inequalities sections of Chapter 3, "Algebra and Functions."

When the height of a triangle is one of the sides, the triangle is known as a *right triangle*, because it has a right angle. The longest side of a right triangle is known as the *hypotenuse*, while the shorter sides are called *legs*. The Pythagorean theorem lets you find the length of the hypotenuse or one of the legs when you know the other two sides.

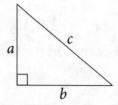

The Pythagorean theorem states that the sum of the squares of the legs equals the square of the hypotenuse, or $a^2 + b^2 = c^2$. You can plug in any two sides and solve for the missing one. For instance, if you know that a triangle has legs of length 3 and 4, just plug those in for a and b and solve for c: Substitute into the formula: $3^2 + 4^2 = c^2$

Evaluate the exponents: $\qquad\qquad$ $9 + 16 = c^2$

Add: $\qquad\qquad\qquad\qquad\qquad$ $25 = c^2$

Take the square root of each side: $\qquad$ $5 = c$

Remember, the hypotenuse is always c. Be sure to substitute the sides of the triangle into the correct places in the theorem.

 If you don't know how to find a length in a figure, just eyeball it. Use the other lengths marked in the figure to work out about how long the missing length is, then eliminate any answer choices that don't match.

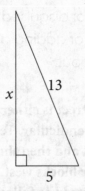

What is the length of the side of the right triangle marked x?

A   8

B   10

C   12

D   14

 Right triangles with sides in the ratios 5:12:13 or 3:4:5 appear frequently on the CAHSEE.

The hypotenuse of this triangle is marked 13, and one leg is marked 5, so you have enough information to find the other leg. Substitute into the formula: $x^2 + 5^2 = 13^2$

Evaluate the exponents: $\qquad\qquad\qquad\qquad x^2 + 25 = 169$

Subtract 25 from each side: $\qquad\qquad\qquad x^2 = 144$

Take the square root of each side: $\qquad\qquad x = 12$

Choice **C** is correct. Choice D is the result of using the values of 5 and 13 for the legs of the triangle. Also, in this question, you can tell from eyeballing the figure that x is longer than 5 and shorter than 13. That lets you rule out choice D, giving you a better chance of guessing correctly if you need to guess.

Sometimes, familiar shapes can be hidden or disguised. If it's not clear what's going on in a problem, try drawing a figure or adding a line or two to a given figure to create a shape you know more about.

The streets in Terry's town form a grid. Each street is either east-west or north-south, and all the intersections are perpendicular. Terry can get home from school either by walking four blocks west and then three blocks south, or by walking three blocks south and then four blocks west. If Terry could walk in a straight line from school to home instead of following the streets, how long would his walk home be?

A Five blocks

B Seven blocks

C Eight blocks

D Fourteen blocks

If you're not quite sure what's going on in a geometry problem, try drawing a picture. Terry can get home by walking four blocks west, then three blocks south, so his home is three blocks south and four blocks west of the school. If he could walk there directly, he would be walking in a straight line between the two points:

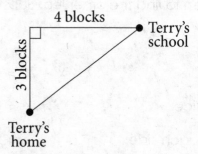

This figure should look familiar—it's a right triangle. The straight line from Terry's school to his home is the hypotenuse of a triangle with legs of length 3 and length 4.

Substitute into the formula: $3^2 + 4^2 = c^2$

Evaluate the exponents: $9 + 16 = c^2$

Add: $25 = c^2$

Take the square root of each side: $5 = c$

The distance is 5 blocks, or choice **A**. Choice B is the result of simply adding the length of the blocks he could walk when walking west and then south ($3 + 4 = 7$). Choice D is the result of doubling the value in choice B.

QUADRILATERALS

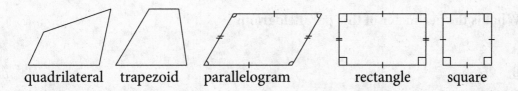

quadrilateral　　trapezoid　　parallelogram　　rectangle　　square

Quadrilaterals are polygons that have four sides and four angles. *Trapezoids* are quadrilaterals that have one pair of parallel sides (*parallel* lines travel in the same direction without crossing each other, like railroad tracks). *Parallelograms* have two pairs of parallel sides. Each side in a pair is the same length as the other side, and opposite angles are equal. *Rectangles* are parallelograms that have four right angles, and *squares* are rectangles that have four equal sides.

What type of geometric shape is shown in this picture?

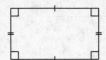

A Hexagon

B Rectangle

C Square

D Triangle

This shape has two pairs of parallel sides and four equal angles. It is a rectangle, which is a type of parallelogram. Choice **B** is correct. A hexagon has six sides, and a triangle has three sides, so these shapes look very different from the figure shown. A square is a special type of rectangle in which both pairs of parallel sides are the same length; in this figure the two pairs are different lengths, so this rectangle is not a square.

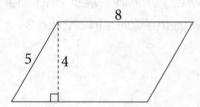

What is the perimeter of this parallelogram?

A   24

B   26

C   32

D   40

The perimeter is the distance around the figure. Each pair of a parallelogram's sides is the same length, so the unlabeled sides are 5 and 8 units long. The perimeter is 8 + 5 + 8 + 5 = 26, which is choice **B**. Choice C is the area of the figure. Choice D is the area of the figure if it were incorrectly found by multiplying a height of 5 times a base of 8.

The area of a parallelogram is the base times the height, $A = bh$.

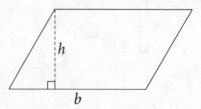

As in triangles, the height is the perpendicular distance from the base to the top of the parallelogram, not necessarily the length of a side. In rectangles, the height is the length of a side, but this is not true for other parallelograms.

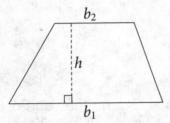

The area of a trapezoid is $\frac{1}{2}h(b_1 + b_2)$. If you need this formula on the test, it will be given in the question.

 The formula for the area of a parallelogram, $A = bh$, will not be given on the test. Be sure you have it down cold beforehand.

Mr. Abrams is putting grass seed on his rectangular lawn. The lawn is 8 yards long and 10 yards wide, and grass seed costs \$0.50 per square foot. How much will Mr. Abrams pay for enough grass seed to cover his lawn?

A \$40.00

B \$200.00

C \$360.00

D \$720.00

Notice that the dimensions of the lawn are given in yards, but the cost of grass seed is given in square feet. The first thing to do is convert the measurements into feet. One yard is 3 feet, so 8 yards are 8 yards $\times \frac{3 \text{ feet}}{1 \text{ yard}} = 24$ feet and 10 yards are 10 yards $\times \frac{3 \text{ feet}}{1 \text{ yard}} = 30$ feet. The area of the rectangular lawn is 24 ft $\times$ 30 ft = 720 ft^2, and the cost is 720 ft$^2 \times$ \$0.50 per ft^2 = \$360.00. Choice **C** is correct. Choice A may have been selected if you did not convert yards into feet before finding the area. Choice D is incorrect because the cost is \$0.50 per square foot, not \$1.00 per square foot.

The perimeter of a square is 20 centimeters. What is the area of the square?

A   20 cm²

B   25 cm²

C   80 cm²

D   400 cm²

The perimeter is the distance around the square. Because all four sides of a square are the same length, each side is $\frac{20\ cm}{4}$ = 5 cm long. The area of a square is the base times the height. Each side is the same length, so the area is 5 cm × 5 cm = 25 cm², or choice **B**. You may have selected choice A if you thought that the area of the figure would be the same as the perimeter. Choice C is the result of multiplying the perimeter of the square by 4. Choice D is the result of squaring the perimeter of the square to find the area.

Chloe has a wallet-sized picture in her scrapbook. Its entire back surface is covered with glue. If Chloe enlarges the picture so that it is three times as long and three times as wide, how many times as much glue will it take to completely cover the back surface of the enlarged picture?

A $1\frac{1}{2}$

B   3

C   6

D   9

Call the length and width of the wallet-sized picture *l* and *w*. The length of the enlarged picture is three times the length of the original picture, so it's 3*l*. The width is three times the original width, so it's 3*w*. The glue covers the back surface of the picture, so the amount of glue is the area of the picture. The original area is *lw*, and the enlarged area is 3*l*(3*w*) = 9*lw*. That's 9 times the original area. Choice **D** is correct. Choice B is the result of making just one of the sides three times as large.

Circles

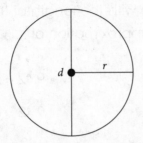

A *circle* is a shape formed by all the points that are the same distance from the center. This distance is called the *radius* of the circle and is used to calculate many other important measurements. The *diameter*, or distance across the circle through the center, is twice the radius, or 2*r*, and the *circumference*, or distance around the circle, is 2π*r*.

The number π represents the ratio between the circumference of a circle and its diameter. It is approximately equal to $\frac{22}{7}$ or 3.14, but if you're estimating to rule out wrong answer choices, all you need to know is that π is a little more than 3. If you are supposed to use one of these approximations, it will be provided in the question. If no approximation is given, treat π as you would treat a variable and leave it in the answer.

 The circumference of a circle is like the perimeter of a polygon. You'll need to memorize the formula for the circumference of a circle, $C = 2\pi r = \pi d$. It won't be given on the test.

Joey measured the circumference of a soup can by wrapping a piece of string around it and then using a ruler to measure the string. He found that the string was 9.42 inches long. Approximately how many inches is the radius of the can? (π ≈ 3.14)

A   1.5

B $\sqrt{3}$

C   3

D   6

The circumference of a circle is $2\pi r$, so you can find the approximate value of r by setting up an equation with the length of the string (the circumference of the can) and the given approximation of π.

Substitute the values:	$9.42 = 2(3.14)r$
Multiply:	$9.42 = 6.28r$
Divide each side by 6.28:	$\dfrac{9.42}{6.28} = r$
Round:	$\dfrac{9}{6} = r$
Simplify:	$\dfrac{3}{2} = r$
Convert to decimal form:	$1.5 = r$

The radius of the can is about 1.5 inches, which is choice **A**. You may have selected choice C if you did not multiply the radius by 2 in the formula.

The area of a circle also depends on π. It is π times the square of the radius, $A = \pi r^2$. It's easy to get circumference and area mixed up, so be sure you know which one you're looking for.

A sprinkler waters a circular area with a radius of 10 feet. How many square feet does the sprinkler water? ($A = \pi r^2$)

A 10π

B 20π

C 25π

D 100π

The radius is 10 feet, so the area is $\pi(10 \text{ ft})^2 = 100\pi \text{ ft}^2$. That's choice **D**. Choice A is the result of simply multiplying the length of the radius by π to find the area. Choice B is the circumference of the circle. Choice C may be selected if you take half of the radius of 10 and square that amount to find the area.

Compound Figures

Some CAHSEE questions include figures made up of several different shapes. These should be no problem as long as you're comfortable with circles, quadrilaterals, and triangles, but they can be a little tricky to get started on. Just don't get overwhelmed by extra information—if you break the figure into simpler shapes, you also break the problem into simpler pieces. Solve each piece one at a time by applying the concepts you already know.

Margaret is placing carpet in her apartment. The diagram below shows the carpeted part of Margaret's apartment.

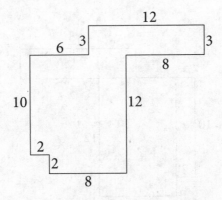

All the angles are right angles, and the distances shown are measured in feet. How many square feet of carpet will Margaret need to carpet her apartment?

A   66

B   144

C   152

D   270

 Diagrams can usually be broken up in several ways. In the question about Margaret's carpet, you could also find the area of a large rectangle and subtract the areas of smaller rectangles.

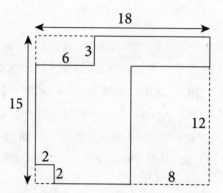

Because all the angles are right angles, the diagram can be divided into rectangles.

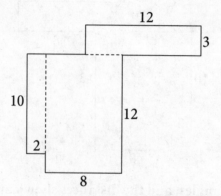

The area of each rectangle is base × height, so the area of all three rectangles is (2 × 10) + (8 × 12) + (12 × 3) = 20 + 96 + 36 = 152 square feet. That's choice **C**. Choice D is the result of multiplying 15 by 18, which is the area of the rectangular shape that surrounds the irregular figure.

Any time you see a circle, or part of a circle, you know you'll need the radius at some point. Find it first, then calculate whatever measurement you're looking for.

A stained glass window is in the shape shown below. The top of the window is a semicircle.

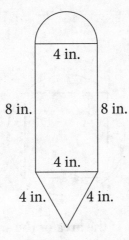

What is the perimeter of the window to the nearest inch? (π ≈ 3.14)

A   24 inches

B   28 inches

C   30 inches

D   36 inches

The perimeter of the window is the distance around the outside. The straight sides are labeled with their lengths, but you'll need to calculate the curved side. The curved side is half of a circle with a diameter of 4 inches. The radius of the circle is 2, and the length of the curved side is half of the circumference of the circle. The curved side is $\frac{1}{2}(2\pi r) = \frac{1}{2}(2\pi(2)) = \frac{1}{2}(4\pi) = 2\pi$ inches long. Because π ≈ 3.14, that's about 2(3.14) = 6.28 inches. Add the lengths of the other sides of the window to get the perimeter: 6.28 + 8 + 8 + 4 + 4 = 30.28 inches. Round that to the nearest inch to get 30 inches, choice **C**. Choice A is the perimeter without the curved section that is equal to half of a circle. Choice B is the result of using 4 inches as the length of the top portion of the figure, instead of finding the distance around the half circle.

Look for or sketch in line segments that are part of more than one shape to move information from one part of the figure to another.

Inscribed means that the vertices, or corners, are on the circle.

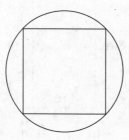

A square is inscribed in a circle. If the area of the square is 4, what is the area of the circle?

A   2π

B   4π

C   4π + 4

D   16π

The area of a square is the length of a side squared, so you know that the lengths of the sides of this square are $\sqrt{4} = 2$. But what does that tell you about the circle? You know that to get any information about the circle, you'll need to find its radius or diameter. Do you see any way to add one of those to the figure that will also be part of the square?

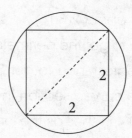

The diameter of the circle is the same as a diagonal of the square. That divides the square into two right triangles, so you can use the Pythagorean theorem to find the length of the diameter.

$$2^2 + 2^2 = c^2$$
$$4 + 4 = c^2$$
$$8 = c^2$$
$$\sqrt{8} = c$$
$$2\sqrt{2} = c$$

The radius of the circle is half of this, or $\sqrt{2}$. The area of a circle is πr^2, so the area of this circle is $\pi(\sqrt{2})^2 = 2\pi$. That's choice **A**.

Estimation can also get you to the answer. You know that π is a little more than 3, so 2π is a little more than 6, 4π is a little more than 12, and so on. You can see from the figure that the area of the circle is larger than the area of the square, but not much larger. It's clearly less than twice the area of the square, so it must be more than 4 but less than 8. The only answer choice that fits is choice **A**.

SOLID GEOMETRY

CAHSEE geometry includes more than just figures in the plane. Solid objects like cereal boxes and soup cans can also be described geometrically. Solids add depth to the two-dimensional shapes you already know.

If you submerged an object in a full glass of water, the water would spill over the top of the glass. The amount of water that spills out is the *volume* of the object, the amount of space the object takes up. Volume is measured in cubic units, such as cm^3. The outside of the object, all the parts that get wet when the object is underwater, is called the *surface area*. The surface area is the sum of the areas of all the faces of the object and is measured in square units. You'll need to know how to find the surface area and volume of rectangular prisms (like boxes) and cylinders (like cans) to score your best.

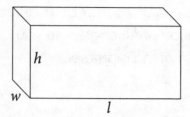

The surface area of a prism is the sum of the areas of all of its sides. The left and right sides of this rectangular prism each have an area of *wh*, the top and bottom are each *lw*, and the front and back are each *lh*. The total surface area of a rectangular prism is $2lh + 2lw + 2wh$.

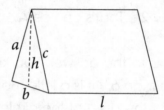

Triangular prisms are less regular but just as easy to understand. The surface area of a triangular prism is the area of each rectangular side plus the area of the two identical triangles on each end. That's $la + lb + lc + bh$.

Don't worry about memorizing either of these surface area formulas. Just find the area of each side of the object and add them all up.

 The formula for the volume of a rectangular prism, *V* = *lwh*, won't be given on the test. Make sure you know it ahead of time.

The volume of a rectangular prism is equal to the length times the width times the height, or $V = lwh$. A *cube* is a special rectangular prism in which the length, width, and height are all the same. The volume of a cube is the length of a side cubed, $l \times l \times l = l^3$. This is why we sometimes refer to taking something to the third power as "cubing it."

A sugar cube is 20 millimeters on each side.

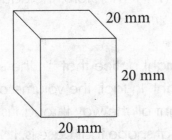

20 mm

20 mm

20 mm

What is the volume of the sugar cube in cubic centimeters?
(1 cm³ = 1,000 mm³)

A   2 cm³

B   8 cm³

C   200 cm³

D   8,000 cm³

The simplest way to solve this problem is to start by converting the lengths to centimeters: 20 mm × $\frac{1 \text{ cm}}{10 \text{ mm}}$ = 2 cm. The cube is 2 cm on a side, so its volume is 2 cm × 2 cm × 2 cm = 8 cm³, or choice **B**. Choice A is the length of one side in centimeters. Choice D may have been selected if you did not change the units to centimeters before multiplying.

You can also find the volume first, then convert: 20 mm × 20 mm × 20 mm = 8,000 mm³ = 8,000 mm³ × $\frac{1 \text{ cm}^3}{1,000 \text{ mm}^3}$ = 8 cm³.

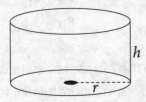

h

r

A *cylinder* is a solid formed by stretching a circle vertically into three dimensions. The surface area of a cylinder has two parts: the circular top and bottom, which each have an area of πr² and the curved surface. The area of the curved surface is similar to what you would get if you peeled the label off a can. It's a rectangle with the same height as the cylinder (*h*) and a length that's the circumference of the cylinder (2π*r*). Therefore, the equation for the total surface area of a cylinder is 2π*rh* + 2π*r*².

The volume of a cylinder is π*r*²*h*. You might notice that it's the same as the area of the circular base times the height. In fact, the volume of any three-dimensional figure that's the same height all the way through is the area of the base times the height, no matter what shape that base is. It works for cylinders, rectangular prisms, triangular prisms, and any other solid of uniform height. (If you need these equations, they'll be provided in the question, so don't worry about memorizing them.)

The surface area of a cylinder is 2π*rh* + 2π*r*². What is the surface area of a cylinder with a diameter of 2 meters and a height of 3 meters?

A   8π m²

B   20π m²

C   30π m²

D   36π m²

The diameter of the cylinder is 2 meters, so the radius is 1 meter. To find the surface area, substitute the values into the formula given in the question.

Substitute:	2π(1)(3) + 2π(1)²
Evaluate the exponent:	2π(1)(3) + 2π(1)
Simplify each term:	6π + 2π
Add:	8π

The surface area is 8π *m*², so the correct answer is choice **A**. Whenever you're working with circles or cylinders, be careful not to mix up the radius and the diameter. Choice B is the result of using 2 meters (the diameter) as the radius of the cylinder.

Compound Solids

Just as simple two-dimensional shapes can be combined to make compound figures, three-dimensional objects can be combined to make compound solids. As with all geometry problems, be sure you know what you're looking for and break these complicated solids down into shapes you know.

 Three-dimensional figures include sides you can't see.

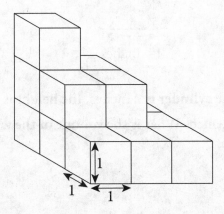

This solid is made of 14 identical cubes, each with a side length of 1 cm. What is the outside surface area of the solid?

A   42 cm²

B   60 cm²

C   72 cm²

D   84 cm²

It's tempting to find the surface area of one cube and multiply by 14, but not all the sides of the cubes are on the outside of the solid. Instead, count up the number of cube faces that are on the outside. Remember to include the back and bottom of the figure along with any other sides you can't see.

The front, sides, and back of the figure each have 6 outside faces (3 along the bottom, 2 in the middle layer, and 1 on the top cube). The bottom has 9 outside faces. Looking down from above the figure, you can see 9 faces as well (1 on the top, 3 on the middle layer, and 5 on the bottom layer). That's a total of 6(4) + 9 + 9 = 24 + 18 = 42 outside faces. Each face has an area of 1 cm × 1 cm = 1 cm², so the total surface area is 42 cm², choice **A**.

A toy car wheel is made of a large cylinder of plastic with a cylindrical hole drilled through the middle.

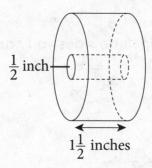

$\frac{1}{2}$ inch

$1\frac{1}{2}$ inches

The diameter of the large cylinder is 2 inches, the height is $1\frac{1}{2}$ inches, and the diameter of the hole is $\frac{1}{2}$ inch. What is the volume of the wheel? ($V = \pi r^2 h$)

A $\frac{45}{32}\pi$ cm³

B $\frac{3}{2}\pi$ cm³

C $\frac{45}{8}\pi$ cm³

D 6π cm³

The volume of the wheel is the volume of the large plastic cylinder minus the volume of the hole, which is also in the shape of a cylinder. The radius of the large cylinder is half the diameter, or $\frac{1}{2}$ × 2 inches = 1 inch, so the volume of the large cylinder is $\pi(1 \text{ in.})^2 \left(1\frac{1}{2} \text{ in.}\right) = 1\frac{1}{2}\pi$ in.³. The radius of the hole is $\frac{1}{2} \times \frac{1}{2}$ in. $= \frac{1}{4}$ in., so its volume is $\pi\left(\frac{1}{4} \text{ in.}\right)^2 \left(1\frac{1}{2} \text{ in.}\right) = \pi\left(\frac{1}{16} \text{ in.}^2\right)\left(\frac{3}{2} \text{ in.}\right) = \frac{3}{32}\pi$ in.³. The volume of the wheel is $1\frac{1}{2}\pi$ in.³ $- \frac{3}{32}\pi$ in.³ $= \frac{48}{32}\pi$ in.³ $- \frac{3}{32}\pi$ in.³ $= \frac{45}{32}\pi$ in.³.

That's choice **A**. Choice B is the volume of the large cylinder only.

COORDINATE GEOMETRY

 To review the basics of plotting points in the coordinate plane, check page 117 in the Graphing Functions section of Chapter 3, "Algebra and Functions."

Coordinate geometry questions can look intimidating, but they're not much different from those in plane geometry. The coordinate plane provides a way to measure the lengths of line segments without having to pull out your ruler or label each one. Because each point has its own location, or pair of coordinates, you can use these numbers to find the distance between any two points.

If two points have the same x- or y-coordinate, you can find the distance between them by subtracting the values that differ and taking the absolute value of the difference.

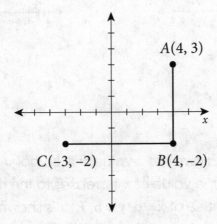

For instance, the distance between A and B is $|3 - (-2)| = |5| = 5$, and the distance between B and C is $|4 - (-3)| = |7| = 7$.

Point Q is located at (3, 5). Point R is three units away from point Q in the positive x direction. Which of the following shows the positions of points Q and R?

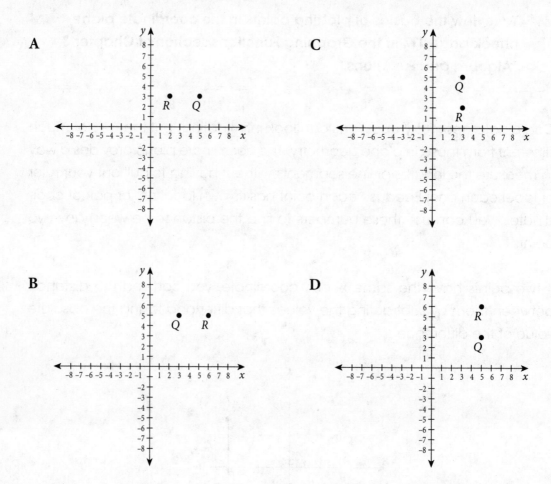

Coordinate pairs always give the x-value first, so point Q is at x = 3, y = 5. The x-axis is horizontal and the value of x increases to the right, so point R is three units to the right of point Q, at x = 6, y = 5. That's shown in the second graph, choice **B**. Choice A shows point Q at (5, 3) and point R at (2, 3). Choice C shows point Q at (3, 5) and point R at (3, 2). Choice D shows point Q at (5, 3) and point R at (5, 6).

To find the distance between points that *don't* lie along a vertical or horizontal line, use the Pythagorean theorem.

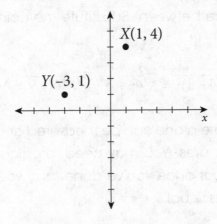

Find the distance between X and Y by using the fact that $\overline{XY}$ is the hypotenuse of a right triangle with vertical and horizontal legs:

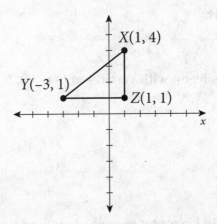

This new point, Z, lets you easily calculate the vertical and horizontal distances. Just substitute these into the Pythagorean theorem to find the direct distance between X and Y. The vertical distance is $4 - 1 = 3$ units. The horizontal distance is $1 - (-3) = 4$ units. The Pythagorean theorem is $a^2 + b^2 = c^2$.

Substitute into the formula:	$3^2 + 4^2 = c^2$
Evaluate the exponents:	$9 + 16 = c^2$
Add:	$25 = c^2$
Take the square root of each side:	$5 = c$

The distance between the points (1, 4) and (–3, 1) is 5 units. You can also plug the points directly into the distance formula, $d = \sqrt{(x_1 - x_2)^2 + (y_1 - y_2)^2}$. The values (x_1, y_1) and (x_2, y_2) represent the coordinates of the points that you are finding the distance between. Substitute the point (1, 4) for (x_1, y_1) and (–3, 1) for (x_2, y_2):

$$d = \sqrt{[1 - (-3)]^2 + (4 - 1)^2} = \sqrt{4^2 + 3^2} = \sqrt{16 + 9} = \sqrt{25} = 5$$

Shapes in the coordinate plane can be measured and manipulated just like shapes without coordinates. You may need to calculate side lengths from coordinate pairs first, but once you've done that, you can find the area or perimeter of a shape as usual.

 Polygons in the coordinate plane are often defined by their vertices. Plot those points and then connect them to find out what the shape is.

What is the area of the polygon with vertices at (–4, –1), (–4, 4), (2, 0), and (2, 5)?

A   15 square units

B   20 square units

C   30 square units

D   32 square units

Sketch a coordinate grid and plot the points to see what kind of polygon the question describes.

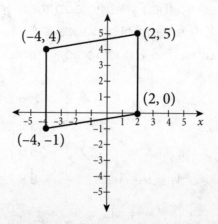

This is a parallelogram. The area, which is the base times the height, will be easiest to calculate if you call the vertical side the base. That side is 4 – (–1) = 5 units long. The height is the perpendicular distance between the bases. Because the base is vertical, the height is horizontal. Find the difference between the x-values of the points on each side. The height is 2 – (–4) = 6 units.

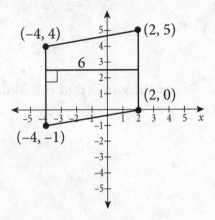

The area of the parallelogram, then, is 5 × 6 = 30 square units. That's choice **C**. Choice A is the result of using the incorrect formula for the area and taking one-half of the area. Choice B and choice D could be the result of finding an incorrect base or height for the figure.

A few questions may combine coordinate geometry (shapes in the coordinate plane) with linear functions (lines graphed in the coordinate plane). If something looks odd, remember the equation of a line, $y = mx + b$, and the definition of slope, $m = \dfrac{y_2 - y_1}{x_2 - x_1}$. Identifying specific points to work with is often a good place to get started.

 To review linear functions, see page 123 in the Graphing Functions section of Chapter 3, "Algebra and Functions."

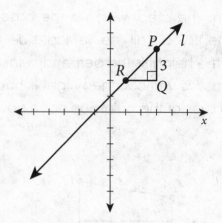

The *x*-intercept of line *l* is –2, and the *y*-intercept is 2. What is the area of triangle PQR in the figure above?

A   2 square units

B   3 square units

C $4\frac{1}{2}$ square units

D $7\frac{1}{2}$ square units

To find the area of the triangle, you'll need the base and the height. The height is given, but it'll take some work to find the base. The *x*- and *y*-intercepts provide convenient points for you to use to calculate the slope of the line, $m = \frac{y_2 - y_1}{x_2 - x_1} = \frac{2 - 0}{0 - (-2)} = \frac{2}{2} = 1$. For every unit that *x* increases, *y* also increases one unit. Whatever point *R* is, point *P* is the same distance above it as it is to the right; the base and the height of the triangle are the same. Because both the base and the height are 3 units, the area is $A = \frac{1}{2}bh = \frac{1}{2}(3)(3) = \frac{9}{2} = 4\frac{1}{2}$ square units. That's choice **C**. Choice B may have been selected if the area was found by multiplying the height of 3 units by the slope of 1.

Transformations

Transformations are ways of changing a shape drawn on the coordinate plane. If the original coordinates were *A*, *B*, and *C*, then the new coordinates are written *A′*, *B′*, and *C′*. Marking the coordinates in this way shows that they correspond to the original coordinates, but that they have changed in some way.

Translations move a shape from one place to another without rotating or stretching it. Translating a shape is like sliding it to a new location. When you translate a shape, you add some constant value to each coordinate's *x*-value, *y*-value, or both. Adding a positive number to the *x*-coordinate moves the shape that many units to the right, while adding a negative number moves it to the left. Adding a positive number to the *y*-coordinate moves the shape up, and adding a negative number moves it down. Both kinds of translation can happen simultaneously.

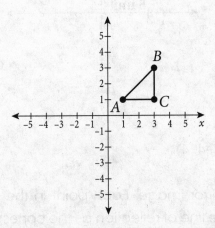

The figure above is translated 5 units to the left and 3 units up to form *A′B′C′*. What are the coordinates of *A′*?

A (−5, 3)

B (−4, 4)

C (1, 1)

D (6, 4)

To move a point 5 units to the left, subtract 5 from the *x*-value: 1 – 5 = –4. There-fore, choice **B** has to be the correct answer. To check, you can calculate the *y*-coordinate: the figure also moved 3 units up, so the new *y*-coordinate is 1 + 3 = 4. Again, that only matches choice **B**. Choice A is the number of units the figure will move during the translation, not the coordinates of the point *A'*. Choice C is the original coordinates of point A. Choice D is the result of translating the points 5 units to the right and 3 units up.

If you're not sure whether to add or subtract, drawing a sketch can make the situation much clearer.

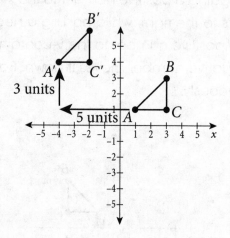

You can see that *A'* is (–4, 4).

A *reflection* is like a mirror image. Each point in the reflection must be the same distance from the line of reflection as the corresponding original point. To reflect a shape across a line, measure how far each point is from the line, then plot a point that distance from the line on the other side. If the figure is reflected across a horizontal line, only the *y*-values will change. If it is reflected across a vertical line, only the *x*-values will change.

The figure that has the vertices $W(-6, 4)$, $X(-3, 6)$, $Y(-1, 1)$, and $Z(-4, 1)$ is reflected across the line $x = 1$. Which of the following shows the reflection of $WXYZ$?

A

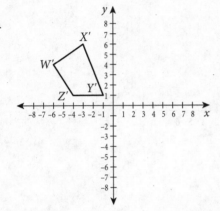

B

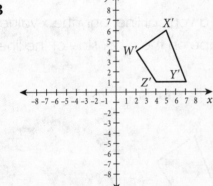

C

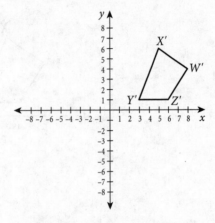

D

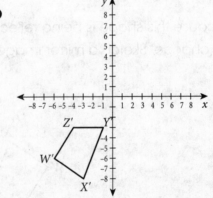

Sketch a graph of *WXYZ* to make the situation clear:

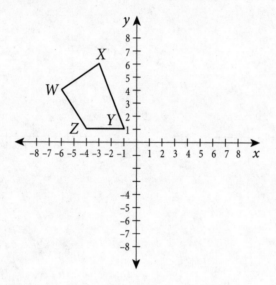

Because this shape is being reflected across a vertical line, only the *x*-values will change. Sketch a mirror image of the shape on the other side of the line:

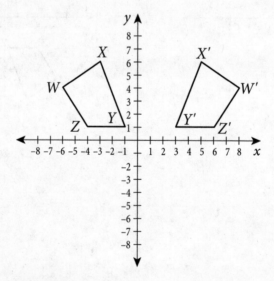

That's choice **C**. Choice A is just the original figure with the prime marks added to each letter. Choice B is a translation 8 units to the right. Choice D is a reflection over the line *y* = –1.

SUMMARY

After reading this chapter, you should be able to do the following:

- Convert measurements between different units.
  - Know the metric system.
  - Know common customary units.
  - Use given conversion factors.
- Find lengths from scale drawings.
- Use dimensional analysis to solve problems with multiple units.
- Solve problems about plane geometry.
  - Find the perimeters of polygons and the circumferences of circles.
  - Identify congruent shapes, sides, and angles.
  - Find the areas of triangles, parallelograms, and circles.
  - Use given formulas to find the areas of other shapes.
  - Use the Pythagorean theorem, $a^2 + b^2 = c^2$, to find sides of right triangles.
  - Identify various types of quadrilaterals.
  - Break up diagrams to find the areas and perimeters of compound figures.
  - Estimate distances to double-check your answers.
- Solve problems about solid objects.
  - Find the surface area and volume of rectangular prisms and cylinders.
  - Break compound solids into simpler shapes.
- Work with shapes in the coordinate plane.
  - Plot points in the coordinate plane.
  - Find the distance between points by using the equation $d = \sqrt{(x_1 - x_2)^2 + (y_1 - y_2)^2}$.
  - Find the areas and perimeters of shapes in the coordinate plane.
  - Translate shapes to a different position in the coordinate plane.
  - Reflect shapes across a vertical or horizontal line.

Measurement and Geometry Quiz

Measurement and Geometry Quiz

1. **A rectangular solid has length 2 feet, width 18 inches, and height 1 foot. What is the volume of this solid, in cubic feet?**

   A 3 ft^3

   B 13 ft^3

   C 36 ft^3

   D 112 ft^3

2. **How many square inches are in 4 square yards?**

   A 12 in^2

   B 36 in^2

   C 144 in^2

   D 5,184 in^2

3. **Which of the following shows a reflection of the polygon over the *y*-axis?**

A

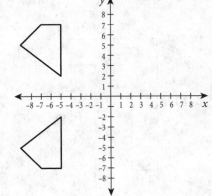

C

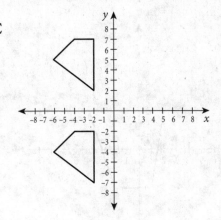

B

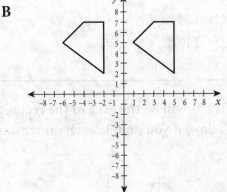

D

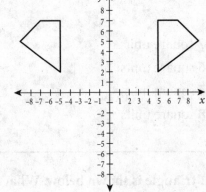

4. What is the area of the trapezoid shown below? $[A = \frac{1}{2}h(b_1 + b_2)]$

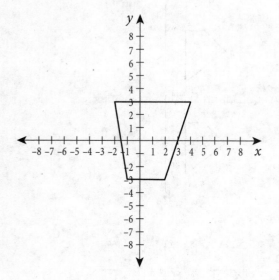

   A   27 square units

   B   36 square units

   C   54 square units

   D   108 square units

5. A right triangle is shown below. What is the value of the variable x?

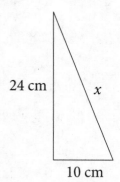

   A   17 cm

   B   26 cm

   C   34 cm

   D 338 cm

6. Carly has a dog run in the irregular shape shown below. What is the area of the dog run?

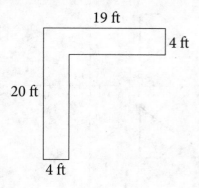

   A   47 ft^2

   B   78 ft^2

   C 124 ft^2

   D 140 ft^2

7. What will be the area of the rectangle below, if you double each dimension?

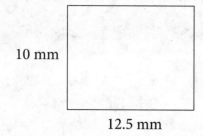

   A   90 mm^2

   B 125 mm^2

   C 250 mm^2

   D 500 mm^2

8. Polygon *ABCDE* is transformed to *A'B'C'D'E'* as shown on the coordinate grid below. The transformation is

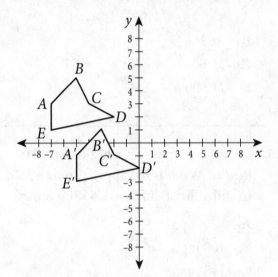

   A a reflection over the *x*-axis.

   B the translation T$_{(-2,4)}$.

   C the translation T$_{(2,-4)}$.

   D a reflection over the *y*-axis.

9. What is the area of a circle with a diameter of 16 inches? Use 3.14 for π.

   A 25.12 in²

   B 50.24 in²

   C 200.96 in²

   D 803.84 in²

10. The answer choices below show the measures of the three sides of different triangles. Which answer choice represents the side measures of a right triangle?

   A 7, 8, 12

   B 8, 15, 17

   C 10, 13, 20

   D 15, 20, 24

11. There are 15 female voices for every 10 male voices in the community choral group. If there are a total of 100 members in the group, how many of the members are female?

   A 15

   B 40

   C 60

   D 67

12. The cellular phone company needs to attach a wire brace to the utility tower as represented in the figure shown below. If the wire is 13 feet long and the wire is attached 12 feet up the tower, how far is the wire stake from the base of the tower?

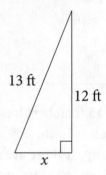

A   1 ft

B   5 ft

C   12.5 ft

D   17.7 ft

13. A blueprint for a rectangular classroom has a width of 2.8 cm and a length of 4.2 cm. If the actual width of the classroom is 20 feet, what is the length of the classroom, in feet?

A   13 ft

B   18.6 ft

C   21.4 ft

D   30 ft

14. A computer printer can print 1 page in 6 seconds. How many pages can be printed in 1 hour?

A   10

B   360

C   600

D   21,600

15. Logan is driving on a highway at 115 km/hr. What is his approximate speed in miles/hr? (1 mile ≈ 1.6 kilometers)

A   70 mph

B   100 mph

C   115 mph

D   184 mph

16. The two rectangles shown below are congruent. What is the measure of side *FE*?

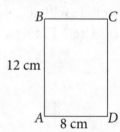 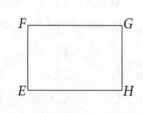

A   4 cm

B   8 cm

C   12 cm

D   20 cm

17. The area of the square below is 25 cm². What is the approximate circumference of the inscribed circle? Use 3.14 for π.

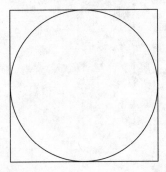

    A   15.7 cm

    B   19.625 cm

    C   31.4 cm

    D   78.5 cm

18. Ravi wants to build a deck around his hot tub, as shown in the shaded region below. What will be the approximate area of the deck? Use 3.14 for π.

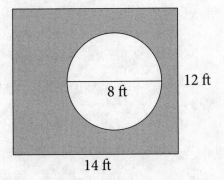

    A   32.96 ft²

    B   52 ft²

    C   118 ft²

    D   168 ft²

19. What is the surface area of the rectangular solid shown below?

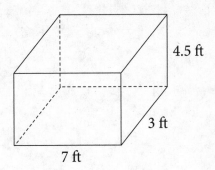

    A   21 in²

    B   31.5 in²

    C   94.5 in²

    D   132 in²

20. What is the area of the triangle shown below?

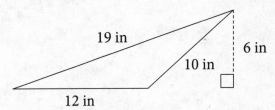

    A   36 in²

    B   41 in²

    C   60 in²

    D   360 in²

Answers and Explanations

1. A

To find the volume of a rectangular solid, you multiply length times width times height. Notice that in this problem, your answer should be in square feet, and one of the measurements, the width, is given in inches. First, convert 18 inches to 1.5 feet. Now multiply: $2 \times 1.5 \times 1 = 3$ square feet, choice A. If you chose C, you forgot to convert the width to feet.

2. D

To convert from square yards to square inches, you can first convert square yards to square feet, and then convert square feet into square inches. Because there are 3 feet in a yard, there are $3^2 = 9$ square feet in 1 square yard. Use this fact to convert 4 square yards to square feet: $9 \times 4 = 36$ square feet. Because there are 12 inches in a foot, there are $12^2 = 144$ square inches in 1 square foot. Convert 36 square feet to square inches: $36 \times 144 = 5,184$ square inches. If you chose A, you probably multiplied 4 square yards by 3 and forgot to convert to square inches. If you chose B, you found the number of inches in a yard instead of the square inches in a square yard.

3. D

A reflection of a polygon over the y-axis is a flip of the figure over the vertical axis. The reflection will be a mirror image to either the left or the right of the original polygon. This is shown in choice D. Choice A is a reflection over the x-axis. Choices B and C are not flips but slides (translations).

4. A

You are given the formula to find the area of a trapezoid, $A = \frac{1}{2}h(b_1 + b_2)$. The bases, b_1 and b_2, are the parallel horizontal sides. The height, h, is the vertical segment perpendicular to and connecting the two bases. Count the spaces to find the lengths of each of these measures. The bases are 6 and 3 spaces long, and the height is 6 spaces long.

Write the formula: $A = \frac{1}{2}h(b_1 + b_2)$

Substitute in the values: $A = \frac{1}{2} \times 6 \times (6 + 3)$

Using order of operations, evaluate the parentheses: $A = \frac{1}{2} \times 6 \times 9$

Multiply across, from left to right: $A = 27$ square units

Choice C may have been selected if you forgot to multiply by $\frac{1}{2}$ in the formula. You may have selected choice D if you multiplied the values within the parentheses instead of adding them.

5. B

The triangle shown is a right triangle, so use the Pythagorean theorem, $a^2 + b^2 = c^2$, to find the missing hypotenuse, x. The legs of the triangle are 10 cm and 24 cm.

Write the Pythagorean theorem: $a^2 + b^2 = c^2$

Substitute in the given values: $10^2 + 24^2 = x^2$

Evaluate the exponents: $100 + 576 = x^2$

Add on the left-hand side: $676 = x^2$

Take the square root of each side: $\sqrt{676} = \sqrt{x^2}$

The missing side is: 26 cm $= x$

Choice D is the result of dividing by 2 in the last step instead of taking the square root.

6. D

You can break up the irregular shape into two rectangles, as shown below:

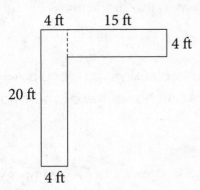

There are now two rectangles, so find the area of each by multiplying the length and width, then add the areas together. The left-hand rectangle has an area of 20 × 4 = 80 ft². The right-hand rectangle has an area of 15 × 4 = 60 ft². The total area is 80 + 60 = 140 ft². Choice A is the sum of the numbers labeled in the figure. Choice B is the perimeter of the shape, or the distance around the figure.

7. D

If you double each of the dimensions of a polygon, its area will increase by a factor of 2 × 2 = 4. Find the area of the original rectangle by multiplying the length and width: 10 × 12.5 = 125 mm². The area of the new rectangle will be 4 × 125 = 500 mm², answer choice D. An alternate way to solve this problem is to double each dimension and then calculate the area. The new rectangle will have dimensions of 10 × 2 = 20 mm and 12.5 × 2 = 25 mm. The new area is thus 20 × 25 = 500 mm². Choice B is the area of the original figure. Choice C is the result of only doubling one dimension when finding the area.

8. C

The polygon is shifted to the right and down, so this is a translation in the direction of positive *x* and negative *y*. Choose one of the points, like *A*, and count the distance it has moved to *A′*. To move from *A* to *A′* takes a shift of +2 in the horizontal direction and –4 in the vertical direction. This is the transformation $T_{(2,-4)}$. In choice A, a reflection over the *x*-axis would flip the figure over to the right into the first quadrant. In choice B, a translation of $T_{(-2, 4)}$ would move the figure 2 units to the left and up 4 units. In choice D, a reflection over the y-axis would flip the figure down into the third quadrant and would not shift it to the right as shown in the diagram.

9. C

The area of a circle is found by using the formula $A = \pi r^2$, where r is the radius of the circle. The radius is one half of the diameter, or $16 \div 2 = 8$ inches. Write the formula:

$$A = \pi r^2$$

Substitute in: $\qquad A = (3.14)(8)^2$

Evaluate the exponent: $\qquad A = 64(3.14)$

Multiply: $\qquad A = 200.96$ square inches

Choice A is the result of multiplying 3.14 by 8 inches. You may have selected this answer choice if you confused finding the area of the circle with finding the circumference, because the formula for circumference is $C = \pi d$. Choice B is the correct circumference of the circle. Choice D is the result of using a radius of 16 inches, instead of the correct radius of 8 inches, to find the area.

10. B

If the sides of a triangle satisfy the relationship such that the longest side squared is equal to the sum of the squares of the other two sides, then the triangle is a right triangle. This fact is the converse of the Pythagorean theorem. Take each answer choice and test. Let c represent the longest side and a and b represent the other two sides. Test answer choice A: $7^2 + 8^2 = 49 + 64 = 113$. The longest side squared, $12^2 = 144$, is not equal to 113. Therefore, choice A is not a right triangle. Now test choice B: $8^2 + 15^2 = 64 + 225 = 289$. The longest side squared is $17^2 = 289$. Therefore, choice B represents a right triangle, because the Pythagorean theorem holds true for these measures.

11. C

The problem states that for every 15 females, there are 10 males. Therefore, for every 25 total members, 15 are female. Set up a proportion of $\frac{female}{total} = \frac{female}{total}$, and cross multiply to find n, the number of females in the chorus.

Set up the proportion: $\frac{15}{25} = \frac{n}{100}$

Cross multiply: $25n = 1500$

Divide both sides by 25: $\frac{25n}{25} = \frac{1500}{25}$

Simplify: $n = 60$

Choice A is the result of using the number of females from the ratio for the total number of females in the whole group. Choice B is the number of males in the group. If you selected Choice D, you may have used the incorrect proportion $\frac{10}{15} = \frac{n}{100}$.

12. B

This problem situation can be represented by a right triangle, where the wire is the hypotenuse of the right triangle and the tower is one of the legs. Use the Pythagorean theorem, $a^2 + b^2 = c^2$, to find the missing leg. In the theorem, the variable c is the hypotenuse, and a and b are the legs.

Write the formula: $a^2 + b^2 = c^2$

Substitute in the given values: $12^2 + b^2 = 13^2$

Evaluate the exponents: $144 + b^2 = 169$

Subtract 144 from both sides: $144 - 144 + b^2 = 169 - 144$

Simplify: $b^2 = 25$

Take the square root of both sides: $\sqrt{b^2} = \sqrt{25}$

Simplify: $b = 5$

Choice A is the result of simply subtracting the two given sides of the triangle. Choice C is the result of dividing by 2 in the last step instead of taking the square root. Choice D is the result of using 12 feet and 13 feet for the legs of the hypotenuse.

13. D

A blueprint is a scale drawing. In a scale drawing, the rectangle on the drawing is similar to the actual rectangular classroom, so the sides are in proportion. Let n represent the length of the classroom and set up a proportion of $\frac{\text{scale}}{\text{actual}} = \frac{\text{scale}}{\text{actual}}$.

Set up the proportion:	$\dfrac{2.8}{20} = \dfrac{4.2}{n}$
Cross multiply:	$2.8n = 84$
Divide both sides by 2.8:	$\dfrac{2.8n}{2.8} = \dfrac{84}{2.8}$
Simplify:	$n = 30$

Choice A is the result of using an incorrect proportion.

14. C

The printer can print pages at a rate of 1 page every 6 seconds. To find out how many pages can be printed in 1 hour, first determine how many pages can be printed every minute. There are 60 seconds in each minute, and $60 \div 6 = 10$, so 10 pages can be printed every minute. There are 60 minutes in every hour, so $10 \times 60 = 600$ pages can be printed each hour. Choice A is the number of pages that can be printed in 1 minute. Choice D is the number of seconds in 6 hours.

15. A

To find Logan's speed in miles per hour, convert 115 kilometers to miles. It is given that there are approximately 1.6 kilometers in every mile. Divide to find the number of miles: $115 \div 1.6 = 71.875$ miles. Choice A is the approximate speed in miles per hour. If you multiplied instead of dividing, you arrived at choice D.

16. B

It is given that the rectangles are congruent, but notice that the right-hand rectangle is rotated 90°. Find the side that corresponds to side *FE*. This is side *AD* or side *BC*, of length 8 cm. Choice C is the length of sides *AB*, *CD*, *FG*, and *EH*.

17. A

The circle is inscribed in the square, so the diameter of the circle is equal to the length of a side of the square. The area of the square is given as 25 cm². Because the area of a square is found by the formula $A = s^2$, where s is a side of the square, the length of a side is $\sqrt{25}$ = 5 cm. This is also the diameter of the circle. The formula to find the circumference is $C = \pi d$, or $C = \pi \times 5$. Substituting in 3.14 for π, the circumference is approximately 15.7 cm. Choice B is the area of a circle with radius 2.5 cm. Choice C is the circumference of a circle with diameter 10 cm. Choice D is the area of a circle with radius 5 cm.

18. C

To find the area of the shaded region, find the area of the inner circle and subtract it from the area of the outer polygon. The area of a circle is found by the formula $A = \pi r^2$, where r is the radius of the circle. The diameter is given as 8 feet, so the radius is one-half of this, or 4 feet. The area of the circle is thus $A = \pi \times 4^2 = 3.14 \times 16 = 50.24$ ft². The outer polygon is a rectangle, and the area of a rectangle is found by multiplying the length and width, so $A = 14 \times 12 = 168$ ft². Therefore the area of the deck, the shaded region, is $168 - 50.24 = 117.76$ ft², or approximately 118 ft², choice C. Choice A is the result of using 8 feet as the radius of the circle and finding the difference between its area and the area of the rectangle. Choice D is the area of the entire rectangular region.

19. D

The surface area of a rectangular solid can be found by using the formula $SA = 2lw + 2wh + 2lh$, where l is the length, w is the width, and h is the height of the solid. Referring to the figure, $l = 7$ m, $w = 3$ m and $h = 4.5$ m.

Write the formula:	$SA = 2lw + 2wh + 2lh$
Substitute in the given values:	$SA = 2(7)(3) + 2(3)(4.5) + 2(7)(4.5)$
Multiply left to right:	$SA = 42 + 27 + 63$
Now add to find the surface area:	$SA = 132$ m²

Choice A is the area of the bottom and top sides of the figure. Choice B is the area of the front and back sides of the figure. Choice C is the volume of the rectangular solid.

20. A

The area of a triangle is found by using the formula $A = \frac{1}{2}bh$, where b is the base of the triangle and h is the height of the triangle. Do not be confused by the fact that all three side lengths are given for the triangle; the base is 12 inches, and the height is the perpendicular length, 6 inches.

Write the formula: $\qquad\qquad\qquad\qquad A = \frac{1}{2}bh$

Substitute in the given values: $\qquad\qquad A = \frac{1}{2} \times 12 \times 6$

Multiply left to right to find the area: $\quad A = 36 \text{ in}^2$

Choice B is the result of adding the values 19 + 12 + 10 from the figure. Choice C may have been selected if an incorrect height of 10 was used to find the area. Choice D is the result of multiplying the correct area by 10.

Chapter 5

Mathematical Reasoning

ANALYZING A PROBLEM

Mathematical reasoning describes the logical thinking skills you use to set up and solve math problems. The problems in this chapter don't cover any new topics; instead, mathematical reasoning problems look at number sense, algebra and functions, statistics, data analysis, probability, and geometry and measurement in new ways. These problems may be a little different from most of the math problems you've seen before. Rather than finding a particular answer, mathematical reasoning is all about how you arrange the given information to figure out whether you can find the answer and, if so, how you would do that.

 Filling in the units can make word problems clearer.

Bob hiked 4 miles in 1 hour and 15 minutes. Which of the following expressions shows Bob's average speed in miles per hour?

A 4 × 1.15

B 4 × 1.25

C 4 ÷ 1.15

D 4 ÷ 1.25

Average speed is a rate, miles per hour. The basic formula is rate $= \dfrac{\text{distance}}{\text{time}}$. You need to divide the number of miles (4) by the number of hours (1.25). That's choice **D**. Don't be fooled by choice C. Because an hour has 60 minutes, 15 minutes is a quarter of an hour; the divisor is 1.25, not 1.15.

Mathematical reasoning questions might ask you identify information in a problem that you don't need.

Suzanne is buying pumpkins to decorate for the Fall Festival. Orange pumpkins cost $0.23 per pound, and white pumpkins cost $0.59 per pound. Suzanne buys two orange pumpkins and one white pumpkin for each of the 23 tables set up at the festival. All together, the orange pumpkins weigh 236 pounds and the white pumpkins weigh 53 pounds. Which of this information is not necessary to find the total cost of the pumpkins Suzanne bought?

A   The cost per pound of the orange pumpkins

B   The number of white pumpkins per table

C   The total weight of the orange pumpkins

D   The total weight of the white pumpkins

Because the pumpkins are priced per pound, the number of pumpkins that Suzanne uses does not help you figure out how much she pays. You need to know the cost per pound of each type of pumpkin (one of which is given in choice A) and the total weight of each type of pumpkin (given in choices C and D). The number of white pumpkins, choice **B**, doesn't help to solve the problem, so it is unnecessary.

This type of question may also ask you to figure out what information is missing.

Brooke drove 40 miles in 45 minutes. At this speed, her car travels an average of 25 miles per gallon of gas. What additional information do you need to find out how much the gas Brooke used on the trip cost?

A How much Brooke paid for each gallon of gas

B The number of gallons of gas used on the trip

C How many minutes Brooke spent at the gas station

D The number of gallons of gas the car started with

To find out how much the gas cost, you need to know how much Brooke paid for it. From the number of miles she drove and the miles per gallon the car gets, you can find the number of gallons that were used. The missing information you need is the price per gallon, choice **A**. Because choice B can be calculated based on the information in the question, you don't need that information to solve the problem. The number of minutes Brooke spent at the gas station (choice C) and the number of gallons of gas the car started with (choice D) are also unnecessary to calculate the cost of gas.

Many mathematical reasoning questions will ask you to apply the method for finding a solution to one question to a different problem. In other cases, you could be asked to identify the general rule you would follow to solve a type of problem. It's helpful to write down your method for solving the first problem so that you can more easily compare it to the answer choices.

> **Martin is packing 400 T-shirts into boxes. Each box can hold 25 T-shirts. How many boxes will Martin use?**

The problem above can be solved by using the same arithmetic operation as which of the following problems?

A   Carol will sing 5 songs at a concert. The average length of each song is 4 minutes long. How long will Carol sing at the concert?

B   Michael is filing papers. Every folder can hold 50 pieces of paper. How many pieces of paper can Michael file in 25 folders?

C   Marsha wrote a story that was 6 pages long in 4 hours. What was the average number of hours it took Marsha to write each page?

D   Cameron is swimming laps. Each lap is 25 meters. How far has Cameron swum after swimming 30 laps?

To find the number of boxes Martin used to pack 400 T-shirts, you would divide the number of T-shirts (400) by the number of T-shirts in each box (25). The arithmetic operation used to solve the problem is division. See which of the problems in the answer choices can also be solved by division.

A   The total amount of time Carol will spend singing at the concert is the sum of the lengths of the songs. If the songs average 4 minutes long, Carol will sing for $5 \times 4 = 20$ minutes. This problem is solved by multiplication, not division.

B   The number of pieces of paper Michael can file is the product of the number of folders and the number of pieces of paper each folder can hold. This problem is also solved by multiplication.

C   The average number of hours each page took is the total number of hours (4) divided by the number of pages (6). This problem is solved by division, so it uses the same arithmetic operation as the original problem. Choice **C** is correct.

D   The total distance Cameron has swum is the sum of the lengths of all the laps, or $30 \times 25 = 750$. This problem is solved by multiplication, not division.

For problems that involve formulas, you'll need to plug in numbers or variables and simplify the resulting expressions. These problems usually include examples to help you along if the directions are confusing, so they're not as complicated as they look.

Karen converted 68 degrees Fahrenheit to degrees Celsius by using the following procedure.

1. Subtract 32.	$68 - 32 = 36$
2. Multiply by 5.	$36 \times 5 = 180$
3. Divide by 9.	$180 \div 9 = 20$

According to Karen's procedure, what is the temperature in degrees Celsius when the temperature in degrees Fahrenheit is F?

A $\dfrac{5F - 32}{9}$

B $\dfrac{5F}{9} - 32$

C $\dfrac{F - 160}{9}$

D $\dfrac{5F - 160}{9}$

> ✎ **To review the order of operations and how it affects expressions, see page 91 in the Simplifying Expressions section of Chapter 3, "Algebra and Functions."**

Plug the given temperature in degrees Fahrenheit into the procedure, following each step in order.

1. Subtract 32.	$F - 32$
2. Multiply by 5.	$(F - 32)5$
3. Divide by 9.	$\dfrac{(F - 32)5}{9}$

Then simplify this expression:

$$\frac{(F - 32)5}{9} = \frac{5F - 160}{9}$$

That's choice **D**. If you got choice B, you multiplied by 5 and divided by 9 before subtracting 32, which is not the correct order of operations. If you selected choice C, you probably forgot to use parentheses around *F* – 32 in the formula or didn't distribute the 5 correctly.

ESTIMATION

You've been using estimation all along to narrow down the answer choices and make sure your calculated solutions are reasonable. Some CAHSEE questions will specifically ask you to estimate, not to solve the problem accurately.

If the question asks you to round to a particular place value (for example, hundreds or tenths), make sure you round to that place value. Round up if the number in the next place is 5 or greater and round down if it is 4 or less.

Sean needs 627 rubber balls for a science project. Each ball costs 39 cents. Which of the following will produce the most reasonable estimate of the cost of the balls in dollars?

A 600×0.30

B 620×0.30

C 630×0.30

D 630×0.40

The number of balls in the answer choices is rounded to the nearest 10 or the nearest 100. The nearest 10 will produce a more accurate estimate. Because 7 is greater than 5, round 627 up to 630. Similarly, 39 cents should be rounded up to $0.40. Choice **D** would produce the best estimate.

 If you're having trouble estimating, you don't always need to solve the problem the way the test writers expect. Instead, solve the problem accurately and then round that answer, instead of rounding each value before performing the operation.

A museum was open for 63 days during the summer. The average number of visitors per day was 792. About how many people visited the museum over the summer?

A   900

B   42,000

C   48,000

D   80,000

The museum was open for about 60 days and had about 800 visitors per day. That makes a total of 60 × 800 = 48,000 visitors over the summer, or choice **C**. You may have selected choice A if you rounded the values to 100 days and 800 visitors and then added them together. Choice B is the result of rounding the values to 60 days and 700 visitors and then multiplying them. Choice D is the result of rounding the values to 100 days and 800 visitors and then multiplying.

Extending a line on a graph is another way to estimate a value that's difficult or impossible to calculate. If you're having trouble seeing where the line goes, use your answer sheet as a straight edge to make the line clearer.

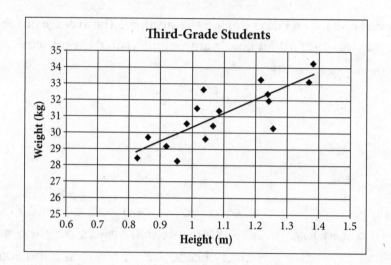

The graph above shows the heights and weights of a group of third-graders. Using the line of best fit shown, about how much should a third-grader who is 0.6 meters tall weigh?

A   26 kg

B   27 kg

C   28 kg

D   29 kg

Extend the line until it reaches a point directly above 0.6 on the *x*-axis.

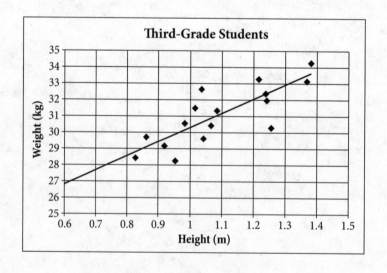

You can see that when a student is 0.6 meters tall, that child's weight should be about 27 kilograms. That's choice **B**. Choice C is the weight for a height of about 0.75 meters. Choice D is the weight for a height of about 0.85 meters.

PATTERNS

Some CAHSEE questions ask you to find patterns. The most common patterns result from adding or multiplying by the same number repeatedly. If you don't see a pattern right away, look for a pattern in the differences between terms.

$$13\frac{1}{2}, 4\frac{1}{2}, 1\frac{1}{2}, \frac{1}{2}, \frac{1}{6}, \frac{1}{n}$$

What is the most likely value of n in the pattern above?

A $\dfrac{1}{18}$

B $\dfrac{1}{8}$

C 12

D 18

Each number in the pattern is the previous number times $\frac{1}{3}$. This pattern may be easier to see if you change each mixed number to an improper fraction. The sequence can be written as $\frac{27}{2}, \frac{9}{2}, \frac{3}{2}, \frac{1}{2}, \frac{1}{6}, \frac{1}{n}$. Each term is one-third the previous term, so multiply by $\frac{1}{3}$ to get the next term in the pattern: $\frac{1}{n} = \frac{1}{6} \times \frac{1}{3} = \frac{1}{18}$. Because $\frac{1}{n} = \frac{1}{18}$, $n = 18$, or choice **D**. A common mistake is to pick choice A, which is the value of the next term instead of the value of n.

Finding patterns in a list of numbers is more difficult when you don't have all the terms. Pattern questions that have tables showing the relationship between two different things often don't include all the terms you might need to spot the pattern in the same way you would looking at a simple list. However, these questions usually ask for an equation describing the relationship between the two things instead of just having you predict the next value. That means you can use the answer choices to solve the problem instead of having to work out the pattern on your own.

If you don't see a relationship between the two things right away, try plugging a few pairs of values into the equations to eliminate the ones that are wrong. Usually, each incorrect answer choice will work for at least one pair of numbers in the chart, so don't stop testing too soon. Only one equation will describe *all* the values given in the question.

 Test every answer choice when you're picking numbers or plugging in values from a chart.

Donald grew plants with different amounts of fertilizer and noticed a pattern in their growth.

Milliliters of fertilizer (f)	Height of plant in centimeters (h)
1	10.5
5	12.5
7	13.5
8	14
10	15

Which of the following equations best describes the relationship between the amount of fertilizer in milliliters (f) and the height of the plants in centimeters (h)?

A $h = 9 + \dfrac{3f}{2}$

B $h = 9.5 + f$

C $h = 10 + \dfrac{f}{2}$

D $h = \dfrac{3f}{2}$

The easiest way to solve pattern problems with tables is to plug in a few values from the table. Try $f = 10$, because it's easy to work with.

A $h = 9 + \dfrac{3(10)}{2} = 9 + \dfrac{30}{2} = 9 + 15 = 24$

That doesn't match the value of 15 shown in the table, so you know choice A is not right.

B $h = 9.5 + 10 = 19.5$

That doesn't match either, so choice B can also be eliminated.

C $h = 10 + \dfrac{10}{2} = 10 + 5 = 15$

That does match, but try choice D as well in case more than one equation happens to work for this particular pair of numbers.

D $h = \dfrac{3(10)}{2} = \dfrac{30}{2} = 15$

Because both choice C and choice D work for this pair of values, try another pair to see which one is correct. $f = 1$ is also easy to evaluate.

C $h = 10 + \dfrac{1}{2} = 10.5$

D $h = \dfrac{3(1)}{2} = 1.5$

Only choice **C** works for all the points in the chart.

NUMBER PROPERTIES

Number properties are patterns that fit all integers (whole numbers) or all real numbers. You know that multiples of 2, like 2, 4, 6, and 8, are even and that the other integers are odd. You know that every number greater than 0 is positive and every number less than 0 is negative. Questions about number properties test how well you understand these patterns.

 Sometimes you'll need to pick several numbers to show that certain answer choices aren't true.

The best way to solve questions about number properties is to pick numbers. Because the patterns apply to all numbers, looking at a few examples will usually let you find the rule. Test all of the answer choices—don't stop when you find one answer choice that works. Sometimes several answer choices can work for a particular number, but only one will work for all numbers. Remember, as always, that the numbers you pick must match any restrictions given in the question.

If x is an odd number and y is an even number, which of the following is always an odd number?

A $x + y$

B $\dfrac{x}{y}$

C $\dfrac{y}{x}$

D $x \cdot y$

Because x is an odd number and y is an even number, you'll need to pick one of each and plug them into the correct locations. Say x is 3 and y is 2, then see which of the answer choices produces an odd number.

A $3 + 2 = 5$

B $\dfrac{3}{2} = 1.5$

C $\dfrac{2}{3} = 0.\overline{6}$

D $3 \cdot 2 = 6$

Choices B and C aren't integers, so they are neither even nor odd. Choice D is an even integer. The only odd number produced by $x = 3$ and $y = 2$ is choice **A**.

The number 1 is not a prime number, because its only factor is itself. The number 2 is the only even prime number; all the other even numbers are multiples of 2, so they have at least three factors.

Questions about number properties may involve some specialized vocabulary. An integer that is divisible by another integer is a *multiple* of that integer. The *factors* of a number are the positive integers that divide evenly into that number. Every positive integer is both a factor and a multiple of itself. For example, $5 \times 2 = 10$, so 10 is a multiple of 5 and 2, and 5 and 2 are factors of 10. A *prime* number, like 2 or 7, has exactly two factors: 1 and itself. The *remainder* is the part of a number that does not divide evenly, or what is left over after dividing. For instance, if 10 is divided by 3, the result is 3 with a remainder of 1.

36
48
60
84
132
144

What do all the numbers in the table above have in common?

A   They are all multiples of 12.

B   They are all multiples of 16.

C   They are all multiples of 18.

D   They are all multiples of 20.

Each of these numbers is a multiple of 12.

$$36 = 12 \times 3$$
$$48 = 12 \times 4$$
$$60 = 12 \times 5$$
$$84 = 12 \times 7$$
$$132 = 12 \times 11$$
$$144 = 12 \times 12$$

Although some of the numbers in the table are multiples of the other numbers listed in the answer choices ($48 = 16 \times 3$, $36 = 18 \times 2$, and $60 = 20 \times 3$), they are all multiples of only 12 among the answer choices. Choice **A** is correct.

SUMMARY

After reading this chapter, you should be able to do the following:

- Use logical thinking skills to analyze CAHSEE questions.
  - o Identify information needed to solve a problem.
  - o Set up a problem without solving it.
  - o Use a problem-solving method from one situation in a different type of problem.
- Estimate reasonable answers to mathematical situations.
  - o Round numbers correctly.
  - o Extend a line on a graph to estimate values.
- Identify common patterns in lists and tables.
- Pick numbers to answer questions about number properties.

Mathematical Reasoning Quiz

1. Micah typed 4,950 words in 1 hour and 30 minutes. What computation will give Micah's average typing speed in words per minute?

   A Divide 4,950 by 1.5.

   B Divide 4,950 by 90.

   C Multiply 4,950 by 1.5.

   D Multiply 4,950 by 90.

2. Which of the following is the best estimate of 8,930 ÷ 9.6?

   A   90

   B   900

   C   9,000

   D 90,000

The speed limit on the highway is 65 miles per hour. At this rate, how long will it take to drive 215 miles on the highway?

3. Which of the following problems would be solved using the same arithmetic operation as would be used to solve the problem above?

   A Brendon drove for 6 hours at a constant speed of 65 miles per hour. How far did he travel?

   B Jingwen earns $5.50 per hour for babysitting. How much will she earn if she works for 4.25 hours?

   C The senior class officers will reserve buses for the class trip. There are 410 seniors, and each bus seats 42 students. How many buses should be reserved?

   D There are 12 water bottles in each package and 24 packages in each carton. How many water bottles are in each carton?

4. Marta is taking a car trip and wants to estimate her gasoline expense. She will travel 460 miles and gasoline costs $2.85 per gallon.

   What *other* information is needed for Marta to estimate her gasoline expense?

   A   The speed limit on the highway
   B   The cost of gasoline for each gallon
   C   The number of hours she will travel
   D   The average number of miles that Marta's car can travel for each gallon of gasoline

5. If you double the side lengths of a 3 × 3 × 3 cube, how does the volume change?

   A   The volume stays the same.
   B   The volume doubles.
   C   The volume will be four times larger.
   D   The volume will be eight times larger.

6. The square and the parallelogram below have the same area. What is the length of a side of the square?

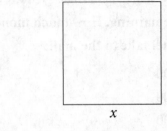

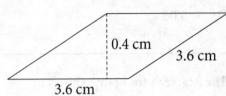

   A   1.2 cm
   B   1.44 cm
   C   3.6 cm
   D   6.48 cm

7. If the area of the right triangle below is 30.25 mm², the height is approximately

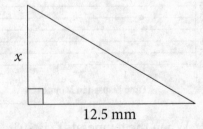

   A   0.5 mm.
   B   2.5 mm.
   C   5 mm.
   D   17.75 mm.

8. Miguel went shopping at the mall. He spent $\frac{1}{2}$ of his money on a skateboard. He then spent $\frac{1}{4}$ of his remaining money on wheel bearings. He had $15.00 remaining. How much money did Miguel take to the mall?

A $15.00

B $30.00

C $40.00

D $80.00

9. The scatter plot below shows a relationship between time and temperature. Based on this data, which statement is <u>not</u> true?

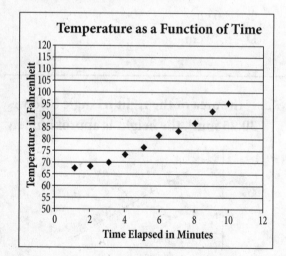

A When the temperature is 70° Fahrenheit, the time elapsed is approximately 3 minutes.

B As the time elapsed increases, the temperature increases.

C As the time elapsed increases, the temperature decreases.

D The temperature at 5 minutes of elapsed time would be approximately 76° Fahrenheit.

10. A triangle has a base length of $b = 15$ mm and a height of $h < 15$ mm. Which of the following could be the area of the triangle?

A 110 mm²

B 113 mm²

C 225 mm²

D 450 mm²

11. Which equation below would require the same arithmetic operation in the first step of solving it as the equation $5x - 7 = 33$?

A $x - 5 = 33$

B $5x + 7 = 33$

C $5(x - 7) = 33$

D $\frac{x}{5} = 33$

12. If n is any even number, which of the following is not always true of $3n$?

A It is an even number.

B It is divisible by 3.

C It is divisible by 2.

D It is an odd number.

13. If 5 oranges cost $2.99, the cost of 18 oranges is approximately

A $6.00.

B $8.00.

C $11.00.

D $15.00.

14. If a and b are both negative numbers, which of the expressions below is always greater than zero?

   A ab

   B $a + b$

   C $a - b$

   D $-a + b$

15. Which table below would represent the function $y = \frac{1}{2}x - 3$?

   A

x	y
−2	−4
−1	−3.5
0	−3
1	−2.5
2	−2

   B

x	y
−4	−2
−3.5	−1
−3	0
−2.5	1
−2	2

   C

x	y
−2	−2
−1	−2.5
0	−3
1	2.5
2	2

   D

x	y
4	5
6	6
8	7
10	8
12	9

16. In 1994, the math club had 4 members. In 1998, the club had 16 members. In 2000, the club had 22 members. If the club attendance rises at this same rate, what is the best estimate of the number of members in the year 2008?

   A 26

   B 28

   C 46

   D 64

17. Juan, a 10th-grade student, works part-time at the hardware store. He works 4 hours a day for 4 days each week. He earns $6.50 for each hour worked. He sells an average of $800.00 worth of merchandise each week.

   Which information pieces are necessary to determine Juan's average sales for each hour of work?

   A The hourly pay and the average merchandise sales

   B The hours worked each day, the days worked each week, and the hourly pay

   C The hours worked each day, the days worked each week, and the average merchandise sales

   D The hours worked each day, his grade in school, and the average merchandise sales

Fraction	Decimal Equivalent
$\frac{1}{9}$	$0.\overline{1}$
$\frac{3}{9}$	$0.\overline{3}$
$\frac{15}{99}$	$0.\overline{15}$
$\frac{205}{999}$	$0.\overline{205}$

18. Using the fraction-to-decimal conversion examples above, and assuming the pattern is consistent, what would be the decimal equivalent of $\frac{1554}{9999}$?

   A $0.\overline{154}$

   B $0.\overline{1554}$

   C $0.155\overline{4}$

   D $15.\overline{54}$

The amount of fabric needed to construct a pair of trousers is $1\frac{7}{8}$ yards. A bolt of wool fabric has enough to make 16 pairs of trousers. How many yards of fabric are on the bolt?

19. Which problem below would require the same mathematical operation to solve as the given problem above?

   A   If 4 buses can transport 216 passengers, how many passengers can each bus transport?

   B   What is the area of a rectangular family room, if the width is 12 feet and the length is 26 feet?

   C   A 2" by 4" piece of lumber is 6 feet long. How many 1.5-foot-long boards can be cut from this lumber?

   D   Raaka earned $30.25 for babysitting. If she earns $5.50 per hour, how many hours did she babysit?

---

20. If a is an odd prime number and b is an odd number, which of the following is always true?

   A   The expression ab is an odd number.

   B   The expression ab is a prime number.

   C   The expression ab is an even number.

   D   The expression ab is a negative number.

Answers and Explanations

1. B

You are asked to find Micah's average typing speed in words per minute. First, convert 1 hour and 30 minutes to minutes. There are 60 minutes in an hour, so Micah types 4,950 words in 60 + 30 = 90 minutes. The unit rate will be found by dividing 4,950 words by 90 minutes. Choice A would have been correct if you were looking for the average speed in words per hour.

2. B

To estimate a mathematical computation, you can round the numbers so that the computation can be done mentally. Round 8,930 to 9,000 and round 9.6 to 10. You can now mentally divide 9,000 by 10 and get 900. You may have selected choice C if you divided 9,000 by 1 instead of 10. Choice D is the result of adding an extra zero to the estimate.

3. C

The time traveled can be found with the formula $D = RT$, where D is the distance traveled, R is the speed, and T is the time. You would therefore divide both sides of the formula by R to solve for the time: $T = \dfrac{D}{R}$. Now, look at the answer choices and determine which of the problems would be solved by division. Choice A uses the same formula as the given problem, but it asks you to solve for distance, so you would multiply to solve this problem. Choices B and D would also be solved by multiplication. In choice C, to determine how many buses are needed, you would divide the number of passengers by the capacity of each bus. Choice **C** uses the same operation, division, to solve the problem.

4. D

To solve this problem, Marta needs to know the average number of miles that her car can travel for each gallon of gasoline, choice **D**. Choice A, the speed limit, and choice C, the hours she will travel, are not necessary information to calculate the gasoline expense. Choice B, the cost of gasoline for each gallon, is not *other* needed information; it is already given in the question.

5. D

The fact that the cube is originally a 3 × 3 × 3 is not needed information. If you double each of the sides of any rectangular solid, the volume will increase by a factor of 2 × 2 × 2 = 8, because the formula for a rectangular solid is $V = lwh$. The new volume will be 8 times larger. Choice B is the result of doubling one of the sides. Choice C is the result of doubling two of the sides.

6. A

The two polygons are a parallelogram and a square. Find the area of the parallelogram and then determine the length of a side of the square. The formula for the area of a parallelogram is $A = bh$. Substitute in the given measures, and the area of the parallelogram is $A = 3.6 \times 0.4 = 1.44$ cm². The area of a square is found by the formula $A = s^2$. Substitute in the given area of 1.44 and solve for the side of the square, s.

Write the formula:	$A = s^2$
Substitute in the area:	$1.44 = s^2$
Take the square root of each side:	$\sqrt{1.44} = \sqrt{s^2}$
The length of the side is:	1.2 cm $= s$

Choice C is the result of finding the area of the parallelogram by using 3.6 cm as the height and 3.6 cm as the base, then taking the square root of this product.

7. C

You are given the area of a triangle and are asked to find its approximate height. The formula for the area of a triangle is $A = \frac{1}{2}bh$, where A is the area, b is the base length, and h is the height.

Write the formula:	$A = \frac{1}{2}bh$
Substitute in the known information:	$30.25 = \frac{1}{2} \times 12.5 \times h$
Multiply each side by 2:	$2 \times 30.25 = 2 \times \frac{1}{2} \times 12.5 \times h$
Simplify:	$60.5 = 12.5 \times h$
Divide each side by 12.5:	$4.84 = h$

You are asked for an approximate height, so find an answer choice that makes sense. The only choice that when multiplied by 12.5 would approximate 60.5 is answer choice **C**, approximately 5 mm. You may have selected choice B if you did not multiply the base and the height by $\frac{1}{2}$.

8. C

To determine how much money Miguel took to the mall, use the strategy of working backwards. Miguel had $15.00 remaining, and prior to this, he had spent $\frac{1}{4}$ of his remaining money on bearings. This means that the $15.00 was $\frac{3}{4}$ of the remaining money. In other words, $15 \div 3 = 5$ dollars, the money spent on bearings. Therefore, prior to buying the bearings, Miguel had $15 + 5 = $20.00. This was after buying the skateboard. Miguel spent $\frac{1}{2}$ of his original money on the skateboard, so the skateboard cost $20.00. Therefore, Miguel started with $20 + 20 = $40.00. You may have selected choice B if you misread the question and did not consider that he spent $\frac{1}{4}$ of his money on wheel bearings.

9. C

This scatter plot shows an approximately linear relationship between time and temperature. As the time increases, so does the temperature. Therefore, choice **C** is <u>not</u> true. Each of the other choices are true.

10. A

The base of the triangle is 15 mm, and the height is less than 15 mm. Use the formula for the area of a triangle to find out the upper limit of the area.

Write the formula: $\qquad$ $A = \frac{1}{2}bh$

Substitute in the given values: $\qquad$ $A = \frac{1}{2} \times 15 \times 15$

Simplify: $\qquad$ $A = 112.5 \text{ mm}^2$

The triangle's actual height is less than 15 mm, so its area must be less than 112.5 mm². Therefore, choice **A**, 110 mm², is the only possible area for the triangle. Choice C is too large and could be the result of not using $\frac{1}{2}$ in the area formula.

11. A

The given equation is a two-step equation. When you solve a two-step equation, the first step is to undo the addition or subtraction. So the first step is to add 7 to both sides of the equation. Now look through the answer choices to see which of these equations has addition as the first step to solving it. The first step to solve the equation listed as answer choice **A** is to add 5 to both sides of the equation; this is the correct answer choice. The first step in choice B would be to subtract 7 from both sides. For choice C, you would first apply the distributive property and multiply by 5 within the parentheses. For choice D, the first step would be to multiply both sides of the equation by 5.

12. D

It is given that n is an even number. Therefore $3n$ will also be an even number, because an even number times an odd number is always an even product. For the same reason, $3n$ will always be divisible by 2, given that n is even. The expression $3n$ will always be divisible by 3, because 3 is a factor of $3n$. Answer choice **D** is <u>not</u> true of $3n$; because n is even, $3n$ is even, not odd.

13. C

You are looking for an approximate answer. Round $2.99 to $3.00. Because 5 oranges cost $3.00, each orange is approximately $3.00 ÷ 5 = $0.60. Round 18 to 20, and the total cost of the oranges would be about 0.60 × 20 = $12.00. The value 18 was rounded up to 20, so the approximate cost will actually be a little less than $12.00, or $11.00, answer choice **C**. Choice A would be the approximate cost for 10 oranges. Choice D would be the approximate cost of 25 oranges.

14. A

It is given that a and b are both negative numbers. When you multiply two integers with the same sign, the product is a positive number. Therefore, ab, answer choice **A**, is always greater than zero. Answer choice B will always be negative. Choices C and D may be either positive or negative, depending on the absolute values of a and b.

15. A

To determine the correct table, substitute in the value of –2 for x into the given equation: $y = \left(\frac{1}{2} \times -2\right) - 3 = -1 - 3 = -4$. Therefore, when $x = -2$, $y = -4$. This eliminates choices B and C. To test choice D, find the value of y when $x = 4$: $y = \left(\frac{1}{2} \times 4\right) - 3 = 2 - 3 = -1$. According to the equation, when $x = 4$, $y = -1$. This eliminates choice D, and choice **A** is the correct table.

16. C

Between 1994 and 1998, there was an increase of 12 members. This is 12 ÷ 4 = 3 new members each year. This pattern holds, because from 1998 to the year 2000, there was an increase of 6 members, and 6 ÷ 2 = 3 new members each year. If this rate continues, then 8 years from the year 2000, in 2008, there will be 8 × 3 = 24 new members. Add 22 current members and 24 new members to get 46 members in the year 2008. Choice D is the result of multiplying the values of 4 and 16 from the question.

17. C

It is given that Juan sells an average of $800.00 worth of merchandise each week. To determine Juan's average sales for each hour of work, you also need to know the number of hours worked each day and the number of days worked each week. It is not necessary to know that Juan is in the 10th grade or that he earns $6.50 an hour, as is given in the other answer choices.

18. B

Looking at the pattern, the number of 9s in the denominator of the fraction determines the number of digits that repeat in the decimal equivalent. The repeat sequence is the value of the numerator of the fraction. The only answer choice that satisfies these conditions is answer choice **B**. Choice A would be equivalent to the fraction $\frac{154}{999}$. Choice C would be equivalent to the mixed number $15\frac{44}{99}$.

19. B

To solve the given word problem, you would multiply the yardage needed per pair of trousers by the number of pairs of trousers that can be made from a bolt. Find a word problem in the answer choices that requires multiplication to solve. To find the area of a rectangle, you multiply the length and the width, answer choice **B**. Each of the other problems would be solved with division.

20. a

It is given that a is an odd prime number and that b is an odd number, and you are asked to find the statement that is always true. Answer choice A is always true, because the expression ab will always yield an odd number. Answer choice C is never true, because multiplying two odd numbers will always yield an odd number. Answer choice B is not correct; the expression ab can never be a prime number, because it has at least 4 factors, namely 1, a, b, and ab. Prime numbers have 2 factors only. Answer choice D is incorrect because neither a nor b is a negative number, so two positive numbers cannot yield a negative number.

Algebra I

ADVANCED EQUATIONS

This part of the CAHSEE builds on things you learned in Chapter 3, "Algebra and Functions," extending that knowledge to more difficult situations. These questions will ask you to solve complicated, multistep equations and inequalities.

As you know from solving simpler equations, the easiest way to get a variable alone on one side of an equation is to reverse whatever has been done to it on both sides of the equation. Two of the reversals you'll use most often are taking the opposite and taking the reciprocal.

Finding the *opposite* of a number or expression is simple—just reverse the sign. The opposite of x is $-x$, and the opposite of $-x$ is x. If $x = -7$, then $-x = -(-7) = 7$.

Finding the *reciprocal* looks a little more complicated. It is 1 divided by the number or expression. The reciprocal of x is $\frac{1}{x}$, and the reciprocal of $\frac{1}{x}$ is $\frac{1}{\frac{1}{x}} = 1 \cdot \frac{x}{1} = x$. The reciprocal of a fraction $\frac{x}{y}$ is $\frac{y}{x}$.

One common mistake is to find the *negative reciprocal*, or opposite of the reciprocal, when the question only asks for the reciprocal. You may already know how to find the negative reciprocal, because it is used to find the slopes of perpendicular lines, but the CAHSEE does not test this skill. Most CAHSEE questions will only request the reciprocal.

What is the reciprocal of $\dfrac{6p}{7n^3}$?

A $-\dfrac{6p}{7n^3}$

B $-\dfrac{7p}{6n^3}$

C $\dfrac{7n^3}{6p}$

D $\dfrac{7p}{6n^3}$

The reciprocal of any number is 1 divided by the number. For a fraction, that's the same as switching the places of the numerator and the denominator. The reciprocal of $\dfrac{6p}{7n^3}$ is $\dfrac{7n^3}{6p}$, or choice **C**.

 To review the basics of simplifying each side of an equation, see the Simplifying Expressions section of Chapter 3, "Algebra and Functions."

The equations and inequalities found in Chapter 3 only required you to undo a few steps, but the more complicated equations in Algebra I may require many steps. Be sure to consider the order in which you take steps as you work to get x alone on one side of the equation. Usually, you will need to combine terms to simplify the equation, use addition or subtraction to put a multiple of x by itself on one side of the equation, and then use division or multiplication to get x alone.

No matter how complicated an equation or expression looks, you can solve or simplify it by using the rules you already know. The distributive property, $a \times (b \pm c) = ab \pm ac$, will help you simplify complicated equations and re-write them in more usable forms.

Which of the following expressions is equivalent to $\dfrac{5(2 + x) - 2(5 - x)}{(x + 7) - x}$ **?**

A $\quad x$

B $\quad \dfrac{3x}{x + 7}$

C $\quad \dfrac{5x}{7}$

D $\quad \dfrac{10 - x}{x}$

Use the order of operations to simplify the given expression. Because none of the parts of the expression contained in parentheses can be simplified further, use the distributive property to work through the multiplication instead:

$$\frac{5(2 + x) - 2(5 - x)}{(x + 7) - x} = \frac{(10 + 5x) - (10 - 2x)}{(x + 7) - x}$$

Then, rearrange the numerator and denominator so that like terms are together:

$$\frac{(10 + 5x) - (10 - 2x)}{(x + 7) - x} = \frac{10 - 10 + 5x + 2x}{x - x + 7}$$

Add or subtract the like terms, then simplify:

$$\frac{10 - 10 + 5x + 2x}{x - x + 7} = \frac{7x}{7} = x$$

That's choice **A**.

If you have trouble simplifying the expression, picking numbers can make this task easier. Say $x = 1$. Simplify the original expression and the answer choices using this value, then see which of the answer choices matches the original expression:

$$\frac{5(2 + 1) - 2(5 - 1)}{(1 + 7) - 1} = \frac{5(3) - 2(4)}{(8) - 1} = \frac{15 - 8}{8 - 1} = \frac{7}{7} = 1$$

A 1

B $\dfrac{3(1)}{1 + 7} = \dfrac{3}{8}$

C $\dfrac{5(1)}{7} = \dfrac{5}{7}$

D $\dfrac{10 - 1}{1} = \dfrac{9}{1} = 9$

Only choice **A** has the same result as the original expression when $x = 1$, so it is correct.

 If you think you might have made a mistake while solving an equation, check your answer by plugging the number you found back into the original equation. If the number makes the equation true, it's the right answer.

If an equation has variables on both sides, you'll need to add or subtract a term containing the variable to move it to one side. Simplify each side of the equation as much as you can first to make this task easier.

What is the value of w when $6(w - 5) = 3(5 - 16w)$?

A $\dfrac{2}{3}$

B $\dfrac{5}{6}$

C 6

D 15

Write out the equation:	$6(w - 5) = 3(5 - 16w)$
Simplify each side by distributing:	$6w - 30 = 15 - 48w$
Add $48w$ to each side:	$6w + 48w - 30 = 15 - 48w + 48w$
Simplify:	$54w - 30 = 15$
Add 30 to each side:	$54w - 30 + 30 = 15 + 30$
Simplify:	$54w = 45$
Divide each side by 54:	$\dfrac{54w}{54} = \dfrac{45}{54}$
Simplify:	$w = \dfrac{5}{6}$

That's choice **B**.

If the answer choices contain parentheses, you know you won't need to multiply everything out or solve for x.

$$\frac{x-4}{x+1} = \frac{x}{3(x+1)}$$

Which of the following equations is equivalent to the equation above?

A $(x-4) = 3x$

B $3(x-4) = x$

C $3(x-4) = x(x+1)$

D $x(x-4) = 3(x+1)$

Treat this equation as you would any proportion—cross multiply:

$$\frac{x-4}{x+1} = \frac{x}{3(x+1)}$$

$$(x-4) \cdot 3(x+1) = x \cdot (x+1)$$

Because $(x+1)$ appears on both sides of the equation, you can divide both sides by $(x+1)$ and cancel it out.

$$(x-4) \cdot 3(x+1) = x \cdot (x+1)$$

$$\frac{(x-4) \cdot 3\cancel{(x+1)}}{\cancel{(x+1)}} = \frac{x \cdot \cancel{(x+1)}}{\cancel{(x+1)}}$$

$$3(x-4) = x$$

That's choice **B**. There's no need to simplify any further or solve for x.

Which of the following is the solution of $-4(a + 6) > 7(3 - a) - 6a$?

A $a < -9$

B $a < 3$

C $a > 4$

D $a > 5$

 If you multiply or divide by a negative number while you are simplifying an inequality, remember to change the direction of the sign.

Write out the inequality:	$-4(a + 6) > 7(3 - a) - 6a$
Simplify by distributing:	$-4a - 24 > (21 - 7a) - 6a$
Rearrange terms:	$-4a - 24 > 21 - 7a - 6a$
Combine like terms:	$-4a - 24 > 21 - 13a$
Add 24 to both sides:	$-4a > 21 + 24 - 13a$
Add 13a to both sides:	$-4a + 13a > 21 + 24$
Combine like terms:	$9a > 45$
Divide both sides by 9:	$a > 5$

That's choice **D**.

Absolute Value Equations and Inequalities

There are two possible values of x in an equation like $|x| = 1$: either $x = 1$, or $x = -1$. Because the absolute value of a number represents its distance from zero, the number could be either to the right or the left of zero. That is, it could be positive or negative. The first step in solving an equation or inequality involving absolute value is to split it into these two possibilities.

What are the possible values of the integer n in the equation $|6 - n| = 3$?

A $\{-3, 6\}$

B $\{-3, 9\}$

C $\{3, 6\}$

D $\{3, 9\}$

First, split the absolute value equation into the two possible equations without absolute value signs. Either $6 - n = 3$, or $6 - n = -3$. Solve each equation by getting n alone on one side.

The first possibility:	$6 - n = 3$
Subtract 6 from both sides:	$-n = 3 - 6$
Simplify:	$-n = -3$
Divide both sides by -1:	$\dfrac{-n}{-1} = \dfrac{-3}{-1}$
Simplify:	$n = 3$

   OR

The second possibility:	$6 - n = -3$
Subtract 6 from both sides:	$-n = -3 - 6$
Simplify:	$-n = -9$
Divide both sides by -1:	$\dfrac{-n}{-1} = \dfrac{-9}{-1}$
Simplify:	$n = 9$

The integer n could equal 3 or 9. Choice **D** is correct.

If you have any trouble setting up the equations, you can backsolve instead. Plug each number in the answer choices into the given equation and see which answer choice has two numbers that both make the equation true.

If $n = -3$, then $|6 - n| = |6 - (-3)| = |6 + 3| = |9| = 9$. That's not 3, so -3 is not a possible value of n. You can eliminate both choice A and choice B.

Both choices C and D include the number 3, so finding out that it works won't help you figure out which of the two answer choices is correct. Instead, try 6, the other value for choice C. If $n = 6$, then $|6 - n| = |6 - 6| = |0| = 0$. That's not 3, so choice C is incorrect. Choice **D** is the only remaining answer choice, so it must be right.

If $n = 3$, then $|6 - n| = |6 - 3| = |3| = 3$. If $n = 9$, then $|6 - n| = |6 - 9| = |-3| = 3$. Both of these numbers make the equation in the question true, so you know that choice **D** is correct.

Inequalities involving absolute values should be split into two possibilities just like equations. However, in an inequality where you change a number to a negative, you'll also need to change the direction of the inequality sign.

Because absolute value is a distance, $|x - 2| < 3$ means that x is less than 3 units away from 2.

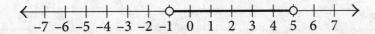

If $x - 2 < 3$, then $x < 5$. If $x - 2 > -3$, then $x > -1$. Both of the new inequalities must be true, so x must be greater than -1 *and* less than 5. An absolute value inequality with ($<$) a less than sign, like this one, indicates that x is within some range. In this case, x is less than 3 units away from 2, or between -1 and 5.

If the inequality sign of the absolute value inequality were reversed, so that $|x - 2| > 3$, then x would be farther than 3 units away from 2.

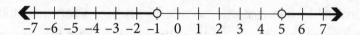

That means $x - 2 > 3$ (and $x > 5$) or $x - 2 < -3$ (and $x < -1$). In other words, x can either be greater than 5 or less than –1, but it can't be both at the same time. With a greater than sign, *either* of the two inequalities produced could be true.

If $|a + 3| < 4$, what are all the possible integer values of a?

A $\{-7, -6, -5, -4, -3, -2, -1, 0, 1\}$

B $\{-7, -6, -5, -4, -3, -2, -1, 0, 1, 2, 3, 4, 5, 6, 7\}$

C $\{-6, -5, -4, -3, -2, -1, 0\}$

D $\{-6, -5, -4, -3, -2, -1, 0, 1, 2, 3, 4, 5, 6\}$

Because $|a + 3| < 4$, you know that $a + 3 < 4$ and $a + 3 > -4$. Solve each inequality, then see which integers make them both true:

$a + 3 < 4$
$\quad a < 1$

AND

$a + 3 > -4$
$\quad a > -7$

The integer values of a are all the integers that are greater than –7 and less than 1. That's –6, –5, –4, –3, –2, –1, and 0, or choice **C**. If the problem used a $\leq$ sign, –7 and 1 would be included, but because it uses <, those numbers are not part of the correct set.

Advanced Word Problems

You've seen quite a variety of word problems already. They're in every chapter of this book! This chapter is no exception: Algebra I can give you a few more tricks to handle the toughest kinds of word problems.

Reciprocals can be helpful when you're setting up a complicated rates problem for dimensional analysis. Use them to turn a rate from miles per hour into hours per mile or gallons of paint per square foot of wall into square feet of wall per gallon of paint.

 To practice simpler rates problems, see the Rates section of Chapter 3, "Algebra and Functions" and the Dimensional Analysis section of Chapter 4, "Measurement and Geometry."

Work problems are among the most difficult rates problems, but your common sense can help! For work problems with multiple people, assume that each person works at the same rate no matter how many other people are helping. Keep your common sense at hand—if people work faster, they'll get the job done sooner, and if more people work together, they'll get the job done more quickly than one person working alone. Usually, the best way to calculate the exact answer to a work problem is to put everything in terms of jobs per hour.

Adrian and Geri are painting a house. Adrian can paint the entire house in 8 hours. Geri can paint the entire house in 10 hours. About how long will it take Adrian and Geri to paint the house if they work together?

A   4 hours and 30 minutes

B   6 hours and 30 minutes

C   7 hours

D   9 hours

First, turn each person's painting time into a rate. Adrian can paint one house in 8 hours, so he can paint $\frac{1}{8}$ house per hour. Geri can paint one house in 10 hours, so she can paint $\frac{1}{10}$ house per hour. That means that together they can paint $\frac{1}{8} + \frac{1}{10} = \frac{10}{80} + \frac{8}{80} = \frac{18}{80} = \frac{9}{40}$ house per hour. One house will take them $\frac{40}{9} = 4\frac{4}{9}$ hours. That's a little less than $4\frac{1}{2}$ hours, so choice **A** is the closest estimate.

Estimation will also get you to the right answer. Because two people are working on the house, you know it will take less time to paint than if either person were working alone. Choice D is longer than it would take Adrian to paint the house himself, so it can't be right. In fact, Adrian and Geri working together will paint the house in less than half the time it would take Geri alone. The two people will be painting for the same length of time and Adrian paints faster than Geri, so Adrian will paint more than half of the house and Geri will paint less than half of the house. That means the two of them can paint the entire house in less time than it would take Geri to paint exactly half of the house, or $\frac{10}{2} = 5$ hours. Choice **A** is the only answer that is less than 5 hours, so it must be correct.

Another type of algebra word problem that can be tricky is the percent mixture problem.

Marcus has 2 pounds of trail mix that is 15% peanuts by weight. He would like to add peanuts so that the finished trail mix is 20% peanuts by weight. How many ounces of peanuts should Marcus add? (1 pound = 16 ounces)

A   0.5 ounces

B   2 ounces

C   5 ounces

D   10 ounces

Because each answer choice is in ounces, start by changing the 2 pounds of trail mix to ounces. Before Marcus adds any peanuts, the trail mix has a total weight of 16 × 2 = 32 ounces and contains 0.15 × 32 = 4.8 ounces of peanuts. If Marcus adds x ounces of peanuts, the weight of peanuts will be 4.8 + x ounces, and the total weight will be 32 + x ounces. Because he wants the final percentage of peanuts to be 20%, the weight of peanuts in the trail mix divided by the total weight will be 0.20 after Marcus has added the correct number of peanuts. Set this up as an equation and solve for x to find how many ounces of peanuts Marcus needs to add.

Set up the equation:	$\dfrac{4.8 + x}{32 + x} = 0.20$
Multiply both sides by (32 + x):	$4.8 + x = 0.20(32 + x)$
Simplify by distributing:	$4.8 + x = 6.4 + 0.2x$
Subtract 4.8 from both sides:	$x = 6.4 - 4.8 + 0.2x$
Subtract 0.2x from both sides:	$x - 0.2x = 6.4 - 4.8$
Combine like terms:	$0.8x = 1.6$
Divide both sides by 0.8:	$x = \dfrac{1.6}{0.8}$
Simplify:	$x = 2$

Marcus needs to add 2 ounces of peanuts to increase the percent of peanuts in the trail mix from 15% to 20%. Choice **B** is correct.

GRAPHING LINEAR EQUATIONS

 To review the basics of graphing lines, see the Linear Functions section of Graphing Functions in Chapter 3, "Algebra and Functions."

As you will recall from Chapter 3, a line can be described by an equation in the form $y = mx + b$. In this equation, m is the slope, and b is the y-intercept. The line is made of all the points that fit this equation, so any point for which the equation is true lies on the line.

Although the slope-intercept form is the easiest to work with, linear equations will not always be presented in this form. You may have to simplify an equation or solve for y to convert the given equation into slope-intercept form, or you may be able to solve the problem by using the equation as it is given.

Which of the following points lies on the line $6x - 3y = 2$?

A $\left(0, \dfrac{2}{3}\right)$

B $\left(\dfrac{1}{3}, 0\right)$

C $\left(\dfrac{2}{3}, 0\right)$

D $(1, 2)$

Plug the given values of x and y into the equation and see which pair makes the equation true. That point lies on the line.

A $\quad 6(0) - 3\left(\dfrac{2}{3}\right) = 0 - 2 = -2$

That doesn't work, so try the next point.

B $\quad 6\left(\dfrac{1}{3}\right) - 3(0) = 2 - 0 = 2$

That works, so choice **B** is correct.

When backsolving, you know there's only one correct answer, so you can stop when you find it. However, you might want to test the other answer choices to double-check your math.

C $\quad 6\left(\dfrac{2}{3}\right) - 3(0) = 4 - 0 = 4$

That doesn't work.

D $\quad 6(1) - 3(2) = 6 - 6 = 0$

That doesn't work either.

If you don't know the equation of the line, you can find the *y*-intercept from the slope and any point on the graph. Plug *m* and the *x*- and *y*-values from any point into the equation *y* = *mx* + *b*, then solve for *b*. Many CAHSEE questions can also be answered by sketching the line and estimating the slope and *y*-intercept.

Which of the following graphs shows the line $\frac{x}{2} + y = 4$?

A
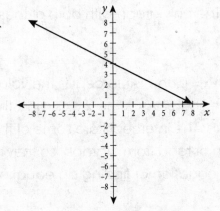

C
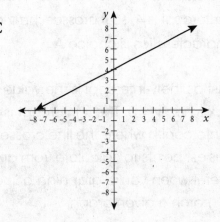

B
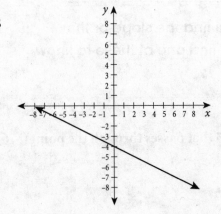

D
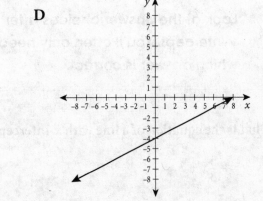

The easiest way to find the graph of a given linear equation is to rewrite the equation in slope-intercept form:

$$\frac{x}{2} + y = 4$$

$$y = -\frac{x}{2} + 4$$

$$y = -\frac{1}{2}x + 4$$

The slope is $-\frac{1}{2}$, so the line must travel down as it goes to the right. The y-intercept is 4, so it crosses the y-axis at 4. The only graph with both of these characteristics is choice **A**.

Just as the y-intercept is the value of y when $x = 0$, the x-intercept is the value of x when $y = 0$. The x-intercept is where the line crosses the x-axis, and the y-intercept is where the line crosses the y-axis. The intercepts are some of the easiest points to calculate from an equation or read from a graph, so they're useful when you're graphing a line from its equation or finding an equation to match a given graph.

 Look at the answer choices after you find the slope or the y-intercept. You'll often only need to find one of these to know which answer is correct.

What is the equation of a line with x-intercept –5 that passes through the point (5, 6)?

A $\quad y = -\frac{5}{3}x + 3$

B $\quad y = \frac{3}{5}x - 5$

C $\quad y = \frac{3}{5}x + 3$

D $\quad y = \frac{5}{6}x - 5$

The definition of slope is rise over run, or $m = \frac{y_2 - y_1}{x_2 - x_1}$. The x-intercept is $(-5, 0)$, so use this in the slope formula with the given point $(5, 6)$. The slope is $m = \frac{6 - 0}{5 - (-5)}$ $= \frac{6}{10} = \frac{3}{5}$, so either choice B or choice C could be correct. You can find the correct choice by calculating the y-intercept. The y-intercept is the value of b in the slope-intercept form of the equation $y = mx + b$. Substitute in $x = -5$, $y = 0$, and $m = \frac{3}{5}$, then solve for b:

$$y = mx + b$$
$$0 = \frac{3}{5}(-5) + b$$
$$0 = -3 + b$$
$$3 = b$$

The equation of this line must be $y = \frac{3}{5}x + 3$, choice **C**.

You could also sketch the line with x-intercept -5 that passes through $(5, 6)$ and figure out the slope and y-intercept from the graph.

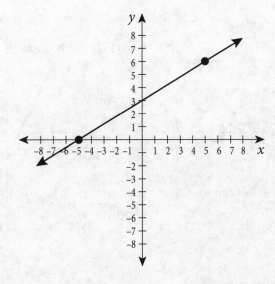

This line clearly has a positive slope and a y-intercept of 3, so it must be choice **C**.

Lines that are *parallel* travel in the same direction without intersecting. Parallel lines have identical slopes. The easiest way to determine whether two equations describe parallel lines is to get them both into slope-intercept form, $y = mx + b$, so that the slopes are easy to compare. Parallel lines must have different *y*-intercepts—if both the slopes and the *y*-intercepts are identical, then the equations are actually describing the same line.

Which of the following is the graph of a line parallel to $2x - 4y = 3$ that has the *x*-intercept –2?

A

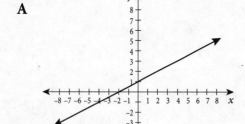

C

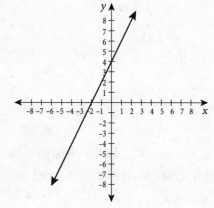

B

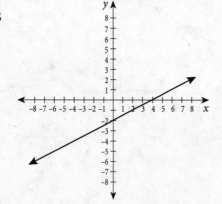

D

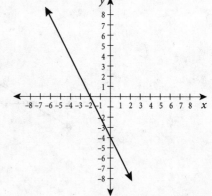

Choices A, C, and D all have the *x*-intercept –2, so to figure out which one is correct, you'll need to know their slopes. Because the correct line is parallel to $2x - 4y = 3$, it will have the same slope as that line. The easiest way to find the slope of $2x - 4y = 3$ is to rewrite the equation in slope-intercept form with *y* on one side of the equation:

$$2x - 4y = 3$$
$$-4y = -2x + 3$$
$$y = \frac{-2x}{-4} + \frac{3}{-4}$$
$$y = \frac{1}{2}x - \frac{3}{4}$$

The slope of the line is $\frac{1}{2}$. That's positive but less than 1, so the line rises slowly as it goes to the right. The only line with an *x*-intercept of –2 that rises slowly as it goes to the right is choice **A**. The graph in choice C shows a line with a steep (greater than 1) slope, and the slope of the line in choice D is negative.

Finding Points of Intersection

If two lines in the same coordinate plane are not parallel, then they must intersect at some point. The point of intersection, or solution of the system of equations, is the one point at which the two lines have the same *x*-value and the same *y*-value. Equations describing parallel lines will have no solutions in common, while equations describing the same line will have an infinite number of solutions in common (for every value of *x*, they will have the same value of *y*).

 To solve for two variables, you need two different equations.

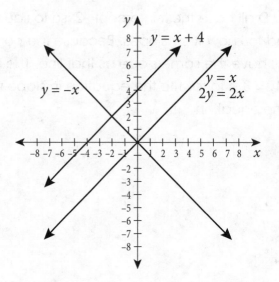

In this figure, you can see that the equations $y = x$ and $2y = 2x$ describe the same line. Every point on the line is a solution to the system of both equations $y = x$ and $2y = 2x$. The lines $y = x$ and $y = x + 4$ are parallel. They have no points in common, so the system of equations $y = x$ and $y = x + 4$ has no solutions. The line $y = -x$, however, is neither identical nor parallel to the line $y = x + 4$. It intersects it once, so there is exactly one point the two lines have in common. You can find that point by using substitution or combination.

 You might have learned "combination" as *elimination* **or** *adding the equations.* **These are just different names for the same technique.**

Substitution is solving either equation for one variable in terms of the other, then substituting that into the other equation. Because $y = -x$ already has y in terms of x, you can replace y in $y = x + 3$ with $-x$ and solve for x to find the x-value of the intersection:

$$-x = x + 3$$
$$-2x = 3$$
$$x = -\frac{3}{2}$$

Then, plug this value of x into either of the equations to find the y-value:

$$y = -x$$

$$y = -\left(-\frac{3}{2}\right)$$

$$y = \frac{3}{2}$$

The lines $y = -x$ and $y = x + 3$ intersect at the point $\left(-\frac{3}{2}, \frac{3}{2}\right)$.

Combination is adding or subtracting the equations. Your goal is to eliminate (cancel out) either x or y; you might need to multiply one of the equations by a constant to make this possible. To solve the system of equations $y = -x$ and $y = x + 3$ by combination, add the two equations so that x cancels out:

$$\begin{array}{r} y = -x \\ + \ y = \ x + 3 \\ \hline 2y = \quad 3 \end{array}$$

Then simplify:

$$2y = 3$$

$$y = \frac{3}{2}$$

Now plug this value into one of the original equations and solve for x:

$$y = x + 3$$

$$\frac{3}{2} = x + 3$$

$$\frac{3}{2} - 3 = x$$

$$\frac{3}{2} - \frac{6}{2} = x$$

$$-\frac{3}{2} = x$$

This method gives you the same result: the two lines intersect at $\left(-\frac{3}{2}, \frac{3}{2}\right)$.

Don't forget the technique of picking numbers and backsolving. There are many ways to solve any CAHSEE problem.

$$\begin{cases} 3x + y = 1 \\ 2x - 2y = 14 \end{cases}$$

What is the solution of the system of equations shown above?

A $(-5, 14)$

B $(-4, -11)$

C $(2, -5)$

D $(3, -8)$

Use substitution. First, find y in terms of x.

$$3x + y = 1$$
$$y = 1 - 3x$$

Now substitute that value for y into the equations:

$$2x - 2y = 14$$
$$2x - 2(1 - 3x) = 14$$
$$2x - 2 + 6x = 14$$
$$8x = 16$$
$$x = 2$$

Finally, use the numeric value of x to solve for y:

$$y = 1 - 3x$$
$$y = 1 - 3(2)$$
$$y = 1 - 6$$
$$y = -5$$

The graphs of the equations $3x + y = 1$ and $2x - 2y = 14$ intersect at the point $(2, -5)$.

Or you can use combination to solve this system of equations. Multiply the first equation by 2 so that the y terms will cancel out: $2(3x + y) = 2(1)$, so $6x + 2y = 2$. Now add the two equations:

$$\begin{array}{r} 6x + 2y = 2 \\ + 2x - 2y = 14 \\ \hline 8x = 16 \end{array}$$

Simplify:

$$8x = 16$$
$$x = 2$$

Substitute the numeric value of x into one of the equations to find y:

$$2x - 2y = 14$$
$$2(2) - 2y = 14$$
$$4 - 2y = 14$$
$$-2y = 10$$
$$y = -5$$

Again, the solution is $(2, -5)$.

If you try backsolving with $3x + y = 1$...

A $3(-5) + 14 = -15 + 14 = -1$

That doesn't match, so eliminate choice A.

B $3(-4) + (-11) = -12 - 11 = -23$

That doesn't match, either, so choice B is also incorrect.

C $3(2) + (-5) = 6 - 5 = 1$

That does match, but try the other equation, $2x - 2y = 14$, in case it's a coincidence.

C $2(2) - 2(-5) = 4 + 10 = 14$

That matches too, so $(2, -5)$ is a solution of both equations. Choice **C** is correct. We'll try choice D anyway, to make sure.

D $3(3) + (-8) = 9 - 8 = 1$

That matches, so check the other equation.

D $2(3) - 2(-8) = 6 + 16 = 22$

That doesn't match, so choice D is incorrect.

Systems of equations can be solved algebraically or by graphing the lines described by the equations and seeing where they intersect. However, to find all the possible solutions of a system of inequalities, you must graph the inequalities and shade the part of the graph that fulfills both inequalities.

The first step in graphing an inequality is just like graphing an equation. Solve the inequality for y in terms of x to get an inequality of the form $y > mx + b$ or $y < mx + b$, then graph the line marking the edge of the inequality by using m for the slope and b for the y-intercept. If the inequality uses ≤ or ≥, then it includes this line, and you should use a solid line on the graph. If it uses < or >, then it does not include the line, so you should draw a dashed line to show that the line itself is not a solution to the inequality.

Once you have drawn the edge of the inequality, shade the part of the coordinate plane that the inequality describes. If it is in the form $y > mx + b$ (or

$y \geq mx + b$), shade the area above the line. If it is in the form $y < mx + b$ (or $y \leq mx + b$), shade the area below the line.

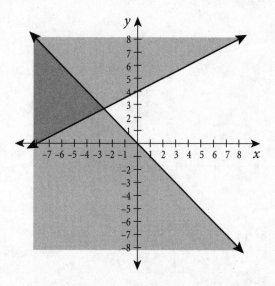

This figure shows the regions that are solutions of the inequalities $y > \frac{1}{2}x + 4$ and $y \leq -x$. The lightly shaded regions are the solutions of each inequality, and the dark region is the solution of the system of inequalities. Points within the dark region, such as (–6, 3), make both inequalities true, while points within each lighter region only make one inequality true.

$$\begin{cases} y < 2x + 3 \\ y > 2x - 2 \end{cases}$$

Which of the following is a solution to the system of inequalities shown above?

A (–1, 1)

B (1, 0)

C (2, 5)

D (3, 3)

Graph each inequality and shade the area that fulfills both inequalities. Draw each answer choice on the coordinate plane so you can see whether or not it is within this region.

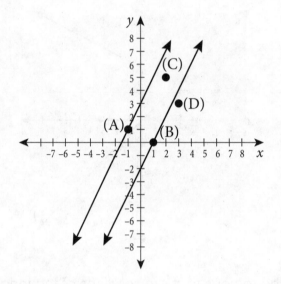

Only choice **C** is within the region described by both inequalities.

You can also use backsolving to see which of the answer choices makes both inequalities true. Let's use $y < 2x + 3$.

A $2x + 3 = 2(-1) + 3 = -2 + 3 = 1$

Therefore, $y = 1$. Because 1 is not less than 1, choice A does not fulfill the first inequality. Eliminate it.

B $2x + 3 = 2(1) + 3 = 2 + 3 = 5$

Because $y = 0$ and $0 < 5$, choice B fulfills the first inequality. Let's try the second, $y > 2x - 2$.

B $2x - 2 = 2(1) - 2 = 2 - 2 = 0$

Because $y = 0$ and 0 is not greater than 0, choice B does not fulfill the second inequality. Eliminate it.

C $2x + 3 = 2(2) + 3 = 4 + 3 = 7$

Because $y = 5$ and $5 < 7$, choice C fulfills the first inequality. Let's try the second.

C $2x - 2 = 2(2) - 2 = 4 - 2 = 2$

Because $y = 5$ and $5 > 2$, choice **C** also fulfills the second inequality. It makes both inequalities true, so it must be correct. Let's backsolve choice D, just to make sure.

D $2x + 3 = 2(3) + 3 = 6 + 3 = 9$

Because $y = 3$ and $3 < 9$, choice D fulfills the first inequality. We'll try the second.

D $2x - 2 = 2(3) - 2 = 6 - 2 = 4$

Because $y = 3$ and 3 is not greater than 4, choice D does not fulfill the second inequality. Eliminate it.

POLYNOMIALS

A *term* is a constant, a variable, or the product or quotient of several constants and variables. *Like terms*, which may have different numerical coefficients but have the same variables, can be added or subtracted by adding or subtracting the coefficients, but *unlike terms* cannot. An algebraic expression with more than one term is called a *polynomial*.

All of the laws of arithmetic operations also apply to polynomials.

Commutative property of addition: $a + b = b + a$

Commutative property of multiplication: $a \times b = b \times a$

Associative property of addition: $a + (b + c) = (a + b) + c$

Associative property of multiplication: $a \times (b \times c) = (a \times b) \times c$

Distributive property: $a \times (b \pm c) = ab \pm ac$

The commutative and associative properties let you simplify polynomials by combining like terms, and the distributive property lets you multiply a polynomial by a constant, a variable, or another polynomial. Keep the order of operations, PEMDAS, in mind to avoid careless errors.

To multiply a polynomial by a *monomial* (a single term), multiply each term in the polynomial by the monomial. For instance, $6a(ab + 3b + 2) = 6a \cdot ab + 6a \cdot 3b + 6a \cdot 2 = 6a^2b + 18ab + 12a$.

To multiply a polynomial by another polynomial, multiply each term in one polynomial by each term in the other polynomial. The most common polynomial multiplication you'll encounter on the CAHSEE is multiplying two *binomials* (polynomials with two terms). To make sure you've multiplied each term in this situation, you can use the mnemonic FOIL—**F**irst, **O**utside, **I**nside, **L**ast. For example, to multiply the binomials $(a + b)(c + d)$, multiply the first terms to get ac, the outside terms to get ad, the inside terms to get bc, and the last terms to get bd. Then add them all together to find that $(a + b)(c + d) = ac + ad + bc + bd$.

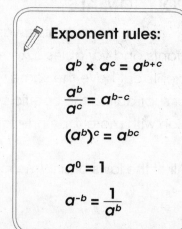

Exponent rules:

$a^b \times a^c = a^{b+c}$

$\dfrac{a^b}{a^c} = a^{b-c}$

$(a^b)^c = a^{bc}$

$a^0 = 1$

$a^{-b} = \dfrac{1}{a^b}$

If $(x + 1)(x + 1) = x^2 + 5$, what is the value of x?

A 2

B 3

C 4

D 5

Use FOIL to simplify the left-hand side of the equation. Then combine like terms so that x is alone on one side of the equation:

$$(x + 1)(x + 1) = x^2 + 5$$
$$x^2 + 1x + 1x + 1 = x^2 + 5$$
$$x^2 + 2x + 1 = x^2 + 5$$
$$2x = 4$$
$$x = 2$$

Choice **A** is correct.

Backsolving is also an excellent way to solve this problem and others like it, or you can backsolve to check your work once you've solved the problem algebraically.

A $(2 + 1)(2 + 1) = (3)(3) = 9$ and $2^2 + 5 = 4 + 5 = 9$.

The two sides of this equation are equal when $x = 2$, so choice **A** is correct.

B $(3 + 1)(3 + 1) = (4)(4) = 16$ and $3^2 + 5 = 9 + 5 = 14$.

The two sides of the equation are not equal when $x = 3$, so choice B is incorrect.

C $(4 + 1)(4 + 1) = (5)(5) = 25$ and $4^2 + 5 = 16 + 5 = 21$.

The two sides of the equation are not equal when $x = 4$, so choice C is incorrect.

D $(5 + 1)(5 + 1) = (6)(6) = 36$ and $5^2 + 5 = 25 + 5 = 30$.

The two sides of the equation are not equal when $x = 5$, so choice D is incorrect.

To divide a polynomial by a monomial, you need to divide each term in the polynomial by the divisor. For instance, $\frac{10x^3 + 5x^2 - 20x}{5x} = \frac{10x^3}{5x} + \frac{5x^2}{5x} - \frac{20x}{5x} = 2x^2 + x - 4$. You can also think of this as factoring the numerator and canceling out:

$$\frac{10x^3 + 5x^2 - 20x}{5x} = \frac{5x(2x^2 + x - 4)}{5x} = 2x^2 + x - 4$$

Which of the following expressions is equivalent to $\frac{abc + ac^2}{4ac}$?

A $\dfrac{a}{4c}$

B $\dfrac{b}{4ac}$

C $\dfrac{b + c}{4}$

D $\dfrac{b + c}{ac}$

Find and cancel out factors common to the numerator and denominator:

$$\frac{abc + ac^2}{4ac} = \frac{\cancel{ac}(b + c)}{4\cancel{ac}} = \frac{b + c}{4}$$

That's choice **C**.

Picking numbers is also a good way to handle complicated algebra questions like this one. If $a = 1$, $b = 2$, and $c = 3$, then $\frac{abc + ac^2}{4ac} = \frac{1(2)(3) + 1(3^2)}{4(1)(3)} = \frac{6 + 9}{12} = \frac{15}{12} = \frac{5}{4}$. Substitute these numbers into the answer choices to see which one also equals $\frac{5}{4}$.

A $\quad \dfrac{a}{4c} = \dfrac{1}{4(3)} = \dfrac{1}{12}$

B $\quad \dfrac{b}{4ac} = \dfrac{2}{4(1)(3)} = \dfrac{2}{12} = \dfrac{1}{6}$

C $\quad \dfrac{b+c}{4} = \dfrac{2+3}{4} = \dfrac{5}{4}$

D $\quad \dfrac{b+c}{ac} = \dfrac{2+3}{1(3)} = \dfrac{5}{3}$

Only choice C has the same value, so it is correct.

Dividing a polynomial by another polynomial is a little more complicated. In this situation, the easiest thing to do is to factor each of the polynomials, then cancel out any common factors. To factor a quadratic expression (an expression that includes an x^2 term), factor out any constants, then use FOIL in reverse. The binomials $(x + a)$ and $(x + b)$ can be multiplied to get $x^2 + (a + b)x + ab$ by FOIL, so the factors of the expression $x^2 + (a + b)x + ab$ are $(x + a)$ and $(x + b)$. To factor the expression $x^2 + 3x + 2$, you'll need to find two numbers that when added together equal 3 and when multiplied together equal 2. The numbers 2 and 1 work, so $x^2 + 3x + 2 = (x + 2)(x + 1)$. You can double-check your answer by multiplying these factors together again: $(x + 2)(x + 1) = x(x) + 1x + 2x + 2(1) = x^2 + 3x + 2$.

Factoring polynomials can be pretty tricky and time consuming, so don't forget the picking numbers and backsolving techniques. These techniques will let you avoid the most difficult parts of the calculations by using the answer choices to your advantage.

 Classic quadratic equations:

$x^2 + 2xy + y^2 = (x + y)^2$

$x^2 - 2xy + y^2 = (x - y)^2$

$x^2 - y^2 = (x + y)(x - y)$

Simplify $\dfrac{x^2 - 4}{3x^2 + 12x + 12}$.

A $\quad\dfrac{x - 4}{3}$

B $\quad\dfrac{x - 2}{x + 2}$

C $\quad\dfrac{x - 2}{3(x + 2)}$

D $\quad\dfrac{x + 2}{3(x + 2)}$

First, factor out any constants in the numerator or denominator:

$$\dfrac{x^2 - 4}{3(x^2 + 4x + 4)}$$

Then, factor the quadratics:

$$\dfrac{(x + 2)(x - 2)}{3(x + 2)(x + 2)}$$

The numbers in the numerator need to add up to 0 and multiply to –4; –2 and 2 work perfectly. The numbers in the denominator need to add up to 4 and multiply to 4, so 2 and 2 work here.

Cancel out common factors:

$$\dfrac{(x - 2)}{3(x + 2)}$$

You're left with choice **C**.

Or try backsolving. Say $x = 1$.

Then $\dfrac{x^2 - 4}{3x^2 + 12x + 12} = \dfrac{1^2 - 4}{3(1^2) + 12(1) + 12} = \dfrac{1 - 4}{3 + 12 + 12} = \dfrac{-3}{27} = -\dfrac{1}{9}$.

Plug $x = 1$ into each of the answer choices to see which one also equals $-\dfrac{1}{9}$.

A $\quad \dfrac{x - 4}{3} = \dfrac{1 - 4}{3} = \dfrac{-3}{3} = -1$

B $\quad \dfrac{x - 2}{x + 2} = \dfrac{1 - 2}{1 + 2} = \dfrac{-1}{3}$

C $\quad \dfrac{x - 2}{3(x + 2)} = \dfrac{1 - 2}{3(1 + 2)} = \dfrac{-1}{3(3)} = -\dfrac{1}{9}$

D $\quad \dfrac{x + 2}{3(x + 2)} = \dfrac{1 + 2}{3(1 + 2)} = \dfrac{3}{3(3)} = \dfrac{1}{3}$

Only choice **C** has the same value, so it is correct.

Polynomials in Word Problems

Polynomials may be combined with geometry or algebra to create complicated-looking, intimidating word problems. But don't be worried! Even though they look complicated, these problems can be solved by using the same skills as any other question. They may take a few more steps than other CAHSEE problems, but these questions don't have anything in them that you don't already know. Just take them step by step until you get to the end.

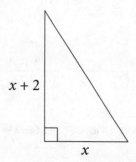

$x + 2$

x

A right triangle has a base that is *x* inches long and a height that is 2 inches longer than the base, as shown in the figure above. What is the area of the triangle in terms of *x* ?

A $\frac{1}{2}x^2 + x$

B $\frac{1}{2}x^2 + 2x$

C $x^2 + 2x$

D $x^2 + 2x + 1$

The area of a triangle is half the base times the height.

Here, that's $\frac{1}{2}x(x + 2) = \frac{1}{2}(x^2 + 2x) = \frac{1}{2}x^2 + \frac{1}{2}(2x) = \frac{1}{2}x^2 + x$, or choice **A**.

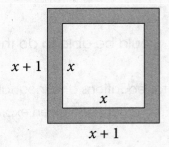

$x + 1$ x

x

$x + 1$

A square painting has a length of x inches per side. It is in a frame that has an outside length of $x + 1$ inches per side, as shown in the figure above. The area of the frame is 7 square inches. How many inches long is a side of the painting?

A   1

B   2

C   3

D   4

The area of the outside square is $(x + 1)^2 = x^2 + 2x + 1$. The area of the painting is x^2. The area of the shaded frame is the difference between these areas, or $x^2 + 2x + 1 - x^2 = 2x + 1$. The question says that the area of the frame is 7 square inches, so set $2x + 1$ equal to 7 and solve for x to find the length of a side of the painting:

$$2x + 1 = 7$$
$$2x = 6$$
$$x = 3$$

Choice **C** is correct.

SUMMARY

After reading this chapter, you should be able to do the following:

- Undo multiple steps to solve equations and inequalities.
  - Find the opposite or reciprocal of a given expression.
  - Simplify expressions.
  - Solve absolute value equations and inequalities.
  - Use equations to solve difficult word problems.
- Graph linear equations.
  - Identify points on a line.
  - Find an equation from a graph or from information about the graph.
  - Identify x- and y-intercepts.
  - Find parallel lines.
  - Use combination or substitution to find the point where two lines intersect.
  - Identify points that fulfill two inequalities.
- Add, subtract, multiply, and divide polynomials and monomials.
  - Use the distributive property to multiply polynomials.
  - Identify and combine like terms.

Algebra I Quiz

1. If x is an integer, then what is the solution to $|2x + 5| = 17$?

   A $\{-11\}$

   B $\{6\}$

   C $\{-11, 6\}$

   D $\{-6, 11\}$

2. Which of the following statements is not true for all real numbers a, b, and c?

   A $a + b = b + a$

   B $a(b + c) = ab + ac$

   C $a \div b = b \div a$

   D $a(bc) = (ab)c$

3. What is the reciprocal of the expression $-\dfrac{x^2y}{6}$?

   A x^2y

   B $\dfrac{x^2y}{6}$

   C $\dfrac{6}{x^2y}$

   D $-\dfrac{6}{x^2y}$

4. What is the value of x in the equation $2x + 3(x - 4) = 18$?

   A $\dfrac{6}{5}$

   B $\dfrac{22}{5}$

   C 6

   D 150

5. Which of the following represents the correct simplification of the inequality below?

   $$-8(2x - 4) - 10 > 38$$

   A $-16x - 4 - 10 > 38$

   B $-16x + 4 - 10 > 38$

   C $-16x - 32 - 10 > 38$

   D $-16x + 32 - 10 > 38$

6. What is the solution to the inequality $-\dfrac{2}{3}x + 14 \leq 22$?

   A $x \leq 12$

   B $x \leq -12$

   C $x \geq 12$

   D $x \geq -12$

7. What is the x-intercept of the linear equation $-6x + 3y = 12$?

   A -2

   B 2

   C 4

   D 18

8. The equation $4(x + 2) + 12 = -8$ is solved correctly below.

> Step 1: $4x + 8 + 12 = -8$
>
> Step 2: $4x + 20 = -8$
>
> Step 3: $4x = -28$
>
> Step 4: $x = -7$

What was done between step 3 and step 4?

A Four was multiplied by x and 2.

B Each side of the equation was divided by 4.

C Twenty was subtracted from each side of the equation.

D Eight and 12 were added.

9. Which of the following points lies on the line $-4x + 5y = 11$?

A $(1, 3)$

B $(0, 11)$

C $(-1, 4)$

D $(2, -2)$

10. What is the perimeter of the pentagon below?

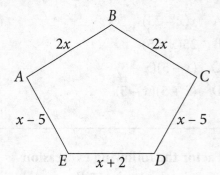

A $4x - 8$

B $7x - 12$

C $7x - 8$

D $7x + 2$

11. What is the slope of a line parallel to the line $y - 5 = -3x$?

A -5

B -3

C $\dfrac{1}{3}$

D 3

12. Simplify $\dfrac{x^2 - 9}{x + 3}$.

A x

B $3x$

C $x - 3$

D $x + 3$

13. What is the result when the expression $x^2 - 25$ is factored completely?

    A $\quad x(x - 25)$

    B $\quad 25(x - 5)$

    C $\quad (x - 5)(x - 5)$

    D $\quad (x + 5)(x - 5)$

14. Factor the following expression completely: $18x^3 - 12x^2 + 6x$.

    A $\quad 3(6x^3 - 4x^2 + 2x)$

    B $\quad 6(3x^3 - 2x^2 + x)$

    C $\quad 6x(3x^2 - 2x)$

    D $\quad 6x(3x^2 - 2x + 1)$

15. Divide $\dfrac{4y^3 + 2y}{2y}$.

    A $\quad 2y^2$

    B $\quad 2y^2 + 1$

    C $\quad 2y^3 + 1$

    D $\quad 4y^3 + 2y$

16. What is the sum of $\dfrac{5x}{y} + \dfrac{9}{2y}$?

    A $\quad \dfrac{10x + 9}{2y}$

    B $\quad \dfrac{5x + 9}{y}$

    C $\quad \dfrac{5x + 9}{2y}$

    D $\quad \dfrac{5x + 9}{3y}$

17. What is the solution set of the equation $x^2 - 2x - 15 = 0$?

    A $\quad \{-3\}$

    B $\quad \{5\}$

    C $\quad \{-5, 3\}$

    D $\quad \{-3, 5\}$

18. It takes 3 hours for Carly to tile a floor. Sam can tile the same floor in 5 hours. If they work together, how long will it take them to tile the floor?

    A $\quad$ 1 hour and 53 minutes

    B $\quad$ 2 hours and 28 minutes

    C $\quad$ 4 hours

    D $\quad$ 8 hours

19. What is the solution to the system of equations graphed below?

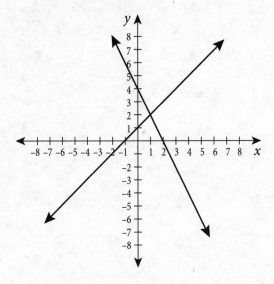

A   (1, 2)

B   (2, 1)

C   (0, 1)

D   (0, 4)

20. What is the solution to the system of equations below?

$$x = -y + 1$$
$$2y - 8 = x$$

A   (2, −3)

B   (−3, 2)

C   (−2, 3)

D   (3, −2)

Answers and Explanations

1. C

This problem presents an absolute value equation. Therefore, the equation will be true when the expression inside the absolute value signs is equal to both 17 and –17. To find all values of x, set the expression equal to both 17 and –17 and solve.

Case I:

Set the expression equal to 17:	$2x + 5 = 17$
Subtract 5 from each side of the equation:	$2x + 5 - 5 = 17 - 5$
The equation becomes:	$2x = 12$
Divide each side of the equation by 2:	$\frac{2x}{2} = \frac{12}{2}$
The variable x is now alone:	$x = 6$

Case II:

Set the expression equal to –17:	$2x + 5 = -17$
Subtract 5 from each side of the equation:	$2x + 5 - 5 = -17 - 5$
The equation becomes:	$2x = -22$
Divide each side of the equation by 2:	$\frac{2x}{2} = \frac{-22}{2}$
The variable x is now alone:	$x = -11$

This equation is true for *x*-values of 6 and –11, so the correct answer is C.

Choices A and B are each just one of the solutions. If you chose D, you added 5 to both sides of the equation instead of subtracting.

2. C

Each of the answer choices is an example of a real number property. Because division is not commutative, the order in which numbers are divided matters and could yield different results. In other words, 10 divided by 5 is 2, but 5 divided by 10 is $\frac{1}{2}$. Therefore, answer choice C is not true for all real numbers. Each of the other answer choices is true for all real numbers *a*, *b*, and *c*. Choice A is an example of the commutative property for addition. Choice B is an example of the distributive property of multiplication over addition. Choice D is an example of the associative property of multiplication.

3. D

The reciprocal of an expression exchanges the numerator with the denominator, and the denominator with the numerator, of a fraction. In this case, the numerator is x^2y, so this expression becomes the denominator of the reciprocal. The denominator of the original fraction is 6, so 6 becomes the numerator of the reciprocal. Thus, the reciprocal is $-\frac{6}{x^2y}$. Note that the original fraction was negative, so the reciprocal is also negative. Choice A is just the original numerator. Choice B is the opposite of the original fraction. If your answer was C, you found the negative reciprocal.

4. C

Solve the equation by getting the variable x alone. The first step in solving the equation is to use the distributive property:

$$2x + 3(x - 4) = 18$$

The equation becomes:

$$2x + 3x - 12 = 18$$

Combine like terms:

$$5x - 12 = 18$$

Add 12 to each side of the equation:

$$5x - 12 + 12 = 18 + 12$$

The equation becomes:

$$5x = 30$$

Divide each side of the equation by 5:

$$\frac{5x}{5} = \frac{30}{5}$$

The variable x is now alone:

$$x = 6$$

If your answer was A, you subtracted 12 from both sides instead of adding. If you chose B, you didn't distribute to the −4 term in parentheses. If your answer was D, you multiplied by 5 instead of dividing in the last step.

5. D

The first step in simplifying this inequality is to use the distributive property. This will eliminate the parentheses. Because $-8(2x - 4) = -8(2x) - (-8)(4) = -16x - (-32) = -16x + 32$, the inequality $-8(2x - 4) - 10 > 38$ becomes $-16x + 32 - 10 > 38$. This is choice D. In choices A and B, the −8 was not distributed to the −4. In choice C, the result of distributing −8 is incorrect; the sign on 32 should be positive.

6. D

Solve the inequality by getting the variable, x, alone.

$$-\frac{2}{3}x + 14 \le 22$$

Subtract 14 from each side of the inequality:

$$-\frac{2}{3}x + 14 - 14 \le 22 - 14$$

The inequality becomes:

$$-\frac{2}{3}x \le 8$$

Multiply each side of the inequality by $-\frac{3}{2}$:

$$\left(-\frac{3}{2}\right)\left(-\frac{2}{3}x\right) \ge \left(-\frac{3}{2}x\right)$$

Remember to switch the direction of the inequality symbol when multiplying or dividing by a negative value. The variable is now alone: $x \ge -12$.

In choice A, the negative sign was ignored. If your answer was B, you forgot to switch the inequality symbol. In choice C, the inequality symbol was switched, but the negative sign was not included.

7. A

The *x*-intercept of a linear equation is the place on a graph where the line intersects, or crosses, the *x*-axis. At this location, the *y*-coordinate is equal to zero. To find the *x*-intercept, substitute $y = 0$ into the equation and solve for *x*.

The equation is:	$-6x + 3y = 12$
Substitute $y = 0$:	$-6x + 3(0) = 12$
Multiply:	$-6x + 0 = 12$
Divide each side of the equation by -6:	$\dfrac{-6x}{-6} = \dfrac{12}{-6}$
The variable *x* is now alone:	$x = -2$

The *x*-intercept is –2. Choice B is the opposite of the *x*-intercept. If your answer was C, you substituted 0 for *x* instead of *y* and found the *y*-intercept. In choice D, you may have added 6 to both sides of the equation instead of dividing by –6.

8. B

To find the correct answer, compare step 3 and step 4. In step 3, the equation is $4x = -28$. Four is being multiplied by *x*. In step 4, the variable is alone; $x = -7$. The inverse of multiplying by 4 is dividing each side by 4. Therefore, to get *x* alone, each side was divided by four. Because $4x \div 4 = x$ and $-28 \div 4 = -7$, this answer checks, and it is true that division by 4 was done on both sides of the equation. Choice A is step 1. Choice C is between steps 2 and 3. Choice D is between steps 1 and 2.

9. A

To find a point that lies on the line, substitute each of the answer choices into the equation and find the ordered pair that makes the equation true. Recall that each ordered pair is in the form (*x*, *y*). First, substitute the point (1, 3).

The equation becomes: $\qquad$ $-4(1) + 5(3) = 11$

Evaluate using the correct order of operations.

Multiply to get: $\qquad$ $-4 + 15 = 11$

Add to get the equation: $\qquad$ $11 = 11$

Because this is a true equation, the point (1, 3) is on the line $-4x + 5y = 11$. If each of the other answer choices were substituted for x and y, it would not make a true equation. For the point (0, 11) in choice B, the equation becomes:

$$-4(0) + 5(11) = 11$$

Multiply to get: $\qquad$ $0 + 55 = 11$

The equation is not true: $\qquad$ $55 \neq 11$

For the point (–1, 4) in choice C,
the equation becomes: $\qquad$ $-4(-1) + 5(4) = 11$

Multiply to get: $\qquad$ $4 + 20 = 11$

The equation is not true: $\qquad$ $24 \neq 11$

For the point (2, –2) in choice D,
the equation becomes: $\qquad$ $-4(2) + 5(-2) = 11$

Multiply to get: $\qquad$ $-8 + -10 = 11$

The equation is not true: $\qquad$ $-18 \neq 11$

10. C

The perimeter of a figure is the sum of the lengths of the sides. Find the perimeter of this pentagon by adding the sides and combining like terms. Because the value of x is unknown, the perimeter will be expressed as a polynomial.

Add the sides: $\qquad$ $2x + 2x + x - 5 + x - 5 + x + 2$

Combine like terms. Recall that $x = 1x$: $\qquad$ $7x - 8$

The perimeter is $7x - 8$. If your answer was A, you may have thought that $x = 0$ and, thus, incorrectly combined to get $4x - 8$. In choice B, $-5 + -5 + 2$ was incorrectly added to get –12 instead of the correct value of –8. If you chose D, you may have ignored the –5 number terms or added them incorrectly to get 0.

11. B

Parallel lines have the same slope. To answer this question, find the slope of the given line. The equation $y - 5 = -3x$ is a linear equation. The slope-intercept form of a linear equation is $y = mx + b$, where m is the slope of the line and b is the y-intercept. Change this equation to slope-intercept form to find the slope of the line (m). That slope will be the same for a line parallel to the given line.

Add 5 to each side of the equation: $\qquad y - 5 + 5 = -3x + 5$

The slope-intercept form of the equation is: $\qquad y = -3x + 5$

The slope (m) of the line is –3, so the slope of the parallel line is also –3. Choice A is the y-intercept of the given line. Choice C is the negative reciprocal of the slope, which is the slope of a line perpendicular, not parallel, to the given line. Choice D is the opposite of the slope.

12. C

To simplify this expression, first factor the numerator and denominator. Then, cancel any common factors to simplify. The numerator $x^2 - 9$ is the difference between two perfect squares. To find the factors, find the square root of x^2 and the square root of 9. Then, write the factors as the product of the sum of the square roots and the difference of the square roots. The factors are $(x + 3)(x - 3)$. The factored expression becomes $\frac{(x + 3)(x - 3)}{x + 3}$. Cancel the common factors of $x + 3$ in the numerator and denominator to get a simplified expression of $x - 3$. Choice A is the simplified result of the fraction $\frac{x^2}{x}$, without regard to the number term. Choice D is the factor that is cancelled.

13. D

The expression $x^2 - 25$ is the difference between two perfect squares. To find the factors, find the square root of x^2 and the square root of 25. Then, write the factors as the product of the sum of the square roots and the difference of the square roots. Therefore, the factors are $(x + 5)(x - 5)$. Choice A is the factored result of the expression $x^2 - 25x$, not $x^2 - 25$. Choice C is the factored result of the expression $x^2 - 10x - 25$.

14. D

To factor the expression, find the greatest common factor (GCF) of each of the terms. Then, write the factors as the product of the GCF and the expression after it as divided by the GCF. The greatest common factor of $18x^3$, $-12x^2$, and $6x$ is $6x$. To divide in the expression, divide the coefficients and subtract the exponents of the common bases. When the expression $18x^3 - 12x^2 + 6x$ is divided by $6x$, the result is $\frac{18x^3}{6x} - \frac{12x^3}{6x} + \frac{6x}{6x} = 3x^2 - 2x + 1$. Thus, the factored expression is $6x(3x^2 - 2x + 1)$. Choice A is an equivalent expression with just the factor of 3 factored out. Choice B is an equivalent expression with just the factor of 6 factored out. If you chose answer choice C, you may have thought that $\frac{6x}{6x} = 0$.

15. B

To divide, place each term of the numerator over the common divisor of $2y$. Then simplify each term. To divide in the expression, divide the coefficients and subtract the exponents of the common bases. For example, $\frac{y^3}{y} = y^{3-1}$ $= y^2$. The expression becomes $\frac{4y^3 + 2y}{2y} + \frac{4y^3}{2y} + \frac{2y}{2y} = 2y^2 + 1$. If you chose choice A, you may have thought that $\frac{2y}{2y} = 0$ instead of 1. If your answer was C, you forgot to factor out one y from the first term of the numerator. Choice D is the numerator of the fraction without regard for the denominator.

16. A

To find the sum, find the least common denominator for the terms in the expression and then add the expressions together. The least common denominator of y and $2y$ is $2y$. Multiply the first fraction by $\frac{2}{2}$ to change to the least common denominator. The expression becomes: $\frac{5x}{y} + \frac{9}{2y} = \frac{2 \cdot 5x}{2 \cdot y} + \frac{9}{2y} = \frac{10x}{2y} + \frac{9}{2y}$. Combine the numerators over the common denominator of $2y$ to get a sum of $\frac{10x + 9}{2y}$. If your answer was B, you added the numerators without finding a common denominator. If your answer was C, you forgot to multiply the first term in the numerator by 2. If you chose D, you added the numerators and added the denominators; this is an incorrect method.

17. D

To solve the equation $x^2 - 2x - 15 = 0$, first factor the expression on the left side of the equation. Then, set each factor equal to zero and solve for x. To find the factors of $x^2 - 2x - 15$, find two numbers with a sum of -2 and a product of 15. These two numbers are -5 and 3. Using x, write these numbers as two binomials. The factors are $(x - 5)$ and $(x + 3)$.

The equation is now: $(x - 5)(x + 3) = 0$

Set each factor equal to zero. $x - 5 = 0$ $x + 3 = 0$

Solve for x. $x - 5 + 5 = 0 + 5$ $x + 3 - 3 = 0 - 3$

$x = 5$ $x = -3$

The solution is $\{-3, 5\}$. Choices A and B each just present one of the two possible solutions. Choice C has the signs reversed for the two values of x.

18. A

Let x = the amount of time it takes Carly and Sam to tile the floor together. Because Carly takes 3 hours to tile the floor, then $\frac{1}{3}$ is the amount of the job she will have completed in 1 hour. Because Sam takes 5 hours, then $\frac{1}{5}$ is the amount of the job he will have completed in 1 hour. It takes them x hours to complete the job together, so $\frac{1}{x}$ is the amount of the job they will finish in 1 hour working together. Write an equation by adding the amount of time it takes Carly and Sam working individually and set it equal to $\frac{1}{x}$. The equation is: $\frac{1}{3} + \frac{1}{5} = \frac{1}{x}$

Solve for x by multiplying each term by the least common denominator of 15x.

$$\frac{1}{3}(15x) + \frac{1}{5}(15x) = \frac{1}{x}(15x)$$

The equation becomes: $5x + 3x = 15$

Combine like terms: $8x = 15$

Divide each side of the equation by 8: $\frac{8x}{8} = \frac{15}{8}$

The variable, x, is now alone: $x = 1.875$

Because the unit is hours, multiply 0.875 by 60 to find the number of minutes.

The correct answer is 1 hour, 53 minutes. If your answer was B, you incorrectly thought that 0.875 represented 1 hour, 28 minutes instead of the correct conversion of 53 minutes. Choice C is the average of the amount of time it took each worker. Choice D is the sum of the amount of time it took each worker. If you chose C or D, you forgot that common sense says they cannot be correct. It will certainly take Carly and Sam less time than 3 hours if they work together, because Carly can do the job alone in 3 hours.

19. A
To find the solution to this system of equations, find the point of intersection of the two lines on the graph. This is the point where the two lines cross. The place where they intersect is 1 unit over to the right on the x-axis and 2 units up on the y-axis. This is the point (1, 2). Choice B has the x and y terms switched. Choice C is the y-intercept of the line with a positive slope. Choice D is the y-intercept of the line with a negative slope.

20. C

To find the solution to this system of equations, use the fact that one side of each equation is equal to x. Set the other sides of the two equations equal to each other and solve for y. To find the x-value, substitute the value of y into either equation and solve for x. Set the two equations equal to each other:

$$-y + 1 = 2y - 8$$

Add y to each side of the equation: $\qquad -y + y + 1 = 2y + y - 8$

The equation becomes: $\qquad\qquad\qquad\qquad 1 = 3y - 8$

Add 8 to each side of the equation: $\qquad\quad 1 + 8 = 3y - 8 + 8$

The equation is: $\qquad\qquad\qquad\qquad\qquad 9 = 3y$

Divide each side of the equation by 3: $\qquad \dfrac{9}{3} = \dfrac{3y}{3}$

The variable, y, is now alone: $\qquad\qquad\quad 3 = y$

Substitute $y = 3$ into either original equation to find the value of x. The first equation becomes:

$$x = -3 + 1$$

Simplify: $\qquad\qquad\qquad\qquad\qquad\qquad x = -2$

The solution is the point (–2, 3).

You can also backsolve to find the correct answer choice. Check choice A by substituting $x = 2$ and $y = -3$ into the first equation: $2 = -(-3) + 1$, and $2 \neq 4$, so choice A can be eliminated. Check choice B by substituting $x = -3$ and $y = 2$ into the first equation: $-3 = -2 + 1$, and $-3 \neq -1$, so choice B can be eliminated. Check choice C by substituting $x = -2$ and $y = 3$ into the first equation: $-2 = -3 + 1$, and $-2 = -2$. This works, so check the second equation: $2(3) - 8 = -2$, and $-2 = -2$, so choice C is the correct answer. Check choice D by substituting $x = 3$ and $y = -2$ into the first equation: $3 = -(-2) + 1$, and $3 = 3$. This works, so check the second equation. $2(-2) - 8 = 3$, and $-12 \neq 3$, so choice D is incorrect.

Full-Length Practice Tests

Full-Length Practice Test 1
Answer Sheet

Remove or photocopy this answer sheet and use it to complete the practice test.

1. Ⓐ Ⓑ Ⓒ Ⓓ   5. Ⓐ Ⓑ Ⓒ Ⓓ   9. Ⓐ Ⓑ Ⓒ Ⓓ   13. Ⓐ Ⓑ Ⓒ Ⓓ   17. Ⓐ Ⓑ Ⓒ Ⓓ
2. Ⓐ Ⓑ Ⓒ Ⓓ   6. Ⓐ Ⓑ Ⓒ Ⓓ   10. Ⓐ Ⓑ Ⓒ Ⓓ   14. Ⓐ Ⓑ Ⓒ Ⓓ   18. Ⓐ Ⓑ Ⓒ Ⓓ
3. Ⓐ Ⓑ Ⓒ Ⓓ   7. Ⓐ Ⓑ Ⓒ Ⓓ   11. Ⓐ Ⓑ Ⓒ Ⓓ   15. Ⓐ Ⓑ Ⓒ Ⓓ   19. Ⓐ Ⓑ Ⓒ Ⓓ
4. Ⓐ Ⓑ Ⓒ Ⓓ   8. Ⓐ Ⓑ Ⓒ Ⓓ   12. Ⓐ Ⓑ Ⓒ Ⓓ   16. Ⓐ Ⓑ Ⓒ Ⓓ   20. Ⓐ Ⓑ Ⓒ Ⓓ

21. Ⓐ Ⓑ Ⓒ Ⓓ   25. Ⓐ Ⓑ Ⓒ Ⓓ   29. Ⓐ Ⓑ Ⓒ Ⓓ   33. Ⓐ Ⓑ Ⓒ Ⓓ   37. Ⓐ Ⓑ Ⓒ Ⓓ
22. Ⓐ Ⓑ Ⓒ Ⓓ   26. Ⓐ Ⓑ Ⓒ Ⓓ   30. Ⓐ Ⓑ Ⓒ Ⓓ   34. Ⓐ Ⓑ Ⓒ Ⓓ   38. Ⓐ Ⓑ Ⓒ Ⓓ
23. Ⓐ Ⓑ Ⓒ Ⓓ   27. Ⓐ Ⓑ Ⓒ Ⓓ   31. Ⓐ Ⓑ Ⓒ Ⓓ   35. Ⓐ Ⓑ Ⓒ Ⓓ   39. Ⓐ Ⓑ Ⓒ Ⓓ
24. Ⓐ Ⓑ Ⓒ Ⓓ   28. Ⓐ Ⓑ Ⓒ Ⓓ   32. Ⓐ Ⓑ Ⓒ Ⓓ   36. Ⓐ Ⓑ Ⓒ Ⓓ   40. Ⓐ Ⓑ Ⓒ Ⓓ

41. Ⓐ Ⓑ Ⓒ Ⓓ   45. Ⓐ Ⓑ Ⓒ Ⓓ   49. Ⓐ Ⓑ Ⓒ Ⓓ   53. Ⓐ Ⓑ Ⓒ Ⓓ   57. Ⓐ Ⓑ Ⓒ Ⓓ
42. Ⓐ Ⓑ Ⓒ Ⓓ   46. Ⓐ Ⓑ Ⓒ Ⓓ   50. Ⓐ Ⓑ Ⓒ Ⓓ   54. Ⓐ Ⓑ Ⓒ Ⓓ   58. Ⓐ Ⓑ Ⓒ Ⓓ
43. Ⓐ Ⓑ Ⓒ Ⓓ   47. Ⓐ Ⓑ Ⓒ Ⓓ   51. Ⓐ Ⓑ Ⓒ Ⓓ   55. Ⓐ Ⓑ Ⓒ Ⓓ   59. Ⓐ Ⓑ Ⓒ Ⓓ
44. Ⓐ Ⓑ Ⓒ Ⓓ   48. Ⓐ Ⓑ Ⓒ Ⓓ   52. Ⓐ Ⓑ Ⓒ Ⓓ   56. Ⓐ Ⓑ Ⓒ Ⓓ   60. Ⓐ Ⓑ Ⓒ Ⓓ

61. Ⓐ Ⓑ Ⓒ Ⓓ   65. Ⓐ Ⓑ Ⓒ Ⓓ   69. Ⓐ Ⓑ Ⓒ Ⓓ   73. Ⓐ Ⓑ Ⓒ Ⓓ   77. Ⓐ Ⓑ Ⓒ Ⓓ
62. Ⓐ Ⓑ Ⓒ Ⓓ   66. Ⓐ Ⓑ Ⓒ Ⓓ   70. Ⓐ Ⓑ Ⓒ Ⓓ   74. Ⓐ Ⓑ Ⓒ Ⓓ   78. Ⓐ Ⓑ Ⓒ Ⓓ
63. Ⓐ Ⓑ Ⓒ Ⓓ   67. Ⓐ Ⓑ Ⓒ Ⓓ   71. Ⓐ Ⓑ Ⓒ Ⓓ   75. Ⓐ Ⓑ Ⓒ Ⓓ   79. Ⓐ Ⓑ Ⓒ Ⓓ
64. Ⓐ Ⓑ Ⓒ Ⓓ   68. Ⓐ Ⓑ Ⓒ Ⓓ   72. Ⓐ Ⓑ Ⓒ Ⓓ   76. Ⓐ Ⓑ Ⓒ Ⓓ   80. Ⓐ Ⓑ Ⓒ Ⓓ

81. Ⓐ Ⓑ Ⓒ Ⓓ   85. Ⓐ Ⓑ Ⓒ Ⓓ   89. Ⓐ Ⓑ Ⓒ Ⓓ
82. Ⓐ Ⓑ Ⓒ Ⓓ   86. Ⓐ Ⓑ Ⓒ Ⓓ   90. Ⓐ Ⓑ Ⓒ Ⓓ
83. Ⓐ Ⓑ Ⓒ Ⓓ   87. Ⓐ Ⓑ Ⓒ Ⓓ   91. Ⓐ Ⓑ Ⓒ Ⓓ
84. Ⓐ Ⓑ Ⓒ Ⓓ   88. Ⓐ Ⓑ Ⓒ Ⓓ   92. Ⓐ Ⓑ Ⓒ Ⓓ

Full-Length
Practice Test 1

This full-length practice test for the CAHSEE has 92 multiple-choice questions. You will not be allowed to use a calculator on the real exam, so make sure you practice without a calculator.

There is no time limit on the CAHSEE, but make sure you pace yourself on the questions. When you have completed your full-length practice exam, turn to page 323 for the answers and explanations.

1. Kelly needs four pieces of fabric to complete a project. Each piece is $\frac{3}{4}$ of a yard in length. What is the total length of all four pieces?

    A 3 yards

    B $3\frac{3}{4}$ yards

    C $5\frac{1}{3}$ yards

    D 12 yards

2. The scores of eight games in a bowling tournament are shown below. What is the mean bowling score?

    121, 152, 185, 97, 87, 90, 121, 251

    A 92

    B 121

    C 138

    D 164

3. $\frac{3}{5} + \left(\frac{1}{10} \div \frac{5}{6} \right) =$

    A $\frac{7}{12}$

    B $\frac{41}{60}$

    C $\frac{18}{25}$

    D $\frac{21}{25}$

Week Number	Price per Gallon
1	$2.15
2	2.21
3	2.27
4	2.33

4. The table above shows the increase in gasoline prices over four weeks. If the prices continue to rise at the same rate, what will be the price in week 6?

    A $2.36

    B $2.39

    C $2.45

    D $2.51

5. Which of the following is the graph of $y = -x$?

A

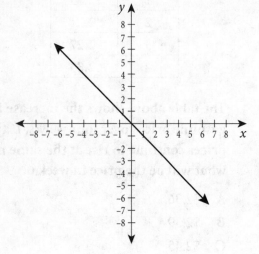

C

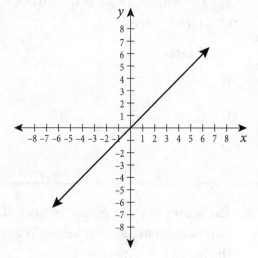

B

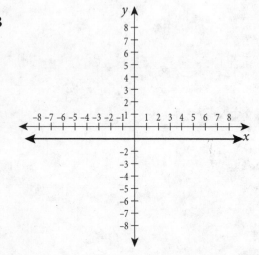

D

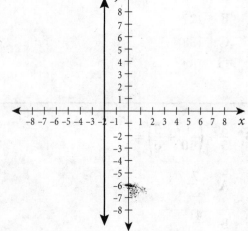

6. Which of the following is equivalent to $\frac{5^9}{5^{-3}}$?

A 5^{-6}

B 5^{-3}

C 5^6

D 5^{12}

7. Kaitlyn buys b books for a total of $20. At this rate, what is the total cost of 7 books?

A $\frac{7b}{20}$

B $\frac{20}{7b}$

C $\frac{140}{b}$

D $\frac{b}{140}$

8. A lion can run at a rate of 44 feet per second. What is this rate in miles per hour (mph)?

A 20 mph

B 30 mph

C 38 mph

D 44 mph

9. A flagpole is 60 feet tall. About how tall is the flagpole in meters, to the nearest hundredth? (1 meter ≈ 1.083 yards)

A 17.05 meters

B 18.47 meters

C 21.66 meters

D 55.40 meters

10. Peter can select a ham, turkey, roast beef, or tuna sandwich. He also needs to choose between mustard and mayonnaise for a condiment, and among sourdough, whole wheat, or rye bread. He can only select one choice from each category. Which of the following tree diagrams represents all of his possible choices?

A
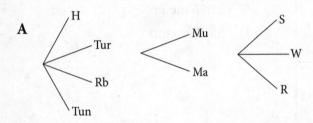

C
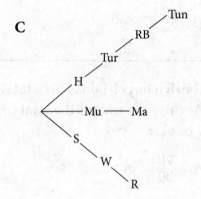

B
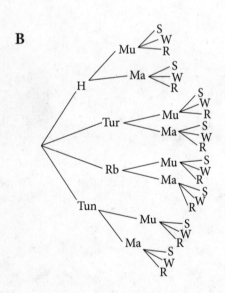

D
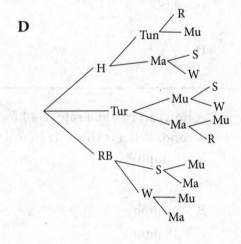

11. The number 0.000861 written in scientific notation is equivalent to which of the following?

    A 0.861×10^{-3}

    B 8.61×10^{-4}

    C 86.1×10^{-5}

    D 861×10^{-6}

12. The heights, in inches, of the players on a basketball team are listed below. What is the median height of the players?

    72, 75, 63, 68, 70, 65, 68, 71, 76, 67

    A   67.5 inches

    B   68 inches

    C   69 inches

    D   69.5 inches

13. Which fraction equals 35%?

    A $\dfrac{1}{35}$

    B $\dfrac{10}{35}$

    C $\dfrac{7}{20}$

    D $\dfrac{100}{35}$

14. Which of the following represents the statement, "Seven more than six times a number, x, is equal to 37"?

    A $7(6x) = 37$

    B $7 = 6x + 37$

    C $6 = 37 + 7x$

    D $6x + 7 = 37$

15. Simplify the expression shown below.

    $$10a^2 + 12b^2 - 8a^2 + 2b^2$$

    A $16a^2b^2$

    B $2a^2 + 14b^2$

    C $18a^2 + 14b^2$

    D $22a^2 - 6b^2$

16. Between which two integers does the square root of 90 lie?

    A   7 and 8

    B   8 and 9

    C   9 and 10

    D   10 and 11

17. What is the volume of the cube in cubic feet (ft.³) shown below?

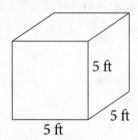

5 ft

5 ft

5 ft

A 15 ft.³
B 25 ft.³
C 100 ft.³
D 125 ft.³

18. A 12-by-18-meter garden is surrounded by a concrete walkway. The total dimensions of the garden and the walkway together are 15 meters by 21 meters. What is the total area, in square meters (m²) of the concrete walkway?

A 99 m²
B 180 m²
C 216 m²
D 315 m²

19. Philip earns 3% simple interest on his bank account. How much interest will he earn in 4 years after depositing $1,500 in his account?

A $45
B $180
C $1,680
D $18,000

20. Which of the following tables best represents the relationship between the values of x and y in the equation $y = 3x + 1$?

A

x	y
1	3
2	6
3	9
4	12

C

x	y
1	2
2	5
3	8
4	11

B

x	y
1	$\frac{1}{3}$
2	$\frac{2}{3}$
3	1
4	$1\frac{1}{3}$

D

x	y
1	4
2	7
3	10
4	13

21. A person driving a car at an average speed of 55 miles per hour stopped after 6 hours. She spent $33.45 on 15 gallons of gasoline but did not fill up her tank. Based on this information, which of the following <u>cannot</u> be determined?

A The total number of miles driven during the 6-hour trip.

B The price per gallon of gasoline that she purchased during the stop.

C The average miles her car gets per gallon of gasoline.

D Each of the above can be determined.

22. Which of the following expressions has a positive value?

    A $(-5) + (-9)$

    B $(-10) - (-2)$

    C $(-4) \times (-3)$

    D $(-20) \div (4)$

23. Simplify the expression shown below.

    $$\frac{x^2 + 3x + 2}{x + 1}$$

    A $x^2 + 2x + 1$

    B $x^2 + 2$

    C $x + 3$

    D $x + 2$

24. Each section of the spinner below is the same size. What is the probability of spinning the spinner once and getting a vowel?

    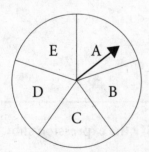

    A $\dfrac{1}{5}$

    B $\dfrac{2}{5}$

    C $\dfrac{1}{2}$

    D $\dfrac{3}{5}$

25. Which of the following are both solutions of the equation $x^2 - 7x + 10 = 0$?

    A $\{-5, 2\}$

    B $\{2, 5\}$

    C $\{-5, 5\}$

    D $\{-2, 2\}$

26. In a school of 875 students, 350 students participate in after-school clubs. What percent of the students participates in clubs?

    A   25%

    B   35%

    C   40%

    D   55%

Chelsea needs to paint a room whose walls have 600 square feet of surface area. Each can of paint she has can cover 50 square feet of wall space. How many cans of paint does she need to paint the room?

27. Which of the following problems could be solved using the same arithmetic operation needed to solve the problem above?

   A   Joe needs to drive 125 miles. His car gets 21 miles to the gallon of gasoline. How many gallons of gas does he need for this trip?

   B   Peter will wallpaper 6 rooms in his house. Each room will take him 1.5 hours to complete. How many hours will it take Peter to wallpaper all 6 rooms?

   C   A certain recipe calls for 2 cups of flour. How many cups of flour are needed if the recipe is tripled?

   D   Lena needs to mix 6 oz of red paint with 3 oz of white paint to make a certain shade of pink paint. What is the total number of ounces of the new shade of paint?

28. Which of the following shows every solution of the equation $|2x - 4| = 20$?

   A $\{-8\}$

   B $\{12\}$

   C $\{-8, 12\}$

   D $\{-12, 8\}$

29. In the first basketball game of the season, Selena scored 24 points. In the second game, she scored 30 points. By what percent did her game score increase?

   A   6%

   B   20%

   C   25%

   D   30%

30. If centimeter cubes form the figure below, what is the total volume of the figure?

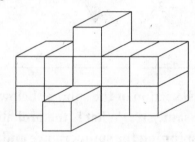

   A   12 cm³

   B   21 cm³

   C   30 cm³

   D   44 cm³

31. Simplify the expression shown below.

   $$(2)^8 \times (2)^{-7}$$

   A $\dfrac{1}{4}$

   B $\dfrac{1}{2}$

   C   2

   D   4

32. A car rental agency offers a special rental of $40 for the first day plus $20 for each day (*d*) *after* the first day, including all taxes and fees. Which equation could be used to find the total number of days the car could be rented if the renter has $140 to spend?

   A $40d + 20 = 140$

   B $20d + 40 = 140$

   C $60d = 140$

   D $40 + 20(d - 1) = 140$

33. Karl swam 50 meters in 45 seconds. At that rate, how many meters (*m*) can he swim in 3 minutes?

   A   100 m

   B   150 m

   C   200 m

   D   750 m

34. What is the area of the shaded region below, rounded to the nearest tenth?

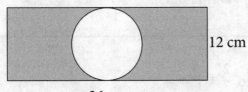

26 cm

12 cm

   A   113.1 cm²

   B   140.4 cm²

   C   198.9 cm²

   D   312.0 cm²

35. When simplifying the expression below, which operation should be performed first?

   $$-16 \div 4 + 4 - 5 \times 3$$

   A   Addition

   B   Division

   C   Multiplication

   D   Subtraction

36. A digital music player that normally sells for $56 is on sale for 30% off the regular price. What is the sale price of the player?

   A $16.80

   B $26.00

   C $29.20

   D $39.20

37. $\sqrt{81a^2b^4c^{16}} =$

   A $9ab^2c^8$

   B $9ab^2c^4$

   C $40.5ab^2c^8$

   D $40.5ab^2c^4$

38. Evaluate the expression $3cd - d$ for $c = -2$ and $d = -5$.

   A   −35

   B   −25

   C   25

   D   35

39. Simplify the expression shown below.

$$(4)^{-2}$$

A −16

B $-\dfrac{1}{16}$

C $\dfrac{1}{16}$

D 16

---

40. A triangle is formed by connecting the points (–2, 7), (2, 7), and (0, 3) on the coordinate grid. What is the area of the triangle?

A 4 square units

B 6 square units

C 8 square units

D 16 square units

---

41. 15 is 12.5% of what number?

A 1.875

B 120

C 125

D 187.5

---

42. The drawing of a car has a scale of 1 cm = 0.5 m as shown below.

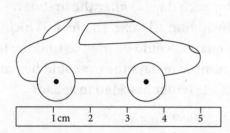

What is the actual length of the car in meters (m)?

A 0.1 m

B 2 m

C 2.5 m

D 10 m

---

43. Jerome can wallpaper a 12-by-7-foot wall in 2 hours. At this rate, how long will it take him to wallpaper a 18-by-7-foot wall?

A 2.5 hours

B 3 hours

C 3.5 hours

D 4 hours

---

44. $\dfrac{2}{7} + \dfrac{3}{14} =$

A $\dfrac{2}{7}$

B $\dfrac{5}{21}$

C $\dfrac{5}{14}$

D $\dfrac{1}{2}$

45. The circle graph below shows Cheryl's expenses for a month.

Cheryl's Monthly Expenses

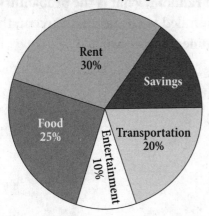

Based on the graph, which of the following statements is true?

A   The amount of money spent on transportation and savings is less than the amount of money spent on rent.

B   The amount of money spent on food and savings is equal to the amount of money spent on rent.

C   The amount of money spent on entertainment and food is the same as the amount of money spent on rent and savings.

D   The amount of money spent on transportation and savings is more than the amount spent on rent.

46. Which number has the least absolute value?

A   −100
B   −25
C   −12
D   10

47. What is the mode of the following numbers?

384, 368, 375, 399, 368, 402, 350

A   368
B   375
C   378
D   399

48. Which of the following scatter plots represents a positive correlation between the data sets?

A
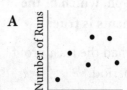

B
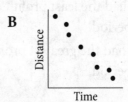

C
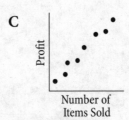

D
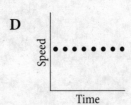

49. The graph below shows the sales profits for three different companies over a period of four months.

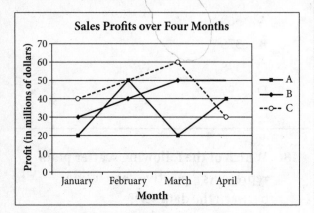

Based on the graph, which of the following statements is true?

A Company A had the least profit during this period.

B Company B had the greatest profit during this period.

C Company B had the least profit during this period.

D Company C had the greatest profit during this period.

50. There are 6 freshmen, 10 sophomores, 12 juniors, and 8 seniors on the math team. If one student is selected at random, what is the probability, rounded to the nearest percent, that the student is a senior?

A 17%

B 22%

C 27%

D 33%

51. The table below shows the total snowfall during a five-year period.

Year	Snowfall (in.)
2002	56
2003	75
2004	50
2005	105
2006	95

Which of the following graphs correctly represents the data in the table?

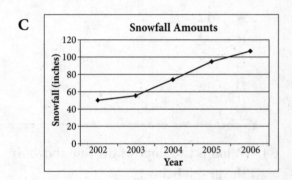

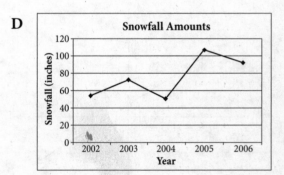

52. Which of the following is equivalent to $(2x^2)(16xy^2)$?

    A $18x^2y^2$

    B $18x^3y^2$

    C $32x^2y^2$

    D $32x^3y^2$

53. Solve the equation below for x.

    $3x - 24 = 18$

    A -12

    B -2

    C 14

    D 16

54. What is the slope of the line shown in the graph below?

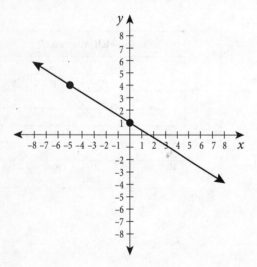

    A $-\dfrac{5}{3}$

    B $-\dfrac{3}{5}$

    C $\dfrac{3}{5}$

    D $\dfrac{5}{3}$

55. The points (2, 1), (6, 1), and (6, 4) plotted on a coordinate grid are the vertices of a right triangle. What is the length of the hypotenuse of this triangle?

    A 5 units

    B 5.5 units

    C 7 units

    D 25 units

56. Simplify the expression shown below.

    $10w - 5(x - 7) + 3y$

    A $10w + 5x - 35 + 3y$

    B $10w - 5x - 35 + 3y$

    C $10w - 5x + 35 + 3y$

    D $10w + 5x + 35 + 3y$

57. When a pair of six-sided dice are rolled once, what is the probability that the sum of the numbers rolled will be less than 3?

    A $\dfrac{1}{36}$

    B $\dfrac{1}{12}$

    C $\dfrac{1}{6}$

    D $\dfrac{1}{2}$

58. Solve the equation below for *x*.

$$10 + 5x \geq 65$$

A $x \geq 11$

B $x \leq 11$

C $x \geq 15$

D $x \leq 15$

59. What is the equation of the graph shown below?

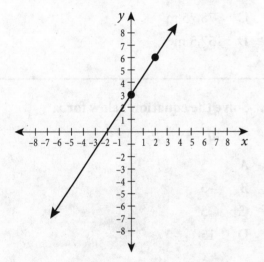

A $y = -\frac{3}{2}x + 3$

B $y = -\frac{2}{3}x + 3$

C $y = \frac{2}{3}x + 3$

D $y = \frac{3}{2}x + 3$

60. Evaluate $12 + (2^3)(7 - 5)$.

A 24

B 28

C 135

D 5,488

61. A jewelry store is running a special on necklaces. A customer can choose between a silver or gold chain; a long or short chain; and a ruby, opal, or emerald stone. How many different necklaces can be selected from for this special?

A 6

B 7

C 9

D 12

62. A taxi service charges $2.50 for the first mile and $1.50 for each mile after the first. What is the greatest distance a passenger can ride for $15?

A 8 miles

B 9 miles

C 10 miles

D 15 miles

63. Which of the following should be the best first step in solving the inequality below?

$$\frac{9x + 7}{4} \leq 8.5$$

A Divide each side of the inequality by 9.

B Subtract 7 from each side of the inequality.

C Divide each side of the inequality by 4.

D Multiply each side of the inequality by 4.

64. What is the y–intercept of the equation $-5 + y = 3x$?

A $\frac{3}{5}$

B $\frac{5}{3}$

C 3

D 5

65. The dimensions of a triangular yard are shown below. What is the total amount of fencing in meters (m) needed to surround the yard?

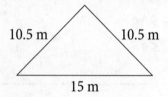

A 36 m

B 72 m

C 78.75 m

D 157.5 m

66. Solve the equation below for x.

$$30 - 3x = 15$$

A −15

B −5

C 5

D 15

67. A number from 0 to 9 is to be selected at random. What is the probability that the number selected will be a prime number?

A $\frac{2}{5}$

B $\frac{4}{9}$

C $\frac{1}{2}$

D $\frac{5}{9}$

68. Which graph represents a line with positive slope?

A

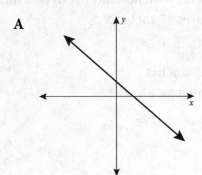

B

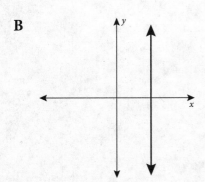

C

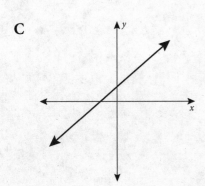

D

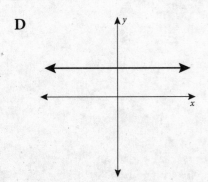

69. During a storm, the snow fell at a rate of 1.5 inches per hour for 6 hours. How many centimeters (cm) of snow fell during the storm? (1 inch ≈ 2.54 centimeters)

  A   3.54 cm

  B   19.05 cm

  C   22.86 cm

  D   28.22 cm

70. What is the surface area of the rectangular prism shown below?

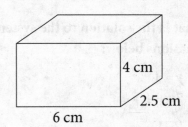

  A   60 cm^2

  B   98 cm^2

  C   120 cm^2

  D   128 cm^2

71. Which of the following combinations of a 60% sugar solution and a 30% sugar solution will result in 50 ounces (oz.) of a 42% sugar solution?

   A   10 oz. of 60% solution and 40 oz. of 30% solution

   B   20 oz. of 60% solution and 30 oz. of 30% solution

   C   25 oz. of 60% solution and 25 oz. of 30% solution

   D   30 oz. of 60% solution and 20 oz. of 30% solution

72. What is the solution to the system of equations below?

$$y = 1$$
$$2y + 4 = -x$$

   A   (6, 1)

   B   (1, −6)

   C   (−1, 6)

   D   (−6, 1)

73. What is the length of the third side of a right triangle of which one side measures 8 inches and the hypotenuse measures 17 inches?

   A   9 inches

   B   15 inches

   C   18.8 inches

   D   112.5 inches

74. Triangle ABC is graphed on the grid below.

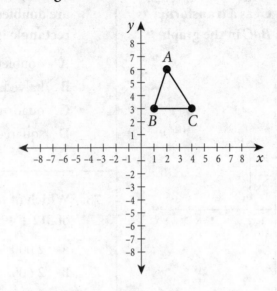

Which of the following represents a translation of triangle ABC by 3 units on the *x*-axis and −4 units on the *y*-axis?

A

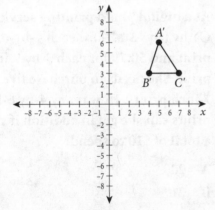

C

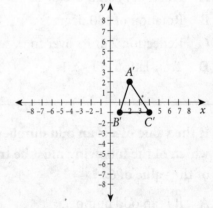

B

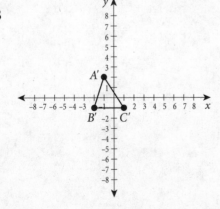

D

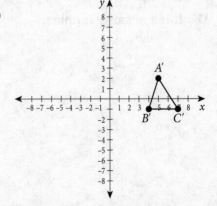

75. Which of the following best describes the figure ΔA′, B′, C′ as a transformation of figure ΔA, B, C in the graph below?

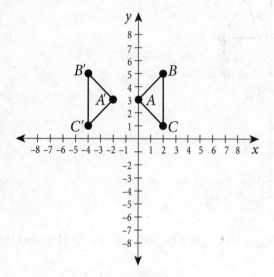

   A   Dilation of scale factor 2

   B   Rotation of 180 degrees

   C   Reflection 2 units over the y-axis

   D   Translation of (–2, 1)

76. If the value of x is an odd number, which of the following must be true of the value of 6x ?

   A   It is an odd number.

   B   It is an even number.

   C   It is a positive number.

   D   It is a negative number.

77. If the length and width of a rectangle are doubled, then the area of the rectangle is

   A   doubled.

   B   halved.

   C   quadrupled.

   D   squared.

78. Which of the follow is the best estimate of 312 + 499 + 1234 + 776?

   A   2,000

   B   2,600

   C   2,800

   D   3,000

79. At a digital photo printing service, Cathy pays $0.29 for each 4-by-6-inch print and $0.79 for each 5-by-7-inch print. She needs to purchase five 5-by-7-inch prints. How many 4-by 6-inch prints can she get in addition if she has a total of $10 to spend?

   A   20

   B   21

   C   31

   D   34

80. When solving the equation below for *x*, which of the following is the correct order of steps?

    $3x - a = b$

    A   Add *A* to each side of the equation, then divide each side by 3.

    B   Subtract *A* from each side of the equation, then multiply each side by 3.

    C   Add *A* to each side of the equation, then multiply each side by 3.

    D   Subtract *a* from each side of the equation, then divide each side by 3.

81. A furniture company produces the same number of chairs each week. If the chairs cost $24 to produce and a profit of $11 is made on each chair sold, what other information is needed to find the total sales for one week?

    A   The amount each chair is sold for this week.

    B   The total number of chairs produced each week.

    C   The number of chairs sold this week.

    D   The number of employees at the company.

82. The steps for solving an equation are shown below.

    Step 1: $3(x + 6) + 5x = 14$
    Step 2: $3x + 18 + 5x = 14$
    Step 3: $8x + 18 = 14$
    Step 4: $8x = -4$
    Step 5: $x = -\dfrac{1}{2}$

    What real number property is used to get from step 1 to step 2?

    A   Associative property of addition

    B   Associative property of multiplication

    C   Inverse property of multiplication

    D   Distributive property of multiplication over addition

83. What is the reciprocal of $-\dfrac{5b^2}{2a}$?

    A $-\dfrac{2a}{5b^2}$

    B $\dfrac{5b^2}{2a}$

    C $\dfrac{2a}{5b^2}$

    D $-\dfrac{2b^2}{5a}$

84. What is the area of the figure below in square centimeters (cm²)?

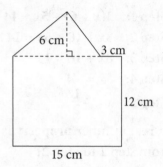

A 72 cm²

B 180 cm²

C 216 cm²

D 252 cm²

85. Which of the following is equivalent to the equation $m = \dfrac{y - y_1}{x - x_1}$?

A $m(y - y_1) = x - x_1$

B $m(x - x_1) = y - y_1$

C $m = \dfrac{x - x_1}{y - y_1}$

D $m = \dfrac{x_1 - x}{y_1 - y}$

86. Sally ordered a meal in a restaurant that costs $10.99. She plans to leave a 15% tip for the server, and she will have to pay 8% sales tax on the meal. Which is the best estimate of the total amount of money she will pay?

A $11.50

B $12.50

C $13.50

D $14.50

87. Which of the following points is on the line $-3y + 12 = 2x$?

A $(-3, 12)$

B $(3, 2)$

C $(3, -6)$

D $(4, 0)$

88. Which of the following corresponds with side $\overline{BC}$ from triangle ABC as a congruent side?

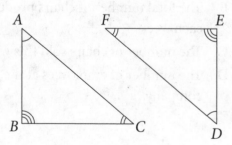

A $\overline{DF}$

B $\overline{DE}$

C $\overline{EF}$

D $\overline{AC}$

89. Simplify the expression shown below.

$$-3x^2 + 4x + 19x^2 - 10x$$

A $16x^2 - 6x$

B $16x^2 + 14x$

C $22x^2 - 14x$

D $10x^3$

90. The graph below shows the average temperature over four months.

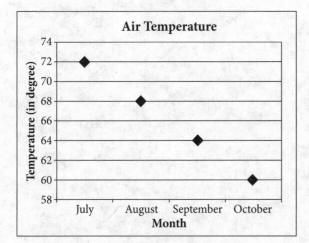

Based on the graph, what is the expected average temperature for December?

A   52 degrees

B   54 degrees

C   56 degrees

D   60 degrees

91. What is the result when the expression $x^2 - 49$ is factored completely?

A $x(x - 7)$

B $x(x - 49)$

C $(x - 7)(x - 7)$

D $(x + 7)(x - 7)$

92. Solve the equation below for x.

$$\frac{1}{x} + \frac{x + 4}{2x} = 2$$

A   1

B   2

C   4

D   6

Answers and Explanations

1. A

To find the total length, multiply the length of each piece by 4: $\frac{3}{4} + 4 = \frac{3}{4} \times \frac{4}{1} = \frac{12}{4} = 3$. She needs a total of 3 yards of fabric. Choice B is the result of adding 3 and $\frac{3}{4}$. Choice C is the result of dividing 4 by $\frac{3}{4}$.

2. C

The mean bowling score is found by dividing the sum of the scores and by the total number of scores in the list. The sum of the scores is $121 + 152 + 185 + 97 + 87 + 90 + 121 + 251 = 1{,}104$. Now, divide this sum by the number of scores in the list: $1{,}104 \div 8 = 138$. The mean score is 138. Choice B is the mode of the data, the value that occurs most frequently. Choice D is the range, the difference between the highest and lowest values in the list.

3. C

To simplify, follow the correct order of operations. First, divide the fractions within the parentheses. To divide by a fraction, multiply by the reciprocal: $\frac{1}{10} \div \frac{5}{6} = \frac{1}{10} \times \frac{6}{5} = \frac{6}{50}$. Next, add $\frac{3}{5} + \frac{6}{50}$. To do this, change the first fraction so it has a common denominator of 50: $\frac{3}{5} \times \frac{10}{10} = \frac{30}{50}$. Then add: $\frac{30}{50} + \frac{6}{50} = \frac{36}{50}$. Simplify the fraction by dividing the numerator and denominator by their greatest common factor, which is 2: $\frac{36 \div 2}{50 \div 2} = \frac{18}{25}$. Choice D is the result of working the operations from left to right, without performing the division within the parentheses first.

4. C

Each week, the price of gasoline increases by $0.06. Because the price at week 4 is $2.33, the price at week 5 can be predicted to be $2.33 + 0.06 = $2.39. Thus, the price at week 6 can be predicted to be $2.39 + 0.06 = $2.45. Choice B is the expected price at week 5 and choice D represents the expected price at week 7.

5. A

The graph of the line $y = -x$ is a linear graph and forms a straight line. The slope of this line is –1, and the y-intercept is the origin (0, 0). This line also contains the points (–1, 1), (–2, 2), and (–3, 3), to name a few. The only graph of a straight line that contains these points is choice A. Choice B is the graph of the line $y = -1$. Choice C is the graph of the line $y = x$. Choice D is the graph of the line $x = -1$.

6. D

When dividing powers with like bases, subtract the exponents and keep the base. In this question, subtract –3 from 9 to get the new exponent: $\dfrac{5^9}{5^{-3}} = 5^{9-(-3)}$ $= 5^{9+3} = 5^{12}$. Choice A is the result of subtracting 9 from 3 instead of subtracting –3 from –9. Choice B is the result of dividing the powers instead of subtracting. Choice C is the result of adding –3 instead of subtracting.

7. C

If she buys b books for a total of $20, then one book costs her $\dfrac{\$20}{b}$. Multiply this value by 7 to get $7 \times \dfrac{\$20}{b} = \dfrac{140}{b}$. Choice A multiplies 7 by the number of books, then divides this amount by $20. Choice B divides $20 by 7 times the number of books. Choice D divides the number of books by the product of 7 and 20, giving the reciprocal of the correct answer.

8. B

To convert from feet per second to miles per hour, multiply by the conversion factors and cancel out the unit labels:

$$\frac{44\ \cancel{\text{feet}}}{1\ \cancel{\text{second}}} \times \frac{60\ \cancel{\text{seconds}}}{1\ \cancel{\text{minute}}} \times \frac{60\ \cancel{\text{minutes}}}{1\ \text{hour}} \times \frac{1\ \text{mile}}{5{,}280\ \cancel{\text{feet}}}.$$

The only unit labels that did not cancel are miles and hours. Multiply the numerators and then the denominators and use the labels that did not cancel.

$$\frac{158,400 \text{ miles}}{5,280 \text{ hours}} \times \frac{30 \text{ miles}}{1 \text{ hours}} = 30 \text{ miles per hour}$$

You may have incorrectly selected choice D if you thought that the rate would be the same, regardless of the unit labels.

9. B

Use the conversion factor of 1 meter ≈ 1.083 yards to answer this question. First, convert 60 feet to yards by dividing 60 by 3; the flagpole is 20 yards high.

Set up the proportion $\frac{\text{meters}}{\text{yards}} = \frac{\text{meters}}{\text{yards}}$.

The proportion becomes $\frac{1 \text{ meter}}{1.083 \text{ yards}} = \frac{x \text{ meters}}{20 \text{ yards}}$.

Cross multiply the proportion to get: $1.083x = 20$

Divide each side of the equation by 1.083: $\frac{1.083x}{1.083} = \frac{20}{1.083}$

The variable, x, is now alone: $x = 18.46722068$

The tree is about 18.47 meters high. Choice C is the result of an incorrect proportion. Choice D is the result of not converting feet into yards and substituting 60 feet into the proportion instead of 20 yards.

10. B

In this case, the correct tree diagram will start with four branches, one each for ham, turkey, roast beef, and tuna. Off of each of those branches will be 2 branches, one for mustard and one for mayonnaise. There are now a total of 8 possibilities. Off of each of those 8, there should be three branches, one each for white, whole wheat, and rye bread. This is a total of 24 possibilities, which is choice B. Choice A shows all of the choices to make for each category but does not list the combinations of selecting one item from each category. Choices C and D do not show all possible combinations.

11. B

Scientific notation is written as the product of a number greater than or equal to 1 and less than 10 and a number that is some power of 10. In this case, the number 0.000861 should be written with 8.61. This moves the decimal point four places to the right, so the exponent on 10 is −4. Therefore, the correct answer is 8.61×10^{-4}. None of the other answer choices has a number greater than or equal to 1 and less than 10 multiplied by a power of 10. In choice A, 0.861 is less than 1. In choices C and D, 86.1 and 861 are each greater than 10.

12. C

To find the median of a set of numbers, first write the set of numbers in order. The list of heights in order is 63, 65, 67, 68, 68, 70, 71, 72, 75, 76. The median number will be the number in the middle of the list. Because there are ten numbers in the list, the middle number is between the fifth and sixth numbers, which are 68 and 70. Find the mean of these two numbers to find the median. This value is 69. Choice A is the result of finding the median of the set without placing the numbers in order first. Choice B is the mode of the data, the value that appears most often. Choice D is the mean of the heights of the players.

13. C

The equivalent fraction to 35% is $\frac{35}{100}$. This fraction can be simplified by dividing the numerator and denominator by their greatest common factor of 5: $\frac{35 \div 5}{100 \div 5} = \frac{7}{20}$. Choice A is approximately 2.85%. Choice B is approximately 28.57%. Choice D is the reciprocal of the correct answer.

14. D

Translate each part of the statement into mathematical symbols. The part "Seven more than" means to add 7 to a quantity. "Six times a number, x" is written as $6x$. Thus, the first part of the statement can be expressed as $6x + 7$. Set this equal to 37 to complete the statement and write the equation $6x + 7 = 37$. Choice A represents the statement "the product of 7 and $6x$ is equal to 37." Choice B represents the statement "the sum of $6x$ and 31 is equal to 7." Choice C represents the statement "6 is equal to the sum of 37 and the product of 7 and a number, x."

15. B

To simplify this expression, combine like terms. Like terms have the same variable(s) and exponent(s). Add or subtract the coefficients of the like terms: $10a^2 - 8a^2 = 2a^2$ and $12b^2 + 2b^2 = 14b^2$. The fully simplified expression is $2a^2 + 14b^2$. In choice A, unlike terms were combined. In choice C, $8a^2$ was added to $10a^2$ instead of subtracted from it. Choice D is the result of incorrectly placing a^2 next to the sum of the first two terms and b^2 next to the sum of the last two terms.

16. C

To find the integers, first find the two perfect squares on either side of 90. These numbers are 81 and 100. Because the square root of 81 is 9 and the square root of 100 is 10, the square root of 90 lies between 9 and 10. Another way to check this answer is to calculate the square root itself. The square root of 90 is approximately 9.49, which is between 9 and 10, or choice C.

17. D

The volume of a cube is found by using the formula volume = (length of an edge)^3, or $V = e^3$. The edge of this cube has length of 5 feet, so the formula is $V = 5^3 = 5 \times 5 \times 5 = 125$ cubic feet. Choice A is the result of adding the dimensions instead of multiplying. Choice B is the result of multiplying only two of the three dimensions.

18. A

Subtract the area of the garden only from the combined area of the garden and the walkway. The area of the garden and the walkway together can be found by using the formula area = length × width, or $A = lw$. Therefore, the area of the garden and walkway together is $A = 15 \times 21 = 315$. The area of the garden is also found by using the formula $A = lw$. The area of the garden only is $A = 12 \times 18 = 216$. Subtract one value from another to find the area of just the walkway: $315 - 216 = 99$. You may have selected choice B if you incorrectly multiplied 12 by 15, the width of walkway and garden together and the width of the garden. Choice C is the area of the garden only. Choice D is the combined area of the garden and the walkway.

19. B

Use the formula interest = principle × rate × time, or $I = prt$, to find the amount of interest he made. He invested $1,500, so the principle, p, is $1,500. He invests for 4 years so time, t, is 4. He earns 3% interest, so change the percent to a decimal by dividing by 100. Thus, the rate, r, is 0.03. Substitute each of these values into the formula: $I = (\$1,500)(0.03)(4) = \$180$. He makes $180 in interest. Choice C is the total balance in the account after the 4 years. Choice D is the result of not changing the percent to a decimal when using it in the formula.

20. D

To represent the equation $y = 3x + 1$, each value of x must result in a value of y that is one more than three times its value. Start by checking each value. An x of 1 should result in a y of $3(1) + 1 = 3 + 1 = 4$. An x of 2 should result in a y of $3(2) + 1 = 6 + 1 = 7$. An x of 3 should result in a y of $3(3) + 1 = 9 + 1 = 10$. The table with the values (1, 4), (2, 7), and (3, 10) is the table in choice D. Choice A is the table for the equation $y = 3x$. Choice B is the table for the equation $y = \frac{1}{3}x$. Choice C is the table for the equation $y = 3x - 1$.

21. C

The distance traveled is equal to 55 miles per hour × 6 hours = 330 miles, so the information in choice A can be determined. The price per gallon can be determined by dividing the total amount of money spent on gasoline by the total number of gallons, so the information in choice B can be determined: $\$33.45 \div 15 = \$2.23$ per gallon. The average miles to the gallon cannot be determined, because she did not fill up her gas tank. So the exact number of gallons used is unknown.

22. C

When multiplying a negative value by a negative value, the result is positive. In choice C, $(-4) \times (-3) = 12$. In choice A, add the absolute values of the numbers and keep the sign. $(-5) + (-9) = -14$. In choice B, change subtraction to addition and change the –2 to 2. Subtract the absolute values and take the sign of the larger absolute value. $-10 + 2 = -8$. In choice D, a negative value divided by a positive value yields a negative value: $(-20) \div (4) = -5$. The only positive result is choice C.

23. D

First, factor the numerator. The expression becomes $\frac{(x + 2)(x + 1)}{x + 1}$.

Cancel the common factor of $x + 1$ in the numerator and denominator: $\frac{(x + 2)(x + 1)}{x + 1}$. The expression simplifies to $x + 2$. Choice A is the result of not factoring the numerator and subtracting a value of x and a value of 1 from the numerator to cancel out the denominator.

24. B

The probability of an event's occurring is

$$P(E) = \frac{\text{number of ways the event can occur}}{\text{total number of possible outcomes}}.$$

There are a total of five sections on the spinner. Two of these sections (A and E) are vowels. Therefore, the probability of getting a vowel is $P(\text{vowel}) = \frac{2}{5}$. Choice D is the probability of *not* getting a vowel: $\left(1 - \frac{2}{5}\right)$.

25. B

Factor the left side of the equation and set each factor equal to zero.

The equation becomes: $(x - 5)(x - 2) = 0$
Set each factor equal to zero. $x - 5 = 0$ or $x - 2 = 0$
Solve for x: $x = 5$ or $x = 2$

The solution set is $\{2, 5\}$. Choice A is the result of confusing the signs when finding the factors of the equation.

26. C

To find the percent, use the proportion $\frac{\text{part}}{\text{whole}} = \frac{\%}{100}$. The part is the 350 students who participate in clubs, and the whole is the 875 total students in the school. You are looking for the percent, so use x to represent the percent and place it over 100 in the proportion.

The proportion becomes:	$\dfrac{350}{875} = \dfrac{x}{100}$
Cross multiply the proportion:	$875x = 35{,}000$
Divide each side of the equation by 875:	$\dfrac{375x}{875} = \dfrac{35{,}000}{875}$
The variable, x, is now alone.	$x = 40\%$

Because 350 is close to but less than one-half of 875, choices A and B are too low, and choice D is too high.

27. A

To find the number of cans of paint she would use, divide the total surface area by the number of square feet each can covers: $600 \div 50 = 12$ gallons. To answer this question, determine which of the other answer choices also require division to solve. In choice A, you would divide the total distance of 125 miles by 21 miles per gallon to find the amount of gasoline needed. In choice B, you would multiply 1.5 hours by the number of rooms to find the total time. In choice C, you would multiply 2 cups of flour by 3. In choice D, you would need to add the number of ounces of each color together to find the total. Only choice A involves division.

28. C

To solve this absolute value equation, make two equations by setting $2x - 4$ equal to 20 and $2x - 4$ equal to -20. Solve for x in each case.

	$2x - 4 = 20$	or	$2x - 4 = -20$
Add 4 to each side or each equation:	$2x - 4 + 4 = 20 + 4$		$2x - 4 + 4 = -20 + 4$
Simplify:	$2x = 24$		$2x = -16$
Divide each side of each equation by 2:	$\dfrac{2x}{2} = \dfrac{24}{2}$		$\dfrac{2x}{2} = \dfrac{-16}{2}$
The variable, x, is now alone:	$x = 12$	or	$x = -8$

The solution set is {–8, 12}. Choice A and choice B each list one of the two solutions, but both need to be listed to have the correct solution set. Answer choice D lists the opposites of the correct answer and could be the result of confusing signs when solving the equation.

29. C

To find the percent of increase, use the proportion $\dfrac{\text{difference in amounts}}{\text{original amount}} = \dfrac{x}{100}$. The change in the number of points scored is $30 - 24 = 6$ points. The original number of points is 24. Thus, the proportion is $\dfrac{6}{24} = \dfrac{x}{100}$. Use this equation to solve for x and find the percent of increase.

Cross multiply the proportion: $\qquad\qquad 24x = 600$

Divide each side of the equation by 24: $\qquad \dfrac{24x}{24} = \dfrac{600}{24}$

The variable, x, is now alone: $\qquad\qquad x = 25$

The percent increase is 25%. Answer choice A is the increase in the number of baskets, not the percent of increase in the number of baskets. Choice B is the result of using 30 as the original number of baskets instead of 24.

30. A

There are 12 centimeter cubes in the figure, so the volume of the figure is 12 cm^3. Be sure to count the cubes that cannot be seen but are underneath other cubes. Choice C is the product of the length, width, and height of the figure. Choice D is the surface area of the figure.

31. C

To simplify this expression, add the exponents. Because $8 + (-7) = 1$, the expression simplifies to 2^1 or 2. Choice B is the value of 2^{-1}. Choice D is the value of 2^2.

32. B

The charge of $40 is for the first day only, and the charge of $20 is for each day after that. Therefore, $20 needs to be multiplied by the number of days after the first, or d. This is written as $20d$. Add 40 to $20d$ and set this expression equal to the total amount that can be spent, $140: $20d + 40 = 140$, which is choice B. Choice A is incorrect because it multiplies 40 by *d* and adds 20, as though the car costs $20 for the first day and $40 for each day after the first. Choice D would be correct if *d* represented the number of days, not the total number of days *after* the first.

33. C

Because the information was given in seconds and the question asks for the distance in minutes, convert 3 minutes into seconds. There are 60 seconds in 1 minute, so multiply: $3 \times 60 = 180$ seconds. Then use the proportion $\frac{meters}{seconds}$ $= \frac{meters}{seconds}$. Because he swam at a rate of 50 meters in 45 seconds, set this equal to $\frac{x}{180}$. Now solve the equation $\frac{50}{45} = \frac{x}{180}$ for *x*.

Cross multiply the proportion: $\qquad\qquad 45x = 9,000$

Divide each side of the equation by 45: $\quad \dfrac{45x}{45} = \dfrac{9,000}{45}$

The variable, *x*, is now alone: $\qquad\qquad x = 200$

Karl can swim 200 meters in 3 minutes.

34. C

To find the area of the shaded region, find the area of the outer region and subtract the area of the inner region. The outer region is a rectangle with a base of 26 cm and a height of 12 cm. The inner region is a circle with a diameter of 12 cm, so the radius is equal to half of this, or 6 cm. Use the formulas for the area of each shape and subtract.

$$A_{shaded} = A_{outer} - A_{inner}$$

$$A_{shaded} = bh - \pi r^2$$

Substitute the values into the formula: $\quad A_{shaded} = (26)(12) - \pi(6)^2$

Evaluate using the correct
order of operations: $\qquad\qquad\qquad A_{shaded} = 312 - 36\pi$

$$A_{shaded} = 312 - 113.0973355$$

Subtract to find the area: $\qquad\qquad A_{shaded} = 198.9026645$

The area of the shaded region is approximately 198.9 cm². Choice A is the area of the inner circle. Choice D is the area of the entire rectangle.

35. B

Follow the correct order of operations, which can be remembered by the acronym PEMDAS:

Parentheses
Exponents
Multiply and **D**ivide (in order from left to right)
Add and **S**ubtract (in order from left to right)

There are no parentheses or exponents, so the division should be done first.

36. D

To find the sale price, find 30% of the regular price and subtract that amount from the original cost. You can find 30% of $56 by multiplying: 0.30 × 56 = $16.80. Then subtract the discount from the original price: $56 – $16.80 = $39.20. The sale price is $39.20. Choice A is the amount of the discount, or the amount you would save when making this purchase. Choice C is $16.80 less than $46.

37. A

To simplify the square root, find the square root of the coefficient and divide each exponent by 2. The square root of 81 is 9, because 9 × 9 = 81. The expression becomes $9ab^2c^8$. Choice B is the result of taking the square root of the exponents of the variables instead of dividing each by 2. Choices C and D each divide 81 by 2, instead of taking the square root of the coefficient.

38. D

To evaluate the expression, first substitute for each variable. Then evaluate using the correct order of operations. The correct order of operations can be remembered as the acronym PEMDAS:

Parentheses
Exponents
Multiply and **D**ivide (in order from left to right)
Add and **S**ubtract (in order from left to right)

Substitute into the expression:	$3(-2)(-5) - (-5)$
Multiply:	$3(10) - (-5)$
	$30 - (-5)$
Change the subtraction to adding the opposite:	$30 + 5$
Add to get the final answer:	35

Choice A is the opposite of the correct answer and could be the result of confusion of the rules for operations with integers. Choice C is the result of subtracting 5 from 30 in the final step.

39. C

To make the exponent positive, find its reciprocal: the expression $(4)^{-2}$ becomes $\frac{1}{4^2}$. Next, apply the exponent: $\frac{1}{4^2} = \frac{1}{4 \times 4} = \frac{1}{16}$. Choice A is the value of $-(4)^2$, which is not the same as $(4)^{-2}$. Choice B is the value of $-(4)^{-2}$. Choice D is the value of 4^2.

40. C

Plot the points on the coordinate grid. The result is the triangle shown below.

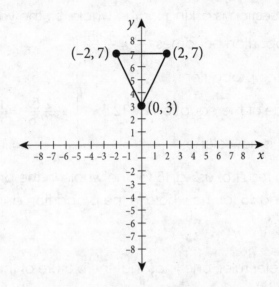

The formula for the area of a triangle is $A = \frac{1}{2}bh$. To find the area, find the base and height of the triangle by counting the units on the grid and substitute those values into the formula. The base of the triangle is 4 units and the height is 4 units.

Substitute the values into the area formula: $A = \frac{1}{2}(4)(4)$

Multiply: $A = \frac{1}{2}(16)$

A is on one side of the equation: $A = 8$

The triangle has an area of 8 square units. Choice A is the result of taking one-half of the area two times. Choice D is the result of not using one-half in the formula.

41. B

Use the proportion $\frac{part}{whole} = \frac{\%}{100}$. In this case, 15 is the part and 12.5 is the percent. The question is asking for the whole, so the variable x can be used for this. The proportion becomes $\frac{15}{x} = \frac{12.5}{100}$.

Cross multiply the proportion: $12.5x = 1,500$

Divide each side of the equation by 12.5: $\frac{12.5x}{12.5} = \frac{1,500}{12.5}$

The variable, x, is now alone: $x = 120$

Choice A is the result of using 15 for the whole in the proportion. Choice D is the result of using 15 for the whole in the proportion and not dividing by 100.

42. C

Using a centimeter ruler, one finds that the picture of the car measures 5 cm. Using the conversion 1 centimeter = 0.5 meters, multiply 5 cm × 0.5 = 2.5 meters. Choice D is the result of multiplying by 2 instead of by 0.5 or $\frac{1}{2}$.

43. B

Find the area of the wall by multiplying base × height: 12 × 7 = 84 square feet. He can wallpaper 84 square feet in 2 hours. The wall he needs to paper has an area of 18 × 7 = 126 square feet.

Use the proportion $\frac{84 \text{ square feet}}{2 \text{ hours}} = \frac{126 \text{ square feet}}{x \text{ hours}}$.

Cross multiply: $84x = 252$

Divide each side of the equation by 84: $\frac{84x}{84} = \frac{252}{84}$

The variable, x, is now alone: $x = 3$

It will take him 3 hours. Choice D is the result of simply doubling the time needed to wallpaper the larger room.

44. D

First, find the least common multiple of the denominators and convert each to an equivalent fraction. The least common multiple of 7 and 14 is 14. The first fraction becomes $\frac{2 \times 2}{7 \times 2} = \frac{4}{14}$, and the second fraction stays the same. Next, add the numerators and keep the common denominator:

$\frac{4}{14} + \frac{3}{14} = \frac{7}{14}$. Simplify the fraction by dividing the numerator and denominator by the greatest common factor of 7: $\frac{7 \div 7}{14 \div 7} = \frac{1}{2}$. Choice B is the result of adding the numerators and denominators without finding the least common denominator. Choice C is the result of adding the numerators and keeping the least common denominator of 14.

45. D

The first step to answering this question is to determine the percentage of money that belongs in the savings category. Because the percents of a circle graph total 100%, add the known amounts and subtract the total from 100%: 30% + 20% + 10% + 25% = 85%, and 100% − 85% = 15% for savings. Examine each answer choice to determine the correct answer. In choice A, the amount spent on transportation and savings is 20% + 15% = 35%, which is more than the amount spent on rent (30%). Choice A is not true. In choice B, the amount spent on food and savings is 25% + 15% = 40%, which is not equal to the amount spent on rent (30%). Choice B is not true. In choice C, the amount spent on entertainment and food is 10% + 25% = 35%, which is not the same as the amount spent on rent and savings (30% + 15% = 45%). Choice C is not correct. Finally in choice D, the amount spent on transportation and savings, 20% + 15% = 35%, is more than the amount spent on rent (30%). Choice D is correct.

46. D

The absolute value of a number is the distance the number is away from zero on the number line. The number 10 is ten units away from zero and, therefore, has the smallest absolute value of the answer choices. In choice A, the number −100 has an absolute value of 100. In choice B, the number −25 has an absolute value of 25. In choice C, the number −12 has an absolute value of 12.

47. A

The mode of a set of numbers is the value that occurs most often. The number 368 appears twice in the set, and each of the other values only appears once, so 368 is the mode. Choice B is the median of this set of data. Choice C is the mean of this set of data. Choice D is simply the fourth number in the set in its present order.

48. C

A positive correlation exists where one set of values tends to increase as the other set of values increases. This is found in choice C. Notice that the points increase as you move across the graph from left to right. Choice A is an example of a data set with no correlation between the sets of data. Choice B is an example of a negative correlation.

49. D

Find the total profit over the four months for each company by adding the amount for each month. Company A had a profit of 20 + 50 + 20 + 40 = $130 million. Company B had a profit of 30 + 40 + 50 + 50 = $170 million. Company C had a profit of 40 + 50 + 60 + 30 = $180 million. Company C had the greatest profit over this period.

50. B

The probability of an event (e) occurring is

$$P(e) = \frac{\text{number of ways the event can occur}}{\text{total number of possible outcomes}}$$

Because there are 8 seniors, and there are a total of 6 + 10 + 12 + 8 = 36 students, the probability is $P(\text{senior}) = \frac{8}{36}$. Change this fraction to a percent by dividing the numerator by the denominator and multiplying by 100: 8 ÷ 36 ≈ 0.2222222, and 0.222222 × 100 = 22.2222%. Choice A is the percent of freshmen on the math team. Choice C is the percent of sophomores on the math team. Choice D is the percent of juniors on the math team.

51. D

The snowfall amounts are graphed correctly in choice D. Choice A graphs each of the amounts in the table backwards, with the amount for 2006 first and the amount for 2002 last. Choice B graphs each of the amounts in order from highest to lowest. Choice C graphs each of the amounts in order from lowest to highest.

52. D

To multiply the expressions, multiply the coefficients and add the exponents of the like bases. The expression $(2x^2)(16xy^2)$ becomes $(2 \times 16)x^{2+1}y^2$. This simplifies to $32x^3y^2$, which is choice D. Choice A shows the sum of the coefficients, rather than their product, and it does not have the correct exponents.

53. C

To solve the two-step equation, get the variable x alone.

First, add 24 to each side of the equation: $3x - 24 + 24 = 18 + 24$

The equation becomes: $3x = 42$

Divide each side of the equation by 3: $\dfrac{3x}{3} = \dfrac{42}{3}$

The variable, x, is now alone: $x = 14$

Choice B is the result of incorrectly subtracting 24 from each side of the equation in the first step.

54. B

To find the slope of a line, write the slope as the change in y over the change in x. In formula form, this looks like slope $= \dfrac{\text{rise}}{\text{run}} = \dfrac{y_1 - y_2}{x_1 - x_2}$. To find the slope of the line, locate two points on the line and substitute the values into the formula. Two points on the line are $(0, 1)$ and $(-5, 4)$. Use the first point for (x_1, y_1) and the second point for (x_2, y_2). Substitute these values into the formula:

$$\frac{y_1 - y_2}{x_1 - x_2} = \frac{1 - 4}{0 - (-5)} = \frac{-3}{0 + 5} = \frac{-3}{5}$$

The slope of the line is $-\dfrac{3}{5}$. Choice A is the reciprocal of the correct slope; you might get that value by finding the ratio of the run to the rise instead of the rise to the run. Choice C is the opposite of the correct slope; you might get that value by subtracting in the wrong order in one part of the ratio.

55. A

When the points are plotted on a grid, a triangle formed is shown in the figure below.

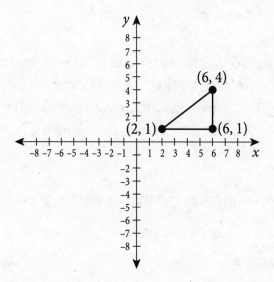

By counting the units on the grid, one finds that the legs of the right triangle are 3 units and 4 units. Use the Pythagorean theorem to find the length of the hypotenuse. The Pythagorean theorem is $a^2 + b^2 = c^2$, where a and b are the leg lengths of the right triangle and c is the length of the hypotenuse.

Substitute ($a = 3$ and $b = 4$) and solve for c:	$3^2 + 4^2 = c^2$
Apply the exponents:	$9 + 16 = c^2$
Add:	$25 = c^2$
Take the square root of each side of the equation:	$\sqrt{25} = \sqrt{c^2}$
The variable, c, is alone on one side:	$5 = c$

Choice C is the result of simply adding the sides of 3 and 4 to find the length of the hypotenuse. Choice D is the result of not taking the square root of 25 in the last step.

56. C

To simplify the expression, use the distributive property. The value of –5 must be multiplied by each of the terms within the parentheses, x and –7. The expression becomes $10w - 5x + 35 + 3y$, which is choice C. Choices A and B each incorrectly use the distributive property, because 35 is negative in these answer choices.

57. A

The probability of an event (*e*) occurring is

$P(e) = \dfrac{\text{number of ways the event can occur}}{\text{total number of possible outcomes}}$.

The only possible sum less than 3 is a sum of 2. This would be the result of getting 1 on each of the two dice, which is one outcome. Because there are six sides to each die, there are a total of 6 × 6 = 36 total outcomes. Thus, the probability of getting a sum less than 3 is $P(\text{sum less than 3}) = \dfrac{1}{36}$. You may have selected choice B if you thought there were 12 total possibilities when rolling two dice, when there are actually 36.

58. A

To solve the inequality, get the variable *x* alone.

First, subtract 10 from each side of the inequality: $\qquad 10 - 10 + 5x \geq 65 - 10$

The inequality becomes: $\qquad\qquad\qquad\qquad\qquad\qquad 5x \geq 55$

Divide each side of the inequality by 5: $\qquad\qquad\qquad \dfrac{5x}{5} \geq \dfrac{55}{5}$

The variable, *x*, is alone: $\qquad\qquad\qquad\qquad\qquad\qquad x \geq 11$

You may have selected choice B if you thought the sign needed to be reversed when solving this inequality. You should take that step only when you divide by a negative number.

59. D

The slope-intercept form of a linear equation is $y = mx + b$, where *m* represents the slope of the line and *b* represents the *y*-intercept. To find the value of the *y*-intercept (*b*), find the place where the line intersects the *y*-axis (the vertical axis). The line intersects the *y*-axis at (0, 3), so the *y*-intercept is 3. The slope of a line is represented by the fraction $m = \dfrac{\text{change in } y}{\text{change in } x} = \dfrac{\text{rise}}{\text{run}}$. Therefore, to find the slope (*m*), start at the *y*-intercept and count up and over until you get to the next point on the line. Lines that slant up to the right have positive slopes, and lines that slant up to the left have negative slopes. In this case, you need to count up three units and over two units to the right to get to the next point

(2, 6). Because you counted up three units and over two units to the right, the slope is $\frac{3}{2}$. The equation, in slope-intercept form, is $y = \frac{3}{2}x + 3$. Choice A has the correct *y*-intercept, but the slope is the opposite of the correct slope. Choice B has the correct *y*-intercept, but the slope is the negative reciprocal of the correct slope. Choice C has the correct *y*-intercept, but the slope is the reciprocal of the correct slope.

60. B

Evaluate the expression using the correct order of operations. The order of operations can be remembered as PEMDAS: Parentheses, Exponents, Multiply, Divide, Add, and Subtract.

Evaluate within parentheses first:	$12 + 2^3(2)$
Apply the exponent:	$12 + 8(2)$
Multiply:	$12 + 16$
Add:	28

Choice C is the result of adding 12 to 8 and multiplying the sum by 7 before subtracting 5. Choice D is the result of incorrectly adding 12 + 2 in the first step, then cubing the sum.

61. D

The Counting Principle tells you to multiply the number of choices for each category to find the total number of outcomes. There are two choices of metal, two choices for the size of the chain, and three choices of stone. This means a total of $2 \times 2 \times 3 = 12$ choices. Choice B is the result of adding the possibilities for each category together instead of multiplying them.

62. B

Subtract $2.50 from $15.00 to get $12.50, the amount she has to spend after the first mile. Then divide $12.50 by $1.50 per mile to get about 8.3 miles. Add the 1 mile paid for by the $2.50 to get a total of 9.3 miles. Because she does not have enough money for 10 miles, the correct answer is B. You might have picked choice C if you left out the additional cost of the first mile.

63. D

Because the expression $9x + 7$ is being divided by 4, the best first step would be to multiply each side by 4: $\frac{9x + 7}{4}(4) \leq 8.5(4)$.

In choice B, 7 should not be subtracted in the first step because that value actually represents $\frac{7}{4}$. Choice C is the inverse, or opposite, of the first step.

64. D

The y-intercept of a linear equation is the place on a graph where the line crosses the y-axis. At this point, the x-coordinate is zero. To find the y-intercept, substitute $x = 0$ into the equation and solve for y.

The equation is:	$-5 + y = 3x$
Substitute 0 for x:	$-5 + y = 3(0)$
Multiply:	$-5 + y = 0$
Add 5 to each side of the equation:	$-5 + 5 + y = 0 + 5$
The variable, y, is now alone:	$y = 5$

The y–intercept is 5. The value in choice C is the slope of the line.

65. A

To find the total amount of fencing, find the perimeter of the yard. The formula for perimeter is $P = $ side + side + side.

Substitute the values into the formula:	$P = 10.5 + 10.5 + 15$
Add to find the perimeter:	$P = 36$

The total amount of fencing needed is 36 meters. You may have selected choice C if you confused area with perimeter and multiplied 10.5 by 15 and divided this value by 2. That is not the correct area, anyway, because 10.5 m is not the height of the triangle.

66. C

Solve for x using the steps for equation solving to get the variable alone.

First, subtract 30 from each side of the equation: $30 - 30 - 3x = 15 - 30$

The equation becomes: $-3x = -15$

Divide each side of the equation by -3: $\dfrac{-3x}{-3} = \dfrac{-15}{-3}$

The variable, x, is alone. $x = 5$

The correct value of x is 5. Choice A is the result of incorrectly adding 30 to each side of the equation in the first step. Choice D is the result of incorrectly adding 30 to each side and disregarding the negative signs when dividing in the second step.

67. A

The probability of an event (e) occurring is

$$P(e) = \dfrac{\text{number of ways the event can occur}}{\text{total number of possible outcomes}}$$

There are a total of ten numbers. Four of these numbers (2, 3, 5, and 7) are prime numbers. Thus, the probability is $P(\text{prime number}) = \dfrac{4}{10}$. Divide the numerator and denominator by the greatest common factor of 2 to get $\dfrac{2}{5}$. Choice C is the probability of *not* selecting a prime number. You may have selected choice B if you thought there were nine digits from 0 to 9 instead of ten.

68. C

Lines with positive slopes slant up to the right. This is true of the graph in choice C. Choice A represents a line with a negative slope. Choice B represents a line with an undefined slope. Choice D represents a line with zero slope.

69. C

First, multiply 1.5 inches per hour by 6 hours to find the total number of inches that fell during the storm: $1.5 \times 6 = 9$ inches. To convert inches to centimeters, use the proportion $\dfrac{\text{inches}}{\text{centimeters}} = \dfrac{\text{inches}}{\text{centimeters}}$. Because 1 inch ≈ 2.54 centimeters, the proportion can be written as $\dfrac{1 \text{ inch}}{2.54 \text{ centimeters}} = \dfrac{9 \text{ inches}}{x \text{ centimeters}}$. Cross multiply the proportion: $x = 22.86$ centimeters. Choice A is the result of dividing 9 inches by 2.54.

70. B

The surface area of a rectangular solid can be found by using the formula $SA = 2lw + 2wh + 2lh$, where l is the length, w is the width, and h is the height of the solid. According to the figure, $l = 6$ cm, $w = 2.5$ cm, and $h = 4$ cm.

Write the formula:	$SA = 2lw + 2wh + 2lh$
Substitute in the given values:	$SA = 2 \times 6 \times 2.5 + 2 \times 2.5 \times 4 + 2 \times 6 \times 4$
Using order of operations, multiply left to right:	$SA = 30 + 20 + 48$
Now add to find the surface area:	$SA = 98 \text{ cm}^2$

Choice A is the volume of the prism as opposed to the surface area.

71. B

Define each variable and write a system of equations to solve for x and y. Let x = the amount of 60% solution and let y = the amount of 30% solution. Because there are 50 ounces in total, the first equation is $x + y = 50$. Solve this equation for y by subtracting x from each side. The equation becomes $y = 50 - x$. Factoring in each percent, the second equation can be written as $0.60x + 0.30y = 0.42(50)$. Substitute the first equation into the second equation for y and solve for x.

The second equation becomes:	$0.60x + 0.30(50 - x) = 21$
Use the distributive property:	$0.60x + 15 - 0.30x = 21$
Combine like terms:	$0.30x + 15 = 21$
Subtract 15 from each side of the equation:	$0.30x + 15 - 15 = 21 - 15$
The equation becomes:	$0.30x = 6$
Divide each side of the equation by 0.30:	$\dfrac{0.30x}{0.30} = \dfrac{6}{0.30}$
The variable, x, is now alone:	$x = 20$

There are 20 ounces of 60% solution. Because there are a total of 50 ounces, there are 50 – 20 = 30 ounces of 30% solution.

Choice C has equal amounts for each solution, which cannot be true because the final solution is not 45%. Forty-five percent is directly between 30% and 60%; this would mean that equal amounts of each were used. Choice D has the correct amounts for each solution reversed.

72. D

To find the solution to the system of equations, substitute the first equation ($y = 1$) into the second equation and solve for x.

The second equation is:	$2y + 4 = -x$
Substitute $y = 1$:	$2(1) + 4 = -x$
Multiply:	$2 + 4 = -x$
Add:	$6 = -x$
Divide each side by -1:	$-6 = x$

Because the value of x is –6 and the value of y is 1, the solution to the system of equations is the point (–6, 1). Choice B has the correct x and y values reversed in the ordered pair.

73. B

Use the Pythagorean Theorem, $a^2 + b^2 = c^2$, to find the missing leg. In the theorem, the variable c is the hypotenuse, and a and b are the legs.

Write the formula:	$a^2 + b^2 = c^2$
Substitute in the given values:	$8^2 + x^2 = 17^2$
Evaluate the exponents:	$64 + b^2 = 289$
Subtract 64 from both sides:	$64 - 64 + b2 = 289 - 64$
Simplify:	$b^2 = 225$
Take the square root of both sides:	$\sqrt{b^2} = \sqrt{225}$
Simplify:	$b = 15$

Choice A is the result of simply subtracting the two known sides of 17 and 8 to find the third side. Choice C is the result of using 8 and 17 as the legs of the right triangle. Choice D is the result of dividing by 2 instead of finding the square root of 225 in the final step.

74. D

A translation is a transformation that "slides" a point or figure in a plane. The image of the triangle that is moved three units to the right and four units down is choice D. Choice A is moved 3 units to the right only. Choice B is moved three units to the left and four units down. Choice C is moved four units down only.

75. C

The image in the figure is reflected, or "flipped," over the y-axis. Therefore, the answer is choice C. In choice A, a dilation of scale factor 2 would make the sides of the triangle twice as large and move it twice as far from the origin. In choice B, a rotation of 180 degrees would turn the triangle halfway around the origin. In choice D, a translation of (–2, 1) would move the triangle two units to the left and one unit up.

76. B

The product of an even number and an odd number is always an even number. Thus, $6x$ will be even. Whether the product is positive or negative, as in choices C and D, cannot be determined.

77. C

If both the length and the width are doubled, this increases each of these dimensions by a factor of 2. Therefore, the entire area is increased by a factor of $2 \times 2 = 4$. The area of the rectangle is multiplied by 4. If just one of the dimensions was doubled, then the area would be multiplied by 2, as in choice A.

78. C

Round each of the values to the nearest hundred to make the numbers easier to add. The sum becomes $300 + 500 + 1,200 + 800 = 800 + 2,000 = 2,800$. Choice B is the result of adding the values in the thousands and hundreds places only to find the estimate.

79. A

Because Cathy needs to purchase five 5-by-7-inch prints, multiply $0.79 by that number: 0.79 × 5 = 3.95. Because $10.00 – 3.95 = $6.05, she has that amount to spend on the smaller prints. Divide $6.05 by 0.29 to find the number of smaller prints: 6.05 ÷ 0.29 = 20.86. Round this amount down to 20 prints. She does not have enough money for 21, so you cannot round up as in choice B.

80. A

To solve this two-step equation,

first add a to each side: $3x - a + a = b + a$

The equation becomes: $3x = b + a$

Then, divide each side of the equation by 3: $\dfrac{3x}{3} = \dfrac{b + a}{3}$

The variable, x, is now alone: $x = \dfrac{b + a}{3}$

81. C

To find the total sales during this one-week period, you would multiply the number of chairs sold during that week by the amount of profit per chair, $11. Each of the other answer choices would not be necessary to find the amount of profit. Note that choice B is the number of chairs produced, not the number of chairs sold.

82. D

To move to the equation in step 2, the parentheses in step 1 were eliminated using the distributive property. The expression $3(x + 6)$ changed to the equivalent expression $3x + 18$. In choice B, the associative property changes the grouping of the values, but the result remains the same.

83. A

The reciprocal of an expression exchanges the numerator and denominator of a fraction. In this case, the numerator is $5b^2$, so this expression becomes the denominator of the reciprocal. The denominator of the original fraction is $2a$, so $2a$ becomes the numerator of the reciprocal. The reciprocal is $-\dfrac{2a}{5b^2}$. Note that the original fraction was negative, so the reciprocal is also negative.

Choice B is the opposite of the original fraction. Choice C is the negative reciprocal of the original fraction.

84. C

This irregular figure consists of a triangle and a rectangle. Find the area of each and add them together to find the total area. Let b = base of the triangle, let h = height of the triangle, let l = length of the rectangle, and let w = width of the rectangle.

Use the formula $\qquad$ $A_{total} = A_{triangle} + A_{rectangle}$

$$A_{total} = \frac{1}{2}bh + lw$$

Because the length of the rectangle is 15 cm and the base of the triangle takes up all but 3 cm of the length, the base has a length of 12 cm (15 cm – 3 cm).

Substitute each value: $\qquad A_{total} = \frac{1}{2}(12 \times 6) + (15 \times 12)$

Multiply: $\qquad A_{total} = \frac{1}{2}(72) + 180$

$$A_{total} = 36 + 180$$

Add: $\qquad A_{total} = 216 \text{ cm}^2$

Choice A is the area of the triangle before taking half. Choice B is the area of the rectangle only. Choice D is the area of the triangle and rectangle together, without taking half the area in the triangle.

85. B

The given equation can also be written as $\dfrac{m}{1} = \dfrac{y - y_1}{x - x_1}$. Cross multiply the proportion to get an equivalent equation. The equation becomes $m(x - x_1) = y - y_1$. This is the equation in choice B. In choice A, the x and y values are switched. Choice C shows the reciprocal of one side of the original equation. Choice D does the same and changes the order of the values of x and y that are being subtracted.

86. C

First, round the cost of her meal to $11.00 to make the estimate easier. Next, find 15% of $11, which is the amount of the tip: 15% of $11 = 0.15 × 11 = $1.65. To calculate the tax, find 8% of $11: 0.08 × 11 = $0.88. The total amount of money spent is $11.00 + 1.65 + 0.88 = $13.53. The closest estimate is $13.50. Choice B leaves out the sales tax.

87. B

To find a point that lies on the line, substitute each pair of values of values in the answer choices into the equation and see which pair makes the equation true. Recall that each ordered pair is in the form (x, y).

First, substitute the point (–3, 12).

The equation becomes: $-3(12) + 12 = 2(-3)$

Evaluate using the correct order of operations.

Multiply to get: $-36 + 12 = -6$

Then add. The equation is not true: $-24 \neq -6$

The equation is not true.
Next, try the point (3, 2) in choice B.

The equation becomes: $-3(2) + 12 = 2(3)$

Multiply to get: $-6 + 12 = 6$

Add to get the equation: $6 = 6$

Because this is a true equation, the point (3, 2) is on the line $-3y + 12 = 2x$. Each of the other answer choices would not make a true equation.

For the point (3, -6) in choice C,
the equation becomes: $-3(-6) + 12 = 2(3)$

Multiply to get: $18 + 12 = 6$

The equation is not true: $30 \neq 6$

For the point (4, 0) in choice D,
the equation becomes: $-3(0) + 12 = 2(4)$

Multiply to get: $0 + 12 = 8$

The equation is not true: $12 \neq 8$

88. C

Because the two triangles are congruent, they are the same shape and size. Their corresponding parts are the sides and angles that will match up if one figure is placed on top of the other. Rotate the second triangle 180 degrees to see that side $\overline{EF}$ corresponds with side $\overline{BC}$. Sides $\overline{DF}$ and $\overline{AC}$ correspond with each other. Side $\overline{DE}$ corresponds with side $\overline{AB}$.

89. A

Like terms have the same variables and exponents. Combine the like terms in the expression by adding the coefficients and keeping the like variables and exponents. Combine the like terms of $-3x^2$ and $19x^2$: $-3x^2 + 19x^2 = 16x^2$. Combine the like terms $4x$ and $-10x$: $4x - 10x = -6x$. The final expression is $16x^2 - 6x$. Choice B is the result of adding $10x$ instead of subtracting $10x$. Choice C is the result of combining like terms but being careless about the signs on the terms. Choice D is the result of combining all of the terms in the expression.

90. A

Following the pattern in the graph, the average temperature decreases by 4 degrees each month. Thus, the average temperature for November can be predicted to be $60 - 4 = 56$ degrees and the average for December to be $56 - 4 = 52$ degrees. Choice C is the expected average temperature for November. Choice D is the expected average temperature for October.

91. D

The expression $x^2 - 49$ is an example of the difference between two perfect squares. To find the factors, find the square root of x^2 and the square root of 49. Next, write the factors as the product of the sum of the square roots and the difference of the square roots. Therefore, the factors are $(x + 7)(x - 7)$.

Choice A shows the factors of $x^2 - 7x$, choice B shows the factors of $x^2 - 49x$, and choice C shows the factors of $x^2 - 14x + 49$.

92. B

Solve for x by getting the variable by itself.

Multiply each side of the equation
by the least common denominator of $2x$: $2x\left(\dfrac{1}{x} + \dfrac{x+4}{2x}\right) = 2x(2)$

The equation becomes: $2 + x + 4 = 4x$

Combine like terms: $x + 6 = 4x$

Subtract x from each side of the equation: $x - x + 6 = 4x - x$

The equation becomes: $6 = 3x$

Divide each side of the equation by 3: $\dfrac{6}{3} = \dfrac{3x}{3}$

The variable, x, is now alone: $2 = x$

Answer choice A is the result of adding the expressions on the left side of the equation without getting a common denominator to get $\dfrac{x+5}{3x} = 2$ and then solving for x.

Full-Length Practice Test 2
Answer Sheet

Remove or photocopy this answer sheet and use it to complete the practice test.

1. Ⓐ Ⓑ Ⓒ Ⓓ   5. Ⓐ Ⓑ Ⓒ Ⓓ   9. Ⓐ Ⓑ Ⓒ Ⓓ   13. Ⓐ Ⓑ Ⓒ Ⓓ   17. Ⓐ Ⓑ Ⓒ Ⓓ
2. Ⓐ Ⓑ Ⓒ Ⓓ   6. Ⓐ Ⓑ Ⓒ Ⓓ   10. Ⓐ Ⓑ Ⓒ Ⓓ   14. Ⓐ Ⓑ Ⓒ Ⓓ   18. Ⓐ Ⓑ Ⓒ Ⓓ
3. Ⓐ Ⓑ Ⓒ Ⓓ   7. Ⓐ Ⓑ Ⓒ Ⓓ   11. Ⓐ Ⓑ Ⓒ Ⓓ   15. Ⓐ Ⓑ Ⓒ Ⓓ   19. Ⓐ Ⓑ Ⓒ Ⓓ
4. Ⓐ Ⓑ Ⓒ Ⓓ   8. Ⓐ Ⓑ Ⓒ Ⓓ   12. Ⓐ Ⓑ Ⓒ Ⓓ   16. Ⓐ Ⓑ Ⓒ Ⓓ   20. Ⓐ Ⓑ Ⓒ Ⓓ

21. Ⓐ Ⓑ Ⓒ Ⓓ   25. Ⓐ Ⓑ Ⓒ Ⓓ   29. Ⓐ Ⓑ Ⓒ Ⓓ   33. Ⓐ Ⓑ Ⓒ Ⓓ   37. Ⓐ Ⓑ Ⓒ Ⓓ
22. Ⓐ Ⓑ Ⓒ Ⓓ   26. Ⓐ Ⓑ Ⓒ Ⓓ   30. Ⓐ Ⓑ Ⓒ Ⓓ   34. Ⓐ Ⓑ Ⓒ Ⓓ   38. Ⓐ Ⓑ Ⓒ Ⓓ
23. Ⓐ Ⓑ Ⓒ Ⓓ   27. Ⓐ Ⓑ Ⓒ Ⓓ   31. Ⓐ Ⓑ Ⓒ Ⓓ   35. Ⓐ Ⓑ Ⓒ Ⓓ   39. Ⓐ Ⓑ Ⓒ Ⓓ
24. Ⓐ Ⓑ Ⓒ Ⓓ   28. Ⓐ Ⓑ Ⓒ Ⓓ   32. Ⓐ Ⓑ Ⓒ Ⓓ   36. Ⓐ Ⓑ Ⓒ Ⓓ   40. Ⓐ Ⓑ Ⓒ Ⓓ

41. Ⓐ Ⓑ Ⓒ Ⓓ   45. Ⓐ Ⓑ Ⓒ Ⓓ   49. Ⓐ Ⓑ Ⓒ Ⓓ   53. Ⓐ Ⓑ Ⓒ Ⓓ   57. Ⓐ Ⓑ Ⓒ Ⓓ
42. Ⓐ Ⓑ Ⓒ Ⓓ   46. Ⓐ Ⓑ Ⓒ Ⓓ   50. Ⓐ Ⓑ Ⓒ Ⓓ   54. Ⓐ Ⓑ Ⓒ Ⓓ   58. Ⓐ Ⓑ Ⓒ Ⓓ
43. Ⓐ Ⓑ Ⓒ Ⓓ   47. Ⓐ Ⓑ Ⓒ Ⓓ   51. Ⓐ Ⓑ Ⓒ Ⓓ   55. Ⓐ Ⓑ Ⓒ Ⓓ   59. Ⓐ Ⓑ Ⓒ Ⓓ
44. Ⓐ Ⓑ Ⓒ Ⓓ   48. Ⓐ Ⓑ Ⓒ Ⓓ   52. Ⓐ Ⓑ Ⓒ Ⓓ   56. Ⓐ Ⓑ Ⓒ Ⓓ   60. Ⓐ Ⓑ Ⓒ Ⓓ

61. Ⓐ Ⓑ Ⓒ Ⓓ   65. Ⓐ Ⓑ Ⓒ Ⓓ   69. Ⓐ Ⓑ Ⓒ Ⓓ   73. Ⓐ Ⓑ Ⓒ Ⓓ   77. Ⓐ Ⓑ Ⓒ Ⓓ
62. Ⓐ Ⓑ Ⓒ Ⓓ   66. Ⓐ Ⓑ Ⓒ Ⓓ   70. Ⓐ Ⓑ Ⓒ Ⓓ   74. Ⓐ Ⓑ Ⓒ Ⓓ   78. Ⓐ Ⓑ Ⓒ Ⓓ
63. Ⓐ Ⓑ Ⓒ Ⓓ   67. Ⓐ Ⓑ Ⓒ Ⓓ   71. Ⓐ Ⓑ Ⓒ Ⓓ   75. Ⓐ Ⓑ Ⓒ Ⓓ   79. Ⓐ Ⓑ Ⓒ Ⓓ
64. Ⓐ Ⓑ Ⓒ Ⓓ   68. Ⓐ Ⓑ Ⓒ Ⓓ   72. Ⓐ Ⓑ Ⓒ Ⓓ   76. Ⓐ Ⓑ Ⓒ Ⓓ   80. Ⓐ Ⓑ Ⓒ Ⓓ

81. Ⓐ Ⓑ Ⓒ Ⓓ   85. Ⓐ Ⓑ Ⓒ Ⓓ   89. Ⓐ Ⓑ Ⓒ Ⓓ
82. Ⓐ Ⓑ Ⓒ Ⓓ   86. Ⓐ Ⓑ Ⓒ Ⓓ   90. Ⓐ Ⓑ Ⓒ Ⓓ
83. Ⓐ Ⓑ Ⓒ Ⓓ   87. Ⓐ Ⓑ Ⓒ Ⓓ   91. Ⓐ Ⓑ Ⓒ Ⓓ
84. Ⓐ Ⓑ Ⓒ Ⓓ   88. Ⓐ Ⓑ Ⓒ Ⓓ   92. Ⓐ Ⓑ Ⓒ Ⓓ

Full-Length Practice Test 2

This full-length practice test for the CAHSEE has 92 multiple-choice questions. You will not be allowed to use a calculator on the real exam, so make sure you practice without a calculator.

There is no time limit on the CAHSEE, but make sure you pace yourself on the questions. When you have completed your full-length practice exam, turn to page 383 for the answers and explanations.

1. **Which of the following shows a reflection over the line $x = 6$?**

A

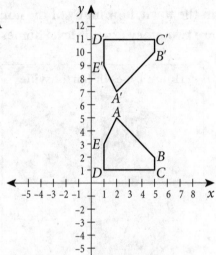

C

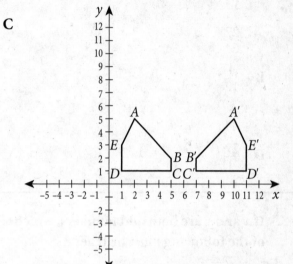

B

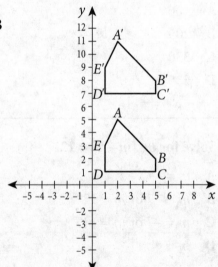

D

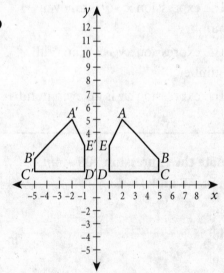

2. Simplify the expression shown below.

$$\left(\frac{3}{4}\right)^3$$

A $\frac{27}{64}$

B $\frac{9}{12}$

C $\frac{3}{64}$

D $\frac{27}{4}$

3. If x and y are both odd numbers, which of the following must be true?

A The expression $x + y$ is an odd number

B The expression $x + y$ is an even number

C The expression $xy + 3$ is an odd number

D The expression xy is an even number

4. Evaluate the expression $100 - 4m \div n^2$, when $m = 8$ and $n = 4$.

A 36

B 48

C 96

D 98

5. The circle graph below shows the percentages of home types in the town of Bartonsville. If there are 500 homes in the town, how many of the homes are two-story or split-level homes?

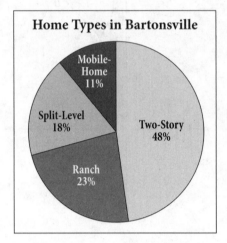

Home Types in Bartonsville

A 66

B 205

C 330

D 355

6. Solve for m: $|m - 5| = 12$.

A $m = -17$

B $m = -7$ or $m = 17$

C $m = -7$ or $m = -17$

D $m = 7$

7. What is the area of the triangle shown below in square millimeters (mm²)?

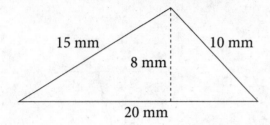

15 mm   10 mm
8 mm
20 mm

- A   45 mm²
- B   80 mm²
- C   160 mm²
- D   200 mm²

8. How many $\frac{3}{4}$ foot length boards can be cut from a 12-foot piece of lumber?

- A   8
- B   9
- C   12
- D   16

9. Which of the following is the best estimate of the area of a circle with a diameter of 19.57 centimeters in square centimeters (cm²)?

- A   30 cm²
- B   60 cm²
- C   300 cm²
- D   1,200 cm²

10. Rachelle is a plumber. She charges $35.00 for a home visit plus $40.00 per hour for labor. Which graph below represents the relationship between the number of hours worked and the charge for labor and home visit?

A

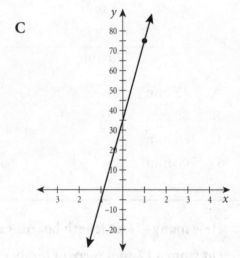

C

B

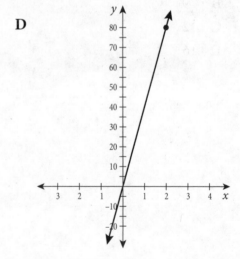

D

11. The bar graph below shows the result of the local school election for class president. Which of the following conclusions is true?

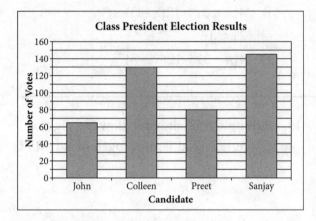

Class President Election Results

A Sanjay had three times as many votes as John.

B Colleen had 50% more votes than Preet.

C Sanjay won with close to 35% of the votes.

D Sanjay won with close to 50% of the votes.

12. Solve: $10n - 5(n - 2) = 35$.

A $n = 3$

B $n = 5$

C $n = 8$

D $n = 9$

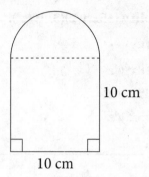

10 cm

10 cm

13. The irregular figure shown above is made up of a square and a semicircle. What is the area of the figure shown above in square centimeters (cm²)?

A $(100 + 12.5\pi)$ cm²

B $(100 + 10\pi)$ cm²

C $(100 + 25\pi)$ cm²

D $(30 + 5\pi)$ cm²

14. Seventeen out of every 20 commuters ride the subway. What percent of the commuters ride the subway?

A 17%

B 37%

C 68%

D 85%

15. Wei walks 5 miles in 75 minutes. Which computation will give Wei's average speed in miles per hour?

A Divide 5 by 0.75

B Divide 5 by 1.25

C Multiply 5 by 1.75

D Multiply 5 by 1.25

16. Simplify $(15x^3y^2z)(3x^2y^2z^2)$.

   A $18x^5y^4z^3$

   B $18x^6y^4z^2$

   C $45x^5y^4z^3$

   D $45x^6y^4z^2$

17. The following line graph shows the number of minutes that Catherine spent exercising over the course of a week. Which day had the greatest decrease in time spent from the previous day?

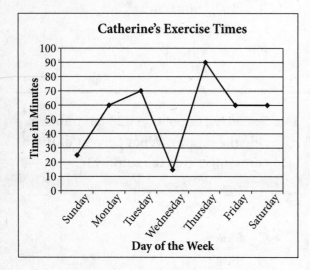

   A   Wednesday

   B   Thursday

   C   Friday

   D   Saturday

18. Which of the following is equivalent to the equation $\frac{x+3}{12} = \frac{x-3}{4}$?

   A $(x+3)(x-3) = 48$

   B $4(x+3) = 12(x-3)$

   C $2x = 16$

   D $4(x-3) = 12(x+3)$

19. Triangle RST shown below is a right triangle. What is the length of side RS?

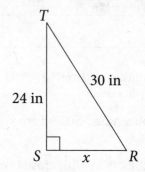

   A   3.46 inches

   B   6 inches

   C   18 inches

   D   38.42 inches

20. Attendance at the school musical rose from 1,500 to 1,850 people from Friday to Saturday. What was the percent increase to the nearest percent?

   A   19%

   B   23%

   C   35%

   D   81%

21. A cookie dough recipe calls for 3 cups of flour, 2 eggs, 1 cup of sugar, and 1 cup of butter. Marissa is using the recipe to prepare cookies for a party and wants to have 3 cookies for each of the 50 guests.

    What other information is necessary to estimate the total amount of flour needed?

    A   The cost of each ingredient
    B   The oven temperature required
    C   The number of cookies the recipe will make
    D   The conversion factor from cups to pints

22. Which equation below represents the sentence "One half of the sum of the numbers x and y is 12"?

    A $\frac{1}{2}x + y + 12$

    B $\frac{1}{2}x + y = 12$

    C $\frac{1}{2}(x + y) + 12$

    D $\frac{1}{2}(x + y) = 12$

23. Shoppers at the mall were asked to name their favorite type of food. The results are shown on the circle graph below.

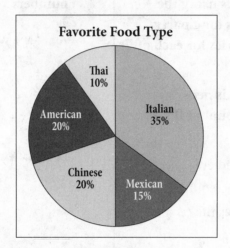

The circle graph represents the data in which table?

A

Favorite Food Type

Type	Number of People
Thai	50
Italian	150
American	100
Chinese	65
Mexican	100
TOTAL	465

C

Favorite Food Type

Type	Number of People
Thai	175
Italian	50
American	100
Chinese	75
Mexican	100
TOTAL	500

B

Favorite Food Type

Type	Number of People
Thai	50
Italian	175
American	100
Chinese	100
Mexican	75
TOTAL	500

D

Favorite Food Type

Type	Number of People
Thai	10
Italian	35
American	15
Chinese	20
Mexican	20
TOTAL	100

24. What is the equation for the line graphed on the coordinate grid below?

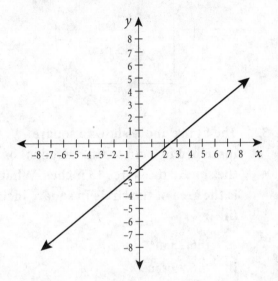

    A $y = \frac{4}{3}x - 2$

    B $y = x - 2$

    C $y = -2x + \frac{3}{4}$

    D $y = \frac{3}{4}x - 2$

25. Which of the following sets of numbers could be lengths of the three sides of a right triangle?

    A   2, 3, 4

    B   9, 15, 17

    C   10, 24, 26

    D   12, 18, 24

26. A restaurant bill totals $36.40. Saba wishes to leave a tip of 18%. What will be the total dinner cost, including the tip?

    A $6.55

    B $29.85

    C $42.95

    D $54.40

27. What is the next number in the sequence below?

    0, 1, 3, 7, 15, . . .

    A   19

    B   20

    C   23

    D   31

28. Simplify $\sqrt{49x^6y^2}$.

    A $7x^3y$

    B $7x^2y$

    C $49x^3y$

    D $49x^2y$

29. The base of a ladder sits 8 feet from the base of a building. The top of the ladder rests 15 feet up the side of the building. What is the length of the ladder?

    A   12.7 feet

    B   17 feet

    C   23 feet

    D   144.5 feet

30. The Grace family is planning a family reunion. All family members gave their opinions on whether the mountains or the beach would be a good location for the event. The results are shown in the Venn diagram below.

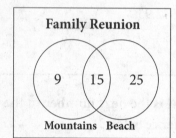

Family Reunion

How many family members would be happy with either the mountains or the beach as locations for the event?

A   6

B   10

C   15

D   49

31. What is the x-intercept of the graph of the equation $3y = 9x - 18$?

A $(3, 9)$

B $(0, -6)$

C $(2, 0)$

D $(9, 3)$

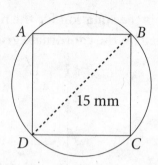

32. The figure above shows a square inscribed in a circle. The diagonal of the square measures 15 inches. What is the area of the circle in square inches (in^2)?

A   56.25 in^2

B   56.25π in^2

C   225 in^2

D   225π in^2

33. Emily deposited $2,200.00 in a savings account with a simple interest rate of 6% per year. How much interest would she earn after 7 years?

A $132.00

B $924.00

C $2,332.00

D $3,124.00

34. **If you roll a pair of standard number cubes, what is the probability of rolling doubles?**

    A $\dfrac{1}{36}$

    B $\dfrac{1}{6}$

    C $\dfrac{1}{3}$

    D $\dfrac{1}{2}$

35. **The graph below shows the costs of sending a package for two freight companies based on the weight of the package in ounces.**

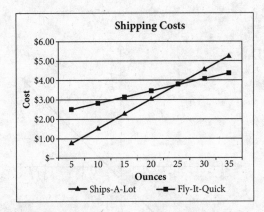

Based on the graph, which of the following statements is true?

A Ships-A-Lot is always more expensive than Fly-It-Quick.

B The cost per ounce is the same for both companies.

C For a package weighing more than 25 ounces, Fly-It-Quick is less expensive.

D For a package weighing more than 25 ounces, Ships-A-Lot is less expensive.

36. **The scatter plot below shows the relationship between money spent on entertainment and money saved.**

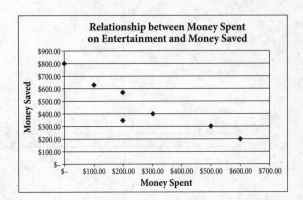

Which of the following statements is supported by the data in the plot?

A There is a negative correlation between the data.

B There is a positive correlation between the data.

C There is no correlation between the data.

D The more money saved, the more money spent.

37. Which of the following graphs has a slope of –1?

A

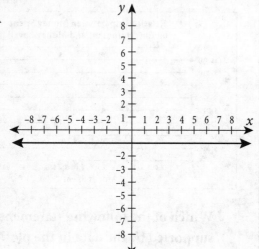

C

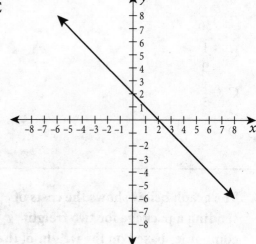

B

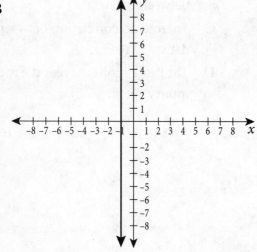

D

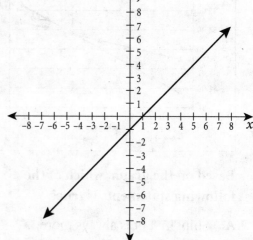

38. Find the area in square millimeters (mm²) of trapezoid *WXYZ*, shown below. Use the formula $A = \frac{1}{2}h(b_1 + b_2)$.

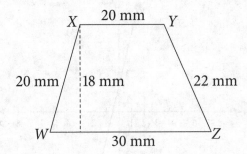

    A   92 mm²

    B   450 mm²

    C   660 mm²

    D   900 mm²

39. Simplify the expression shown below.

    $7^{-3} \div 7^{-5}$

    A 7^{-8}

    B 7^{-2}

    C 7^2

    D 7^8

Determine the perimeter of a parcel of land with dimensions of 300 feet, 324 feet, 462 feet, and 450 feet.

40. Which of the following problems would be solved using the same arithmetic operation as would be used to solve the problem above?

    A   What is the combined cost of a $3.95 sandwich and a $1.35 soda?

    B   What is the area of a room that is 12 feet by 10 feet?

    C   What is the volume of a rectangular solid with dimensions of 2 cm, 3 cm, and 5 cm?

    D   What is the cost of 5 lbs of apples if they cost $1.39 per pound?

41. Which of the following is the graph of the function $y = -2x + 3$?

A
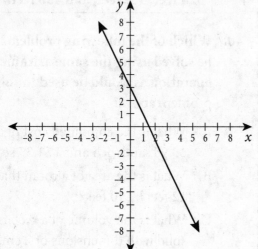

C
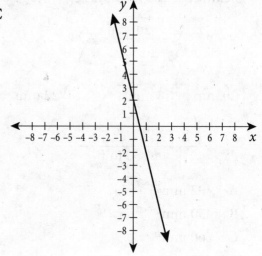

B
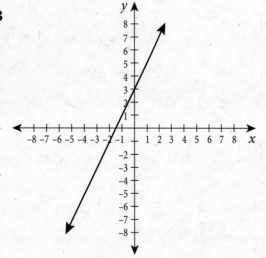

D
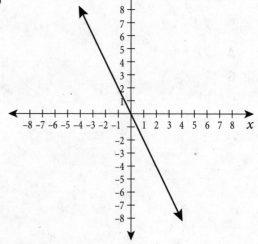

42. What is the probability of rolling a 5 and then rolling an even number on a standard die?

    A $\dfrac{1}{12}$

    B $\dfrac{1}{10}$

    C $\dfrac{1}{8}$

    D $\dfrac{2}{3}$

43. Which of the following points lies on the line $4y = 2x + 6$?

    A $(-3, 0)$
    B $(0, -3)$
    C $(0, 6)$
    D $(6, 0)$

44. Ravi can cycle 15 miles every hour. How far can he cycle in 100 minutes?

    A   6.67 miles
    B   25 miles
    C   250 miles
    D   1,500 miles

45. What is the value of 2^{-3}?

    A -6
    B -5
    C $\dfrac{1}{8}$
    D $\dfrac{1}{6}$

46. Two painters can paint a 40-by-15-feet rectangular room with a height of 12 feet in 3 hours. A gallon of paint covers 100 square feet. Each painter earns $22.00 for every hour worked.

    What other information is necessary to determine the cost of labor and paint?

    A How long the job would take for one painter
    B The perimeter of the room
    C The cost of a gallon of paint
    D The volume of the room

47. What is the slope of the line graphed below?

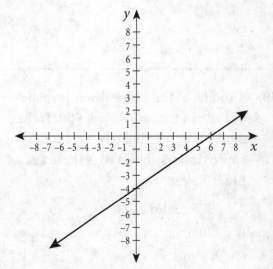

    A -4

    B $\dfrac{2}{3}$

    C $\dfrac{3}{2}$

    D 4

48. A pizza shop offers two sizes of pizza, three kinds of crusts, and five different toppings. How many different one-topping pizzas can be ordered?

    A   5
    B   10
    C   15
    D   30

49. What is the slope of a line parallel to the line $y = \frac{2}{3}x + 5$?

    A -5
    B $-\frac{2}{3}$
    C $\frac{2}{3}$
    D   5

50. A model of the Eiffel Tower is made to scale in the ratio of 1:8,500. If the model is approximately 3.6 cm tall, approximately how tall is the actual Eiffel Tower?

    A   306 centimeters
    B   30.6 meters
    C   306 meters
    D   36 kilometers

51. Simplify $\frac{1}{5} + \frac{7}{20} - \frac{3}{10}$.

    A $\frac{1}{4}$
    B $\frac{8}{20}$
    C $\frac{5}{15}$
    D $\frac{11}{20}$

52. If chicken costs $2.89 per pound, approximately how many pounds of chicken can you buy for $42.00?

    A   14 pounds
    B   21 pounds
    C   84 pounds
    D   126 pounds

53. Solve for x: $2(x - 4) = 12$.

    A   6
    B   8
    C   10
    D   16

54. For every 20 students in the senior class of a high school, 4 are left-handed, and the rest are right-handed. If there are 288 right-handed seniors, how many total students are in the senior class?

    A   230
    B   360
    C   1,440
    D   3,600

55. The data below represents the weight in pounds of babies born at General Hospital last week.

8.2 5.8 9.5 5.8 7.3 7.6 7.0 7.2

What was the median weight of the babies?

A 5.8 lbs.

B 7.25 lbs.

C 7.75 lbs.

D 7.3 lbs.

56. Which of the following is the equation of a line parallel to the line $2y = 6x + 4$?

A $y = 6x - 3$

B $y = 6x + 4$

C $y = 4x$

D $y = 3x + 11$

57. What is the area of the parallelogram below?

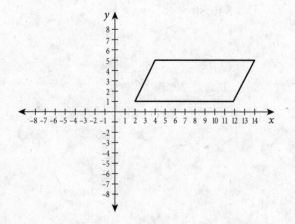

A 14 square units

B 20 square units

C 40 square units

D 80 square units

58. Between which two integers does the value of $\sqrt{160}$ lie?

A 4 and 5

B 12 and 13

C 40 and 41

D 80 and 81

59. Martin can do 30 pushups in 2 minutes. At this rate, how many pushups can he do in 5 minutes?

A 60

B 75

C 90

D 105

60. How many square yards are in 5,184 square inches?

A 4

B 9

C 36

D 144

61. The table below shows the number of points scored by 3 members of the Riverside High School basketball team in each of 5 games. Which of the following is a true statement?

Team Member	Game 1	Game 2	Game 3	Game 4	Game 5
Shante	8	8	14	17	12
Reza	4	8	10	2	6
Paul	0	2	4	8	8

A Reza was the top scorer.

B The mean of the points scored is 11.8.

C The mean is equal to the mode of the data.

D The median is equal to the mode of the data.

62. Which of the following is the solution of the following system of equations?

$$y = 5x + 3$$
$$y = 3x - 1$$

A $(-2, -7)$

B $(-7, -2)$

C $(1, 8)$

D $(1, 2)$

63. What is the volume in cubic centimeters (cm³) of the cylinder shown below?

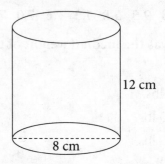

12 cm

8 cm

A 16π cm³

B 64π cm³

C 192π cm³

D 768π cm³

64. A handbag originally priced at $36.00 is on sale at 30% off. What is the sale price of the handbag?

A $10.80

B $25.20

C $30.00

D $46.80

65. Which of the following could be equation of the graph below?

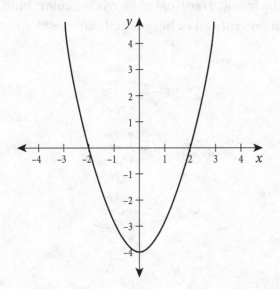

   A $y = x - 4$

   B $y = 2x - 4$

   C $y = x^2 + 4$

   D $y = x^2 - 4$

66. Which of the following sets of numbers is ordered from least to greatest?

   A $9.03 \times 10^{-2}, 7.12 \times 10^{-1}, 4.92 \times 10^2$

   B $1.23 \times 10^{-2}, 4.603 \times 10^{-4}, 9.7 \times 10^{-6}$

   C $5.1 \times 10^{-8}, 5.03 \times 10^{-8}, 5.6 \times 10^{-10}$

   D $2.1 \times 10^2, 2.06 \times 10^2, 2.009 \times 10^2$

67. The inequality $12x + 3 \leq 51$ represents the weight of a carton of a dozen packs of greeting cards in ounces, where x is the weight of a single pack. Which of the following statements is true?

   A   One pack of greeting cards weighs 4 ounces or less.

   B   One pack of greeting cards weighs at least 4 ounces.

   C   One pack of greeting cards weighs 12 ounces or less.

   D   One pack of greeting cards weighs at least 12 ounces.

68. Which expression represents the phrase "Seven less than the product of 5 and a number"?

   A $7 - 5m$

   B $7 - (5 + m)$

   C $5m - 7$

   D $\dfrac{5}{m} - 7$

69. Danielle is shopping for a pattern and fabric to make a dress. At the fabric store, she is choosing between a short-sleeve dress pattern and a long-sleeve dress pattern. She can choose from among satin, cotton, or silk for the fabric. Her final choice is for color: blue, green, yellow, or peach. Which tree diagram represents all of her possible choices?

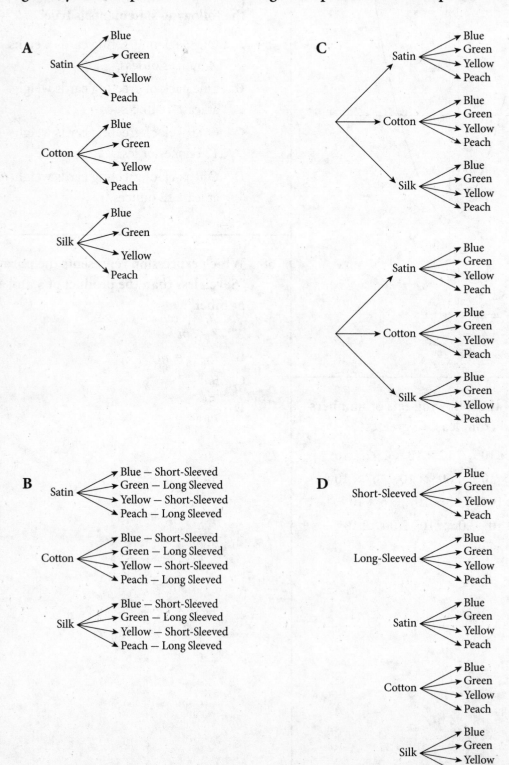

70. Which expression below represents the area of rectangle shown?

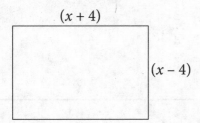

$(x + 4)$

$(x - 4)$

    A $x^2 - 16$

    B $x^2 - 8x - 16$

    C $2x$

    D $4x$

71. Colin is driving on a highway at 65 miles per hour. What is his speed in kilometers per hour? (1 mile ≈ 1.6 kilometers)

    A   40.63 km/hr

    B   65 km/hr

    C   66.6 km/hr

    D   104 km/hr

72. The number 0.003067 written in scientific notation is

    A 30.67×10^{-4}.

    B 3.067×10^{-3}.

    C 3.067×10^{-2}.

    D 3.067×10^{3}.

73. Solve for y: $6y - 3 > 39$.

    A $y < 6$

    B $y > 6$

    C $y < 7$

    D $y > 7$

74. Which of the following represents n^{-4}?

    A $-\dfrac{1}{n} \times -\dfrac{1}{n} \times -\dfrac{1}{n} \times -\dfrac{1}{n}$

    B $\dfrac{1}{n} \times \dfrac{1}{n} \times \dfrac{1}{n} \times \dfrac{1}{n}$

    C $-4n$

    D $-n \times -n \times -n \times -n$

75. Triangle *ABC* is transformed to triangle *A′B′C′* as shown on the coordinate grid below.

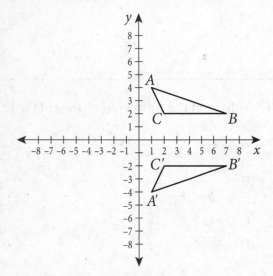

The transformation is

A a reflection over the *y*-axis.

B the translation T$_{(0,4)}$

C a reflection over the *x*-axis.

D the translation T$_{(4,0)}$

76. The dollar figures below represent a salesperson's monthly commissions for the first five months of the year.

$5,200.00 $7,000.00
$6,300.00 $8,450.00
$5,900.00

What is the mean value of the sales commissions?

A $3,250.00

B $6,300.00

C $6,570.00

D $7,000.00

77. Evaluate $|x - 5|$ when $x = 2$.

A –7

B –3

C 2

D 3

78. Janette bought some lemons for $0.45 each and a watermelon for $3.75. If the total price for the lemons and watermelon was $7.80, how many lemons did Janette buy?

A 2

B 9

C 17

D 25

79. What is the diameter of a circle with an area of 49π square inches?

A 7 inches

B 14 inches

C 28 inches

D 49 inches

80. Eighty percent of the 300 students in the senior class attended the spring prom. Ten of those who attended will not attend the senior class trip. Which of the following <u>cannot</u> be determined based on the given information?

   A The number of students in the senior class who attended the spring prom

   B The number of students in the senior class who will not attend the senior class trip

   C The number of students who did not attend the spring prom

   D The number of students attending the prom who will also attend the senior class trip

81. What are the integer solutions to the equation $|x + 1| < 3$?

   A $\{-2, 2\}$

   B $\{0, 2\}$

   C $\{-3, -2, -1, 0, 1\}$

   D $\{-4, -3, -2, -1, 0, 1, 2\}$

82. All of the following expressions are positive numbers except

   A $(-3)^3$

   B $-13 + 20$

   C $2 - (-8)$

   D $|2 - 11|$

83. What is the surface area in square centimeters (cm^2) of the rectangular solid shown below?

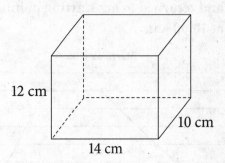

   A   36 cm^2

   B   428 cm^2

   C   856 cm^2

   D 1,680 cm^2

84. Justin can install a carpet in a 40-by-30-foot room in 4 hours. Miguel can do the job in 6 hours. How long will it take them to work on the room together, if each works at a constant rate?

   A 1.5 hours

   B 2.4 hours

   C 4 hours

   D 10 hours

85. The graph below shows Martina's progress on her morning hike. She started her hike at 6:00 AM and returned to her starting point at 10:00 AM.

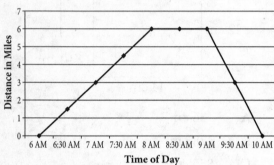

Martina's Hike

Which statement is true of her hike?

A   Martina walked at a constant speed.

B   Martina stopped walking between 8:00 AM and 9:00 AM.

C   Martina started out fast, stopped, and then slowed down.

D   Martina gradually increased her speed between 6:00 AM and 9:00 AM.

86. $4^3 \div 4^5 =$

A $\dfrac{1}{16}$

B   16

C 4^8

D 4^{15}

87. Helena has written a novel and is retyping the 60,750-word manuscript. So far, she has typed 13,500 words in 7.5 hours. At that rate, how many more hours will it take her to finish retyping the manuscript?

A   26.25

B   30.75

C   33.75

D   41.25

88. Two sides of a triangle are 12 cm and 5 cm in length. The third side must be

A   less than 5 cm or greater than 12 cm.

B   between 5 cm and 12 cm.

C   between 7 cm and 17 cm.

D   less than 7 cm or greater than 17 cm.

89. A service that provides digital music for downloading has a $15.00 membership fee. Each song download costs $0.75. Which expression represents the total cost for a potential member of downloading *m* songs, in dollars?

A $75m + 15$

B $15m + 75$

C $0.75 + 15m$

D $0.75m + 15$

90. What is the volume in cubic feet (ft³) of a rectangular swimming pool that is 20 feet wide, 50 feet long, and 6 feet deep?

   A   1,840 ft³

   B   2,000 ft³

   C   2,840 ft³

   D   6,000 ft³

91. There are 10 red, 6 yellow, 7 green, and 7 orange gumballs in a machine. The gumballs are randomly dispensed from the machine one at a time. What is the probability that the next 2 will be a yellow gumball and then a red gumball?

   A $\dfrac{1}{15}$

   B $\dfrac{2}{29}$

   C $\dfrac{79}{145}$

   D $\dfrac{8}{15}$

92. Simplify the expression shown below.

   $$\dfrac{10y^3 - 2y^2 + 6y}{2y}$$

   A $5y^3 - y^2 + 3y$

   B $10y^2 - 2y + 6$

   C $5y^2 - y + 3$

   D $5y^2 - 2y + 3$

Answers and Explanations

1. C

The line $x = 6$ is a vertical line that passes through the x-axis at 6. This will be the line of symmetry for the reflection of the figure. In other words, the figure will be flipped over this line. Choice A shows a figure reflected over the line $y = 6$. Choice B shows a translation in which the x-coordinate remains the same and the y-coordinate shifts up 6 units. Choice D involves a reflection over the y-axis.

2. A

When you have an exponent associated with a fraction, you apply the exponent to both the numerator and the denominator: $\left(\frac{3}{4}\right)^3 = \frac{3^3}{4^3} = \frac{3 \times 3 \times 3}{4 \times 4 \times 4} = \frac{27}{64}$, which is choice A. If you chose choice B, you might have evaluated 3×3 and 4×3, instead of $3 \times 3 \times 3$ and $4 \times 4 \times 4$. If your answer was C, you did not apply the exponent to the numerator. If your answer was D, you did not apply the exponent to the denominator.

3. B

You can demonstrate that the statements are false if you find one example that doesn't work. To test the answer choices, use $x = 3$ and $y = 5$. For choice A, $3 + 5 = 8$, so A is false. Choice B is always true; an odd number added to an odd number is always an even number. This can be shown because odd numbers are of the form $2n + 1$, and $(2n + 1) + (2n + 1) = 4n + 2$, which is even. For choice C, $(3)(5) + 3 = 15 + 3 = 18$, an even number; choice C is false. For choice D, $(3)(5) = 15$, and 15 is odd; choice D is false.

4. D

To evaluate an expression, substitute in the given values and then use the correct order of operations, which can be remembered by the acronym PEMDAS: Parentheses, Exponents, Multiply, Divide, Add, and Subtract.

Write the expression:	$100 - 4m \div n^2$
Substitute in the given values:	$100 - 4 \times 8 \div 4^2$
Evaluate the exponent first:	$100 - 4 \times 8 \div 16$
Next, multiply:	$100 - 32 \div 16$
Now, divide:	$100 - 2$
Finally, perform subtraction:	98

The correct choice is D. If your answer was choice A, you divided, multiplied, evaluated the exponent, and then subtracted. If you chose B, you also did not follow the correct order of operations and just evaluated left to right. If your answer was choice C, you evaluated $4m$ as 48, not as the correct value of 4×8.

5. C

To find the number of homes that are two-story or split-level, add the percents: 48% + 18% = 66%. There are a total of 500 homes, and 66% are either two-story or split-level. Change the 66% to a decimal by dividing by 100 and multiply this by the total number of homes: 0.66 × 500 = 330. Choice A would be the number of homes if there were a total of 100 rather than 500. If you selected choice B, you found the number of homes that are either ranch or split-level. Answer choice D is the number of homes that are two-story or ranch.

6. B

To solve an absolute value equation, you must set up two equations: $m - 5 = 12$ and $m - 5 = -12$. Solve each equation.

Write the equations:	$m - 5 = 12$		$m - 5 = -12$
Add 5 to both sides:	$m - 5 + 5 = 12 + 5$		$m - 5 + 5 = -12 + 5$
Simplify:	$m = 17$	OR	$m = -7$

This is answer choice B. Choice C gives the opposite of each solution, while choices A and D each give one of those opposites.

7. B

The formula for the area of a triangle is found by using the formula $A = \frac{1}{2}bh$, where b is the base of the triangle and h is the height. In this triangle, the base is 20 mm and the height is 8 mm.

Write the formula: $\qquad\qquad\qquad A = \frac{1}{2}bh$

Substitute into the formula: $\qquad\quad A = \frac{1}{2} \times 20 \times 8$

Simplify: $\qquad\qquad\qquad\qquad A = 80 \text{ mm}^2$

This is answer choice B. Choice A is the perimeter of the triangle. If you selected C, you may have forgotten to multiply by $\frac{1}{2}$. If your choice was D, you may have taken half of the square of 20 rather than half of the product of 20 and 8.

8. D

To find the number of $\frac{3}{4}$-foot boards that can be cut from a 12-foot piece, you divide 12 by $\frac{3}{4}$: $\frac{12}{1} \div \frac{3}{4} = \frac{12}{1} \times \frac{4}{3} = \frac{48}{3} = 16$ boards. If you chose B, you multiplied instead of dividing. Answer choice C is the number of 1-foot boards that can be cut.

9. C

To estimate the area, first round the diameter to 20 cm and then use the formula for the area of a circle, $A = \pi r^2$, where A is the area and r is the radius of the circle. The radius is one half of the diameter, or approximately 10 cm. Round the constant π down to 3, The approximate area is $A = 3 \times 10^2 = 3 \times 100 = 300 \text{ cm}^2$. If you chose A, you did not square the radius. Likewise, choice B would result if you used the diameter instead of the radius and did not square that value. If you chose answer D, you may have used the approximate diameter for the value of the radius.

10. C

Rachelle charges a basic fee of $35. That should be the value of y at 0 hours,. Each hour, the y value should increase by $40, so the slope of the graph should be 40. The graph with a y-intercept of 35 and a slope of 40 is found in choice C. The graph in choice A indicates that the total charge is $75, no matter how many hours it takes to do the job. The graph in choice B reflects a fee of $40 plus a charge $35 for each hour worked. The graph in choice D reflects the correct hourly fee but does not account for the basic $35 fee.

11. C

Read the graph to get all of the numbers. John received 65 votes, Colleen received 130, Preet received 80, and Sanjay received 145. Now, determine the truth value of each answer choice. For choice A, three times the number of votes for John is $65 \times 3 = 195$, which is more than Sanjay's votes. The other choices concern percentages. Calculate the percentages for Colleen, Preet, and Sanjay. The total number of votes is $65 + 130 + 80 + 145 = 420$ total votes. Colleen received $\frac{130}{420} \approx 0.31 = 31\%$. Preet received $\frac{80}{420} \approx 0.19 = 19\%$. Sanjay received $\frac{145}{420} \approx 0.345 = 34.5\%$. If you did not look at the actual number values and just estimated by looking at the bars, you may have mistakenly chosen choice A. Choice B is not true; Colleen had 12% more votes than Preet, not 50% more. Choice D is not true. Sanjay did not win with over 50% of the votes; the combined votes for the other candidates exceed the votes for Sanjay.

12. B

Write the equation to solve:	$10n - 5(n - 2) = 35$
First, apply the distributive property:	$10n - 5n + 10 = 35$
Next, combine like terms:	$5n + 10 = 35$
Subtract 10 from both sides:	$5n + 10 - 10 = 35 - 10$
Simplify:	$5n = 25$
Divide both sides by 5:	$\frac{5n}{5} = \frac{25}{5}$
Simplify:	$n = 5$

You might have selected choice C if you got $5n - 5 = 35$ instead of $5n + 10 = 35$ after applying the distributive property. If your answer was choice D, you might have gotten -10 instead of 10 when applying the distributive property.

13. A

This irregular figure consists of a square and one half of a circle. To find the total area, add the areas of each of those figures. The area of a square is $A = s^2$, where s is a side of the square of length 10 cm. The area of a circle is $A = \pi r^2$, where r is the radius of the circle. In this case, the radius is one half of the side of the square, or 5. The area of the entire figure is $10^2 + \frac{1}{2} \times \pi \times 5^2$. Evaluate the exponents to get $100 + \frac{1}{2} \times \pi \times 25$. Now, multiply, and the area is $100 + 12.5\pi$ cm^2, choice A. Choice B is the area of the square portion plus the diameter of the circle. Choice C is the result of not dividing the area of the circle by 2. Choice D is the perimeter of the figure.

14. D

To find the percentage, take the ratio of the part to the whole and multiply this fractional ratio by 100: $\frac{17}{20} = 0.85$, and $0.85 \times 100 = 85\%$, answer choice D. Choice A represents 17 out of 100 commuters, rather than 17 out of 20. The number 37 in choice B is just the sum of 17 and 20. In choice B, you added the coefficients instead of multiplying, and you multiplied the exponents instead of adding. Choice C represents 17 out of 25 commuters.

15. B

Convert 75 minutes to hours by dividing 75 by 60: $75 \div 60 = 1.25$ hours. Now, to find the rate in miles per hour, divide 5 by 1.25. If you chose A, you might have used the number of minutes rather than the number of hours. Choice C uses 0.75, rather than 1.25, as the equivalent of 75 minutes, and it is the result of multiplying instead of dividing.

16. C

To multiply monomials, multiply the coefficients and then each variable term. The coefficients will result in the number $15 \times 3 = 45$. To multiply the variable terms, keep the base and add the exponents: $x^3 \times x^2 = x^{3+2} = x^5$; $y^2 \times y^2 = y^{2+2} = y^4$; and $z \times z^2 = z^{1+2} = z^3$. The resultant product is $45x^5y^4z^3$, choice A. In choice A, the variables and exponents are correct, but the coefficients were added rather than multiplied. The expression in choice B uses the sums of coefficients and the products of the exponents. In choice D, the coefficient is correct, but the exponents were multiplied rather than added.

17. A

To find the greatest decrease, find the steepest downward slope, going from left to right. This occurs between Tuesday and Wednesday, so Wednesday has the biggest decrease from the previous day. Choice B is an increase; the graph goes up when read from left to right. Choice C (between Thursday and Friday) represents a decrease, but it is not as steep as that between Tuesday and Wednesday. Choice D is incorrect, because there was no change in the amount of time from Friday to Saturday.

18. B

To solve a proportion, you can cross multiply and set the product of the means equal to the product of the extremes. This is answer choice B. If you chose choice A, you incorrectly set the product of the numerators equal to the product of the denominators. If you chose choice C, you incorrectly set the sum of the numerators equal to the sum of the denominators. Choice D is incorrect; you cannot multiply the numerator by the denominator of one side and set it equal to this product on the other side.

19. C

Triangle *RST* is a right triangle with a hypotenuse of 30 in. and one leg measuring 24 in. Use the Pythagorean theorem, that is $a^2 + b^2 = c^2$, to find the missing leg, x.

Write the Pythagorean theorem:	$a^2 + b^2 = c^2$
Substitute in the given measures:	$x^2 + 24^2 = 30^2$
Evaluate the exponents:	$x^2 + 576 = 900$
Subtract 576 from both sides:	$x^2 + 576 - 576 = 900 - 576$
Simplify:	$x^2 = 324$
Take the square root of both sides:	$\sqrt{x^2} = \sqrt{324}$
Simplify:	$x = 18$

This is answer choice C. Choice A is the result you would get if you doubled each side's length instead of squaring it. Answer choice B is the difference between the two given side lengths. Answer choice D represents a common error made when working with right triangles, mistaking the hypotenuse for one of the legs of the triangle.

20. B

To find the percent increase, take the ratio of $\dfrac{\text{change in values}}{\text{original value}}$ and then multiply by 100. The change in values is 1,850 – 1,500 = 350. The original value is 1,500. The ratio is $\dfrac{350}{1,500} \approx 0.23$, and 0.23 × 100 = 23%, answer choice B. If you selected choice A, you might have used 1,850 as the original value instead of 1,500. Answer choice D is the ratio of 1,500 to 1,850.

21. C

To determine the amount of flour needed to make 150 cookies for the party, you only need to know the number of cookies the recipe will make. The costs, conversion factor, and temperature will not affect the amount of flour needed for the cookies.

22. D

In this statement, the word *of* means to multiply. The statement refers to one half of the sum, so that sum, $x + y$, must be enclosed in parentheses. The key word *is* indicates an equal sign. The resultant equation is $\frac{1}{2}(x + y) = 12$. Choice A would be the expression for "One half of the number x plus y plus 12." Choice B would be the equation for "One half of the number x plus y is 12." Choice C would be the expression for "One half of the sum of the numbers x and y plus 12."

23. B

Calculate the percentages of the amounts in each table compared to the total responses in each table find which table matches the circle graph. For the table in choice A, the percent of Thai is $\frac{50}{465} \approx 0.108 = 10.8\%$, which does not match the circle graph. For the table in choice B, the percent of Thai is $\frac{50}{500} = 0.10 = 10\%$, which does match the circle graph. The percent for Italian is $\frac{175}{500} = 0.35 = 35\%$, the same as the graph. The percent for American and Chinese is $\frac{100}{500} = 0.20 = 20\%$, and these also agree with the circle graph. Finally, the percent for Mexican is $\frac{75}{500} = 0.15 = 15\%$, also consistent with the graph. Choice B is the correct table. Notice that in the table of choice C, Thai has more votes than Italian. This is not consistent with the circle graph, so choice C is incorrect. Choice D is a tempting choice, but read carefully! The values for American and Mexican are switched, so it does not match the graph.

24. D

To find the equation of a graphed line, determine the slope, m, and the y-intercept, b. The equation will be $y = mx + b$ in slope-intercept form. The y-intercept is the y-value of the point where it crosses the y-axis. In this line, it is at $y = -2$, so $b = -2$. The slope is found as the ratio of $\frac{\text{change in } y \text{ value}}{\text{change in } x \text{ value}}$. Find two points on the graph, such as $(0, -2)$ and $(4, 1)$. Now, calculate the slope: $\frac{1 - -2}{4 - 0} = \frac{3}{4}$. The slope, m, is $\frac{3}{4}$. The equation is therefore $y = \frac{3}{4}x - 2$, choice D. In choice A, the y-intercept is correct, but the slope given is the reciprocal of the correct slope. Choice C has the y-intercept and the slope switched.

25. C

You can plug each set of numbers into the Pythagorean theorem formula. For choice A, see whether $2^2 + 3^2 = 4^2$. Because $4 + 9 \neq 16$, those values cannot be the side lengths of a right triangle. For choice B, see whether $9^2 + 15^2 = 17^2$. Because $81 + 225 \neq 289$, choice B cannot represent a right triangle. For choice C, test $10^2 + 24^2 = 26^2$. Because $100 + 576 = 676$, answer choice C is a right triangle. Finally, test choice D and find out whether $12^2 + 18^2 = 24^2$ is true. Because $144 + 324 \neq 576$, answer choice D is not a right triangle.

26. C

Calculate the tip as 18% of the dinner bill and add the tip to the bill to get the total cost. Writing 18% as a decimal equivalent gives 0.18. The tip is 0.18 × $36.40 = $6.55. Add the tip to the bill to get $6.55 + $36.40 = $42.95. Choice A is the amount of the tip, not the total bill. If you selected choice B, you might have subtracted the tip from the meal's cost instead of adding them. If your choice was D, you might have thought the tip was $18 rather than 18% of the meal's cost.

27. D

To find the next number in the sequence, look at the difference between successive values. The differences are 1, 2, 4, and 8. These are the powers of 2; that is 2^0, 2^1, 2^2, and 2^3. The next difference will be $2^4 = 16$, so the next number in the sequence is 15 + 16 = 31. If you chose answer A, you might have thought each term differed by exactly 4. If you chose C, you might have thought each term differed by 8.

28. A

To simplify a radical, take the square root of each part under the square root sign. To take the square root of the variable terms, divide the exponents by 2. The coefficient, 49, will be $\sqrt{49} = 7$. The x piece will be $\sqrt{x^6} = x^{6÷2} = x^3$. The y part will be $\sqrt{y^2} = y^{2÷2} = y^1 = y$. The result is therefore $7x^3y$. Choice B would be arrived at by incorrectly dividing the exponent on the variable x by 3 instead of by 2. Choices C and D both have an incorrect coefficient; it should be the square root of 49, not 49.

29. B

Draw a picture of the situation.

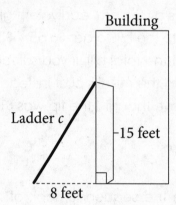

The length of the ladder is the hypotenuse of a right triangle with legs of 8 and 15 feet. Use the Pythagorean theorem, $a^2 + b^2 = c^2$, to find the length of the ladder.

Write the theorem:	$a^2 + b^2 = c^2$
Substitute in the given values:	$8^2 + 15^2 = c^2$
Evaluate the exponents:	$64 + 225 = c^2$
Add on the left side:	$289 = c^2$
Take the square root of both sides:	$\sqrt{289} = \sqrt{c^2}$
Simplify:	$17 = c$

This is choice B. If you selected choice A, you might have thought the hypotenuse was 15 feet, when in fact 15 feet is the length of one of the legs. If your answer was C, you might have multiplied by 2 instead of squaring, and you might have divided by 2 instead of taking the square root. If your answer was D, you might have divided by 2 in the final step instead of taking the square root.

30. C

The number of family members happy with both the mountains and the beach is the number in the area intersection, 15. Choice A is the difference between those that like both and those that like the mountains only. Choice B is the difference between those that like both and those that like the beach only. Choice D is the total number of people who were asked (9 + 15 + 25).

31. C

The x-intercept is the value of x in the equation when $y = 0$. Substitute in the value of 0 for y and solve for x.

Write the equation:	$3y = 9x - 18$
Substitute in 0 for y:	$3 \times 0 = 9x - 18$
Add 18 to both sides:	$0 + 18 = 9x - 18 + 18$
Simplify:	$18 = 9x$
Divide both sides by 9:	$\dfrac{18}{9} = \dfrac{9x}{9}$
Simplify:	$2 = x$

The x-intercept is (2, 0), choice C. The values in choice A are the coefficients for the y and x terms of the equation listed as an ordered pair. Choice B gives the coordinates of the y-intercept of the graph.

32. B

The area of a circle is found by using the formula $A = \pi r^2$, where r is the radius of the circle. The diagonal of the square is also the diameter of the circle, and the radius is one half of the diameter, 7.5 inches. Substitute into the formula, and the area is $A = \pi \times (7.5)^2 = 56.25\pi$ in^2. Choice D is the result of using the diameter of the circle in the formula instead of the radius.

33. B

Use the simple interest formula $I = prt$, where I is the interest earned, p is the principle invested, r is the interest rate, and t is the time in years. Change the interest rate of 6% to 0.06 by dividing by 100.

Write the formula:	$I = prt$
Substitute in the given values:	$I = 2,200 \times 0.06 \times 7$
Simplify:	$I = 924$

Choice A is the interest earned after just 1 year. Choice C is the amount of the savings plus interest after 1 year. Choice D is the amount of the savings plus interest after 7 years, not just the interest earned.

34. B

Probability is found by taking the ratio of $\dfrac{\text{number of ways an event can occur}}{\text{total number of possible outcomes}}$.
When you roll 2 dice, there are 6 × 6 = 36 possible outcomes. Of these, there are 6 ways to roll doubles, that is {(1, 1), (2, 2), (3, 3), (4, 4), (5, 5), (6, 6)}. The probability is therefore $\dfrac{6}{36} = \dfrac{1}{6}$, choice B. If your answer was choice A, you found the correct number of possible outcomes but only accounted for one way to roll doubles. If you chose C, you may have found the probability of rolling a certain number on a standard die, which is $\dfrac{1}{6}$, and then added to get $\dfrac{1}{6} + \dfrac{1}{6} = \dfrac{2}{6} = \dfrac{1}{3}$. If you chose D, you may have thought that there were only 12 possible outcomes, 6 of which were doubles.

35. C

Notice that the lines intersect at the value of 25 ounces. At this weight, the companies charge the same amount. For all other values, the costs differ. To find which company is less expensive when the weight is more than 25 ounces, look to the right of the value 25 and note that Fly-It-Quick is lower. If choice A were true, the graph for Ships-A-Lot would always be above the graph for Fly-It-Quick. If choice B were correct, the two graphs would lie on top of each other. If you selected choice D, you may have matched each line with the wrong company.

36. A

On this scatter plot, as you read the data from left to right, the trend runs downward. This indicates a negative correlation, which means that the more money spent on entertainment, the less money is saved. If choice B were correct, the trend would be upwards when reading the data from left to right. If choice C were correct, the data would not approximate a line; it would be scattered over the entire graph. Choice D would coincide with a graph with a positive correlation.

37. C

A graphed equation with a negative slope runs downward when looking at the graph from left to right. Choice A is the graph of $y = -1$ and has a slope of 0. Choice B is the graph of $x = -1$; it has an undefined slope. Choice D has a positive slope; it slopes upward when read from left to right. Choice C is the graph of $y = -x + 2$, which has a negative slope.

38. B

Use the given formula $A = \frac{1}{2}h(b_1 + b_2)$, where A is the area, h is the height of the trapezoid, given as 18 mm, and b_1 and b_2 are the parallel bases, with given measures of 20 mm and 30 mm.

Write the formula:	$A = \frac{1}{2}h(b_1 + b_2)$
Substitute in the given values:	$A = \frac{1}{2} \times 18 \times (20 + 30)$
Use order of operations and first evaluate within parentheses:	$A = \frac{1}{2} \times 18 \times (50)$
Multiply left to right:	$A = 450$ mm^2

Choice A gives the perimeter of the trapezoid. If you answered choice C, you may have been thinking of a parallelogram and just multiplied 22 and 30. Choice D is the result you would reach if you did not multiply by $\frac{1}{2}$.

39. C

When you divide numbers with the same base, keep the base and subtract the exponents: $7^{-3} \div 7^{-5} = 7^{-3-(-5)} = 7^{-3+5} = 7^2$. Choice A is the product of the two terms; you would get that product by adding the exponents instead of subtracting. If your answer was B, you may have subtracted −3 from −5 instead of −5 from −3. Choice D would be incorrect because you added the absolute values of the exponents.

40. A

To find the perimeter of a polygon, you add up all of the sides. Find a problem situation that requires addition. This is answer choice A. Do not be misled by choices B and C. Even though they also involve measurement, these problems would be solved with multiplication, not addition. Likewise, choice D would be solved by multiplication.

41. A

This function is given in slope-intercept form, $y = mx + b$, where m is the slope of the line and b is the y-intercept. Look for the graph that has a slope of -2 and a y-intercept of 3. A graphed line with a negative slope runs downwards when viewed from left to right. This eliminates choice B, which has a positive slope. Because the y-intercept is 3, look for the graph that crosses the y-axis at 3. The only remaining graph with that feature is found in choice A. Choice C is the graph of the function $y = -3x + 2$, which has a y-intercept of 2 and a slope of -3. Choice D is the graph of the function $y = -2x$, which has the correct slope but a y-intercept of 0.

42. A

Probability is a fractional ratio of $\dfrac{\text{number of ways an event can occur}}{\text{total number of possible outcomes}}$. The probability of rolling a 5 on a standard number cube is therefore $\dfrac{1}{6}$. There are 3 even numbers on a number cube: 2, 4, and 6. The probability of rolling an even number is thus $\dfrac{3}{6} = \dfrac{1}{2}$. To find the probability of one event and then another event, you multiply the probabilities for each together: $\dfrac{1}{6} \times \dfrac{1}{2} = \dfrac{1}{12}$. If your answer was B, you may have taken the probability of rolling a 5 to be $\dfrac{1}{5}$ instead of $\dfrac{1}{6}$. Choice D is the sum of the probabilities, not the product.

43. A

To find a point that lies on a line, substitute the variables from each ordered pair into the equation to find the pair that produces a true statement. Choice A has an x value of -3 and a y value of 0. Use the given equation $4y = 2x + 6$ and test. By substitution, $4 \times 0 = 2 \times -3 + 6$, or $0 = -6 + 6$, resulting in $0 = 0$, a true statement. So the ordered pair $(-3, 0)$ lies on the line $4y = 2x + 6$. Each of the other ordered pairs would result in a false statement. Test choice B by substitution: $4 \times -3 = 2 \times 0 + 6$, or $-12 = 0 + 6$, resulting in $-12 = 6$, a false statement. Test choice C: $4 \times 6 = 2 \times 0 + 6$, or $24 = 0 + 6$, resulting in $24 = 6$, a false statement. Test choice D: $4 \times 0 = 2 \times 6 + 6$, or $0 = 12 + 6$, resulting in $0 = 18$, a false statement.

44. B

It is given that Ravi can cycle 15 miles every hour, which is 15 miles every 60 minutes. To find out how far Ravi can cycle in 100 minutes, you can set up a proportion. Let n represent the number of miles he can cycle in 100 minutes, such that $\frac{15}{60} = \frac{n}{100}$. Cross multiply: $1,500 = 60n$. Divide both sides by 60, and $n = 25$ miles in 100 minutes. If you chose A, you might have gotten the incorrect equation $100 = 15n$. If you chose C, you may have set up the correct proportion but divided by 6 instead of by 60. Choice D is the number of miles Ravi can cycle in 100 hours.

45. C

A number raised to the power of –3 is equal to the reciprocal of the cube of that number. So $(2)^{-3} = \frac{1}{2} \times \frac{1}{2} \times \frac{1}{2} = \frac{1}{8}$, choice C. Choice A is simply the product of 2 and –3. If you chose D, you may have added the denominators instead of multiplying.

46. C

To determine the cost of labor and paint, the other information needed is the cost of a gallon of paint, choice C. As for choice A, it does not matter how long it would take one painter to paint the room, because the two painters are working together. The perimeter and volume of the room, choices B and D, are not needed for this problem. The area will need to be determined, and then the number of gallons to paint will be calculated. Once the cost of a gallon of paint is known, the cost can be determined.

47. B

To find the slope of a graphed line, first find two points on the line. Two points easy to identify are the x and y intercepts, namely (6, 0) and (0, –4). Slope is calculated as the ratio of the change in y values (the rise) to the change in x values (the run): $\frac{\text{rise}}{\text{run}} = \frac{-4 - 0}{0 - 6} = \frac{-4}{-6} = \frac{2}{3}$, choice A. Choice B is the reciprocal of the slope, the ratio of the run to the rise. Choice D is the y-intercept of the line.

48. D

Use the counting principle to find the total number of kinds of pizzas that can be ordered: 2 × 3 × 5 = 30, so there are 30 possibilities. Choice B would be the number of possibilities if there were only one kind of crust. The value in choice C would be the number of possibilities if there were only one size of pizza.

49. C

Parallel lines have equal slopes. Find the slope of the given equation and then choose the answer with the identical slope. The equation is given in the slope-intercept form of $y = mx + b$, where m is the slope and b is the y-intercept. Therefore, the slope of a parallel line is $\frac{2}{3}$. Choice A is the opposite of the y-intercept of the equation. Choice B is the opposite of the value of the slope.

50. C

Use the scale ratio and set up the proportion of $\frac{\text{model}}{\text{real}} = \frac{\text{model}}{\text{real}}$. Let n represent the height of the Eiffel Tower and substitute in the given information: $\frac{1}{8,500} = \frac{3.6}{n}$. Cross multiply to get $n = 3.6 \times 8,500 = 30,600$ cm. To change centimeters to meters, divide by 100: 30,600 cm = 306 m, choice C. Choice A uses the wrong unit. Choice B would be the result of dividing 30,600 by 1,000 instead of by 100. Choice D, 36 km, is 3,600 meters, not 306 meters.

51. A

To add and subtract fractions, first find the least common denominator (LCD) of the fractions and make equivalent fractions with this denominator. The least common multiple of the denominators of 5, 10, and 20 is 20: $\frac{1}{5} = \frac{4}{20}$ and $\frac{3}{10} = \frac{6}{20}$. Rewrite the problem with these equivalent fractions: $\frac{4}{20} + \frac{7}{20} - \frac{6}{20} = \frac{4+7-6}{20} = \frac{11-6}{20} = \frac{5}{20}$. Simplify the answer by dividing the numerator and the denominator by the greatest common factor of 5: $\frac{5}{20} \div \frac{5}{5} = \frac{1}{4}$, choice A. If you selected choice D, you might have forgotten to subtract $\frac{6}{20}$.

52. A

The question is asking for an approximate amount, so round the $2.89 to $3.00 to make the problem easier to calculate. If you have $42.00, and chicken is approximately $3.00 per pound, divide to find the number of pounds you can buy: $42 \div 3 = 14$ pounds of chicken, choice A. If your answer was choice B, you may have thought the price was closer to $2.00 per pound instead of $3.00. For choice C, you may have rounded $2.89 to $2.00 and then multiplied instead of dividing. For choice D, you may have rounded correctly but then multiplied instead of dividing.

53. C

Write the equation to solve:	$2(x - 4) = 12$
First, apply the distributive property:	$2x - 8 = 12$
Add 8 to both sides:	$2x - 8 + 8 = 12 + 8$
Simplify:	$2x = 20$
Divide both sides by 2:	$\dfrac{2x}{2} = \dfrac{20}{2}$
Simplify:	$x = 10$

Choice A is the solution of the incorrect equation $2x = 12$. Choice B is the solution of $2x - 4 = 12$ and might be the results of not distributing the 2 when multiplying 2 by $x - 4$.

54. B

If there are 4 left-handed students for every 20 seniors, there are 16 right-handed students for every 20 seniors.

Set up the proportion of $\dfrac{\text{sample right-handed}}{\text{sample students}} = \dfrac{\text{total right-handed}}{\text{total students}}$ and solve.

Let n represent the total number of students in the senior class and substitute: $\dfrac{16}{20} = \dfrac{288}{n}$. Cross multiply to get $16n = 5{,}760$. Divide both sides by 16 to get $n = 360$ students, choice B. If you selected choice A, you may have set up the correct proportion but cross multiplied incorrectly. Choice C would be the number of students if there were 288 left-handed students.

55. B

To find the median, first order the data from least to greatest:

    5.8   5.8   7.0   7.2   7.3   7.6   8.2   9.5

The median is the middle value. There are 8 data values, so the middle is the average of 7.2 and 7.3, which is 7.25, choice B. Choice A is the mode of the data, the value that appears most often. Choice C is the mean of the data set. Choice D is the fifth entry when the data is ordered, not the middle of the set.

56. D

Two graphed lines that are parallel have the same slope. Take the given equation and put it in the slope-intercept form of $y = mx + b$, where m is the slope of the line and b is the y-intercept. Divide the equation $2y = 6x + 4$ by 2 on both sides to get the correct form: $y = 3x + 2$. The slope is 3. The answer choices are all in slope-intercept form, and choice D is the equation that also has the slope of 3. If you chose answer choices A or B, you may have thought the slope of $2y = 6x + 4$ was 6 instead of 3. If you chose choice C, you might have thought the slope was 4.

57. C

The area of a parallelogram is found by using the formula $A = bh$, where b is the length of the base and h is the length of the height. By counting the squares, $b = 10$ and $h = 4$. The area is $A = 10 \times 4 = 40$ square units, choice C. Choice A would be arrived at by adding the base and height instead of multiplying. If your answer was B, you may have divided the area by 2, confusing the formula of the area of a triangle with the formula for the area of a parallelogram.

58. B

We know that 160 is between the perfect squares 144 and 169. Take the square root of each of these perfect squares: $\sqrt{144} = 12$ and $\sqrt{169} = 13$. Thus, the value of $\sqrt{160}$ lies between 12 and 13. Choice A gives the integers between which the value of $\sqrt{1,600}$ lies.

59. B

To solve a rate problem such as this one, you can find the unit rate and then multiply by the number of minutes. Martin can do 30 pushups in 2 minutes, which is 15 pushups every minute. He therefore can do 15 × 5 = 75 pushups in 5 minutes, choice B. Answer choice A is the number of pushups he can do in 4 minutes. Answer C is the number of pushups he can do in 6 minutes. Choice D is the number he can do in 7 minutes.

60. A

To solve this problem, you can first convert square inches to square feet, then convert square feet to square yards. There are 12 × 12 = 144 square inches in 1 square foot, so divide 5,184 ÷ 144 = 36 square feet. There are 3 × 3 = 9 square feet in 1 square yard, so divide again to find the square yards: 36 ÷ 9 = 4 square yards, choice A. Choice B is the number of square feet in one square yard. Choice C is the number of square feet, rather than the number of square yards, in 5,184 square inches. Choice D is the number of square inches in 1 square foot.

61. D

Take each answer choice and determine its truth value. Choice A is false. Reza, who scored a total of 30 points, is not the top scorer; Shante is the top scorer with a total of 59 points. Choice B is false. The mean of the data is the sum of all of the scores divided by the amount of data. The mean of the data is thus 111 ÷ 15 ≈ 7.4, and 11.8 is the mean of Shante's data only, the data in the first row. Choice C is false; the mean, calculated above as 7.4, is not equal to the mode. The mode is the number that occurs most often, which is 8. Choice D is the only true choice. The mode is 8, as explained. The median is the middle value when the data is arranged from least to greatest. The data arranged from least to greatest is: 0, 2, 2, 4, 4, 6, 8, 8, 8, 8, 8, 10, 12, 14, 17. The middle value is also 8. It is true, therefore, that the median is equal to the mode of the data.

62. A

These two equations are both in the same form. The easiest way to solve this system is to use the substitution method. Both equations are solved for *y*, so set one equation equal to the other and solve for *x*:

The equation is:	$5x + 3 = 3x - 1$
Subtract 3*x* from both sides:	$5x + 3 - 3x = 3x - 1 - 3x$
Combine like terms:	$2x + 3 = -1$
Subtract 3 from both sides:	$2x + 3 - 3 = -1 - 3$
Simplify:	$2x = -4$
Divide both sides by 2:	$x = -2$

The value of the *x*-coordinate of the solution is –2. Substitute this into either equation to find the *y*-coordinate: $5x + 3 = 5 \times -2 + 3 = -10 + 3 = -7$. The solution is (–2, –7), choice A. If you chose B, you may have solved the system correctly but reversed the *x* and the *y* coordinates. If your answer was C, you may have added 3 to both sides of the equation in step 3 above, instead of subtracting 3, and then used the first equation to find the value of *y*. If your answer was D, you might have the same error as explained for choice C but used the second equation to find the value of *y*.

63. C

The volume of a cylinder is given by the formula $V = \pi r^2 h$, where *V* is the volume, *r* is the radius of the base, and *h* is the height. The radius is 4 cm, one half of the diameter, and the height is 12 cm. Substitute these given values into the formula: $V = \pi r^2 h = \pi \times 4^2 \times 12$. Simplify to get $V = \pi \times 16 \times 12 = 192\pi$ cm³, choice C. Choice A is the value of πr^2. Choice D would be the result of using the diameter instead of the radius in the formula.

64. B

To find the amount of the discount, convert 30% to a decimal equivalent and multiply. Because $0.30 \times 36 = 10.8$, the discount is $10.80. Subtract this from the original price to get the sale price: $36.00 − $10.80 = $25.20, choice B. Choice A is the discount, not the sale price. Choice C is the percent, written out as if it were the sale price instead of the sale percentage off. Choice D would be the value if the handbag were marked up by 30% instead of being discounted at that rate.

65. D

This graph is a parabola, and the equation of a parabola is a quadratic equation in the form $ax^2 + bx + c = d$ ($ax^2 + bx + c = 0$ if $d = 0$). Answer choices A and B are equations of linear functions and would be graphed as straight lines. To determine whether the equation is choice C or D, look at the y-intercept, where the graph meets the y-axis. The y-intercept is -4. The value of c in the equation $ax^2 + bx + c = 0$ is the y-intercept, so the correct equation is choice D. The y-intercept of graph choice C is $+4$.

66. A

To order numbers written in scientific notation, look at the exponents on the powers of 10; these exponents should be in increasing order. In answer choice A, the exponents are in the order of -2, -1, and 2. Because $-2 < -1 < 2$, these numbers are in increasing order. Choices B and D have numbers in decreasing order.

67. A

Each answer choice statement asks for the weight of 1 pack of greeting cards, which is the value of x. Solve the inequality for x:

Write the inequality:	$12x + 3 \leq 51$
Subtract 3 from each side:	$12x + 3 - 3 \leq 51 - 3$
Simplify:	$12x \leq 48$
Divide both sides by 12:	$x \leq 4$

Each package of greeting cards must be 4 ounces or less, as stated in choice A. Choice B would be the correct answer if the simplified inequality were $x \geq 4$. If you selected choice C or D, you may have divided by 4 at the end of the solution instead of dividing by 12.

68. C

The key word product is the result of multiplication, so translate "the product of 5 and a number" as $5m$. "Seven less than the product" means that you should subtract 7 from that product. So the correct expression is $5m - 7$, choice C. Choice A represents "Seven less the product of 5 and a number m." Choice B represents "Seven less the sum of 5 and a number m." Choice D represents "Seven less than the quotient of 5 and a number m."

69. C

The total number of choices can be found with the counting principle. For Danielle's dress, the total number of choices is $2 \times 3 \times 4 = 24$. The correct tree diagram will have 24 choices on the rightmost part of the tree. It will start with two branches, for short- or long–sleeved dresses. Off of each of these branches will be 3 branches, 1 for each of the fabric types. There are now 6 branches. Off of each of these will be 4 additional branches for each fabric color, resulting in the 24 total possibilities, tree choice C. Tree A does not take into consideration the length of the sleeves. In tree B, half of the branches are missing. For example, one choice missing is Satin – Blue – Long-Sleeved. Choice D does not show possible combinations of patterns types and materials.

70. A

The area of a rectangle is found by the formula $A = lw$, where l is the length and w is the width. Substitute in the terms, and the area is $A = (x + 4)(x - 4)$. Use the distributive property and multiply: $(x + 4)(x - 4) = x^2 - 4x + 4x - 16 = x^2 - 16$. Choice B would be the area of a square with dimensions of $(x - 4)$ and $(x - 4)$. Choice C would be the result of adding the two dimensions instead of multiplying. Choice D is the perimeter of the rectangle.

71. D

Use the given conversion factor to convert miles to kilometers. Because 1 mile ≈ 1.6 kilometers, you must multiply the miles per hour by 1.6 to find the speed in kilometers per hour. $65 \times 1.6 = 104$ km/hour, choice D. If you had divided instead of multiplying, you would have selected choice A. Choice B is in miles per hour, not kilometers per hour. Choice C is just the sum of 65 and 1.6.

72. B

Numbers written in scientific notation take the form of $m \times 10^n$, where $1 \leq m < 10$ and n is an integer. To express 0.003067 as a number between 1 and 10, you must move the decimal point of the number 3 places to the right to make it 3.067. So the number written in scientific notation is 3.067×10^{-3}, choice B. Choice A is an equivalent number, but it is not in scientific notation. Choice C is the number 0.03067 in scientific notation. Choice D is the number 3,067 in scientific notation.

73. D

Write the inequality:	$6y - 3 > 39$
Add 3 to both sides:	$6y - 3 + 3 > 39 + 3$
Simplify:	$6y > 42$
Divide both sides by 6:	$y > 7$

If you picked choice A or B, you might have subtracted 3 from both sides instead of adding. Choice A also has the inequality sign reversed, as does choice C.

74. B

A number raised to the power of –4 is the reciprocal of the number multiplied by itself 3 times. So $n^{-4} = \dfrac{1}{n} \times \dfrac{1}{n} \times \dfrac{1}{n} \times \dfrac{1}{n}$, choice B. Choice A represents $-n^{-4}$, rather than n^{-4}. Keep in mind that the negative exponent has no effect on the sign of the factors. If you chose C, you multiplied –4 by n instead of treating it as an exponent. Choice D is the value of $-n^4$.

75. C

The triangle is "flipped" over the horizontal axis, making it a reflection over the x-axis, choice C. A reflection over the y-axis, incorrect choice A, would be a side-to-side flip. Translations, choices B and D, "slide" a geometric figure. That kind of transformation does not change the orientation of the figure.

76. C

To find the mean, add up the data values and divide by the number of values. The sum of the 5 commission amounts is $32,850. Divide this total by 5 to get the mean price: $32,850 ÷ 5 = $6,570, choice C. Choice A is the range of the data, the difference between the highest and lowest values. Choice B is the median, or middle, value when the data is arranged in order.

77. D

To evaluate an expression, plug in the given value and then simplify. The given expression is $|x - 5|$. Because $x = 2$, the expression is $|2 - 5| = |-3|$. The absolute value of –3 is 3, choice D. Choice B is simply the value of $x - 5$. Choice C is the value of x, not the value of the expression.

78. B

Write an algebraic equation representing this situation. Let x represent the number of lemons purchased.

Write the equation:	$0.45x + 3.75 = 7.80$
Subtract 3.75 from both sides:	$0.45x + 3.75 - 3.75 = 7.80 - 3.75$
Simplify:	$0.45x = 4.05$
Divide both sides by 0.45:	$x = 9$

Choice A is the number of watermelons that could be bought for $7.80 if no lemons were purchased. Choice C is the number of lemons that could be purchased for $7.80. If your answer was choice D, you might have added 3.75 in the second step above instead of subtracting it.

79. B

The area of a circle is given as 49π square inches. The formula for the area of a circle is $A = \pi r^2$, where r is the radius of the circle. Find the radius: divide the area of 49π by π to get an r^2 of 49; therefore, $r = 7$ inches. Then multiply the radius by 2 to get the diameter: $r \times 2 = 7 \times 2 = 14$ inches, choice B. Choice A is the radius of the circle. If your answer was C, you may have multiplied the radius by 4 instead of by 2. Choice D would be correct if 49π were the circumference of the circle rather than the radius.

80. B

Take each answer choice and decide if you can determine each amount. You are told that 80% of the 300 seniors attended the prom, so you know the amount at issue in choice A. Consider choice B. Although you know that 10 of the prom attendees will not attend the senior class trip, you do not know how many in the entire class will not attend this trip. Choice B is the correct choice because it *cannot* be determined based on the given data. You can also determine choice C, which is just 300 minus the number who did attend. Because you are told that 10 students attending the prom will not attend the senior class trip and you can calculate how many seniors attended the prom, you can determine choice D.

81. C

To solve an absolute value inequality, you must set up two inequalities, $x + 1 < 3$ and $-(x + 1) < 3$. Solve each inequality. Subtract 1 from both sides of $x + 1 < 3$ to get $x + 1 - 1 < 3 - 1$ which simplifies to $x < 2$. Use the distributive property on the second inequality to get $-x - 1 < 3$. Add 1 to both sides to get $-x - 1 + 1 < 3 + 1$. Simplify to get $-x < 4$. Now, divide both sides by -1 and remember to reverse the inequality symbol (because you are dividing by a negative number). The simplified second inequality is $x > -4$. The solution set of the two inequalities is all numbers less than 2 and greater than -4. That includes all integers between, but not including, -4 and 2, which is answer choice C.

If you chose A or B, you may have arrived at the boundary point of 2 and incorrectly assumed that there were two solutions, just -2 and 2 for choice A and 0 and 2 for choice B. In answer choice D, the values of -4 and 2 are included. These would only be in the solution set if the symbols were $\leq$ instead of $<$.

82. A

Test each expression. Choice A, $(-3)^3$, is equal to $-3 \times -3 \times -3 = -27$. This is the correct response. Choice B has a positive value: $-13 + 20 = 7$. Choice C is also positive: $2 - (-8) = 2 + 8 = 10$. Choice D is an absolute value expression, and the absolute value of any expression is always positive.

83. C

The surface area of a rectangular solid can be found by using the formula $S = 2lw + 2wh + 2lh$, where S represents the surface area, l is the length, w is the width, and h is the height. The length is 14 cm, the width is 10 cm, and the height is 12 cm. Substitute these values into the formula to get $S = 2 \times 14 \times 10 + 2 \times 10 \times 12 + 2 \times 14 \times 12$. Multiply and then add to get $280 + 240 + 336 = 856$ cm², choice C. Choice A is the sum of the three dimensions. Choice B is one half of the surface area. Choice D is the volume of the solid, not the surface area.

84. B

If it takes Justin 4 hours to carpet the room, he can do $\frac{1}{4}$ of the job in an hour. Likewise, Miguel can do $\frac{1}{6}$ of the job in an hour. Let h represent the number of hours it will take them working together.

Set up the equation: $\qquad\qquad\qquad\qquad \frac{1}{4}h + \frac{1}{6}h = 1$

Multiply both sides by the LCD: $\qquad 12\left(\frac{1}{4}h + \frac{1}{6}h\right) = 1 \times 12$

Simplify: $\qquad\qquad\qquad\qquad\qquad 3h + 2h = 12$

Combine like terms: $\qquad\qquad\qquad\qquad 5h = 12$

Divide both sides by 5: $\qquad\qquad\qquad\qquad h = 2.4$ hours

Choice C is the time the job would take Justin alone. Choice D is the sum of the times the job would take each of them alone. Keep in mind that carpeting the room will take the two of them less time working together than either one of them working alone.

85. B

The given graph is the story of Martina's hike. The slope of each segment in the graph, the steepness, indicates how fast Martina walked. The steeper the slope, the faster she walked. The flat part of the graph, between 8:00 am and 9:00 am has a slope of 0, indicating that she was at a standstill. Therefore, choice B is correct. Not all portions of the graph have the same steepness, so choice A is incorrect. Martina's speed was greatest at the end of her hike, so choice C is incorrect.

86. A

When you divide powers with the same base, keep the base and subtract the exponents: $4^3 \div 4^5 = 4^{3-5} = 4^{-2}$. Taking a number to the exponent of –2 means to take the reciprocal of the number and then multiply it by itself. In other words, $4^{-2} = \frac{1}{4} \times \frac{1}{4} = \frac{1}{16}$, choice A. Choice B is the value of $4^5 \div 4^3$. Choice C is the value of $4^3 \times 4^5$.

87. A

To solve a rate problem such as this, you can find the unit rate and then multiply by the number of hours. Helena can type 13,500 words in 7.5 hours. Because $13,500 \div 7.5 = 1,800$, she types at a rate of 1,800 words every hour. She still has to type 47,250 words (60,750 – 13,500). So at 1,800 words per hour, it will take her 26.25 hours to finish the job (47,250 ÷ 1,800). Answer choice C is the number of hours to complete the entire job, not the number of hours to finish it. Choice D is the number of hours it would take her to type 74,250 words (60,750 + 13,500).

88. C

In any triangle, the sum of any two sides must be larger than the third side. To find the possible lengths for the third side, take the sum and the difference of the two given sides. 12 + 5 = 17, and 12 – 5 = 7. So the third side must be between 7 and 17 cm, choice C. If your choice was either A or B, you might have taken the side lengths as the boundaries for the third side. However, the third side's length could very well be the shortest or the longest side.

89. D

Each downloaded song costs $0.75, so the cost of m songs would be $0.75m$. There is, however, a one-time membership fee of $15.00. The total cost is $0.75m + 15$, choice D. Choice A represents the cost of a download as $75.00, rather than $0.75. Choice B reflects a $75 membership fee plus $15 per download. Choice C represents a $0.75 membership fee plus $15 for each download.

90. D

The swimming pool is a rectangular solid, so the formula for its volume is $V = lwh$, where V represents the volume, l is the length, w is the width, and h is the height. The length is 50 feet, the width is 20 feet, and the height is 6 feet. Substitute these values into the formula to get $V = 50 \times 20 \times 6 = 6{,}000$ ft³, choice D. Choice A is the sum of the three dimensions. Choice B would be the volume if the depth were 2 feet. Choice C is the surface area of the solid with these dimensions, and choice A is the surface area of the five sides of the pool's interior.

91. B

Before the machine dispenses any gum, it contains 30 gumballs $(10 + 6 + 7 + 7)$. Probability is calculated as the ratio of the $\dfrac{\text{number of ways an event can occur}}{\text{total number of possible outcomes}}$. The probability that her first gumball will be yellow is $\dfrac{6}{30} = \dfrac{1}{5}$. Now, note that dispensing a gumball from the machine is a dependent event, because the machine will have 29 gumballs after it dispenses the first, with only 5 yellow ones remaining. So the probability of Tasha now dispensing a red gumball is $\dfrac{10}{29}$. To find the probability of one event followed by another, multiply the probabilities for each event together: $\dfrac{1}{5} \times \dfrac{10}{29} = \dfrac{10}{145}$. This fraction can be simplified by dividing: $\dfrac{10}{145} \div \dfrac{5}{5} = \dfrac{2}{29}$. Choice A would have been the correct choice if the first gumball were returned to the machine. Choice C would be the result of obtaining the correct probabilities of each event but then adding instead of multiplying. Choice D would have been arrived at if you assumed that the first gumball were returned and if you then added the fractions instead of multiplying.

92. C

To divide this monomial, divide each variable term by $2y$. Divide the first term: $10 \div 2 = 5$, and $y^3 \div y = y^{3-1} = y^2$. The first term is thus $5y^2$. Divide the second term: $-2 \div 2 = -1$, and $y^2 \div y = y^{2-1} = y^1 = y$. The second term is $-y$. Divide the third term: $6 \div 2 = 3$, and $y \div y = 1$. The third term is 3. Putting these three terms together yields the correct simplified expression $5y^2 - y + 3$, choice C. Choice A is the simplified form of $\dfrac{10y^3 - 2y^2 + 6y}{2}$, and B is the simplified form of $\dfrac{10y^3 - 2y^2 + 6y}{y}$. You might have picked choice D if you forgot to divide the second term of the numerator by 2.